THE AMERICAN REVOLUTION

100

THE PEOPLE, BATTLES, AND

EVENTS OF THE AMERICAN WAR

FOR INDEPENDENCE, RANKED

BY THEIR SIGNIFICANCE

BOOKS BY MICHAEL LEE LANNING

- The Only War We Had: A Platoon's Leaders Journal of Vietnam

- Vietnam 1969–1970: A Company Commander's Journal

- Inside the LRRPs: Rangers in Vietnam

- Inside Force Recon: Recon Marines in Vietnam (with Ray W. Stubbe)

- The Battles of Peace

- Inside the VC and NVA: The Real Story of North Vietnam's Armed Forces (with Dan Cragg)

- Vietnam at the Movies

- Senseless Secrets: The Failures of U.S. Military Intelligence from George Washington to the Present

- The Military 100: A Ranking of the Most Influential Military Leaders of All Time

- The African-American Soldier: From Crispus Attucks to Colin Powell

- Inside the Crosshairs: Snipers in Vietnam

- Defenders of Liberty: African-Americans in the Revolutionary War

- Blood Warriors: American Military Elites

- The Battle 100: The Stories Behind History's Most Influential Battles

- Mercenaries: Soldiers of Fortune, from Ancient Greece to Today's Private Military Companies

- The Civil War 100: The Stories Behind the Most Influential Battles, People, and Events in the War Between the States

THE AMERICAN REVOLUTION

100

THE PEOPLE, BATTLES, AND
EVENTS OF THE AMERICAN WAR
FOR INDEPENDENCE, RANKED
BY THEIR SIGNIFICANCE

MICHAEL LEE LANNING

SOURCEBOOKS, INC.®
NAPERVILLE, ILLINOIS

Published by Sourcebooks, Inc.
P.O. Box 4410, Naperville, Illinois 60567-4410
(630) 961-3900
Fax: (630) 961-2168
www.sourcebooks.com

Library of Congress Cataloging-in-Publication Data
Lanning, Michael Lee.
  American Revolution 100 : the battles, people, and events of the American war for independence, ranked by their significance / Michael Lee Lanning.
      p. cm.
  Includes bibliographical references and index.
  1. United States—History—Revolution, 1775-1783—Handbooks, manuals, etc. I. Title. II. Title: American Revolution one hundred.
  E209.L36 2008
  973.3—dc22
                          2008017859

Printed and bound in the United States of America
BG 10 9 8 7 6 5 4 3 2 1

To

The staff of the Hippocrates Health Institute, West Palm Beach,
    Florida, for showing me the way;

Dr. Pamandee Shama of M.D. Anderson Cancer Center, Houston,
    Texas, for her candor and support;

Major General Bernard O. Loeffke (U.S. Army, Retired), Hollywood,
    Florida, for his mentorship in war, in peace, and in health;

and

Linda, for everything.

CONTENTS

INTRODUCTION

We hold these truths to be self evident: That all men are created equal; that they are endowed by their Creator with certain unalienable rights; that among these are life, liberty, and the pursuit of happiness; that, to secure these rights, governments are instituted among men, deriving their just powers from the consent of the governed.

—Declaration of Independence
July 4, 1776

These simple, yet ambitious, words begin the declaration that became the birth certificate of the United States of America—a document that ended any chance that the rebellious colonists and the British king might settle their differences anywhere but on the battlefield. The vastly outnumbered Revolutionaries faced what seemed to be overwhelming obstacles to their independence. Many of their fellow colonists opposed the Rebellion, and others chose neutrality. Great Britain, the most powerful military power in the world at the time, had a large population and almost unlimited resources. The Americans had no united military force, no monetary system, and no governing body to support the newly declared nation. Five years after the founders signed the *Declaration of Independence*, the Americans accepted the surrender of the main British army in America and two years later signed a peace agreement that recognized the independence of the United States.

The opportunity for "life, liberty, and the pursuit of happiness" achieved by the Revolutionary War led to the longest reigning democracy in history. Over the succeeding years, the United States has advanced to the status of the richest country and world's single superpower. Its revolution has served as model to those seeking independence from oppression of all kinds, and the United States remains today a beacon of hope to freedom-loving people everywhere.

Wars can change the course of history. The American Revolution ranks as the most influential conflict of all time. In the thousands of books that have been written about the war since it ended, most authors have focused on combining the divergent political and social issues with battlefield actions. A myriad of others have covered the lives of the individual military and civilian leaders or covered the specific units, battles, or campaigns. Yet, none of these works to date has attempted to rank the war's leaders, battles, and events in terms of their influence on the Revolutionary War itself.

The 100 entries that follow are not necessarily the best, greatest, largest, most powerful, or even the most famous. Rather this list ranks leaders, battles, and events in order of their influence on the war. For the ease of comparison, when one leader, battle, or event refers to another included on the list, the ranking of the referenced entry follows its name, e.g., Nathanael Greene (4), Battle of Bunker Hill (23), and the Boston Massacre (93).

1

GEORGE WASHINGTON

American General

1732–1799

George Washington is the single most influential factor of the American Revolution, his impact on the war far exceeding that of any other person, battle, or event. As the commander of the Continental Army (7), Washington led an assembly of citizen soldiers that he described as "sometimes half starved; always in rags, without pay and experiencing, at times, every species of distress which human nature is capable of undergoing." With this "ragtag" army and political skills equal to the task of appeasing civilian commanders and garnering support from other countries, Washington led the thirteen states to defeat one of the world's foremost military powers. Without his skills and leadership, the Revolution would not have been successful, and there might never have been a United States of America.

Washington, born to a farm family on February 22, 1732, in Westmoreland County, Virginia, mostly educated himself by extensive reading of geography, military history, and agriculture. The young Washington also studied mathematics and surveying, which led him, at age sixteen, to join a survey expedition to western Virginia. In 1749, Washington became the official surveyor of Culpepper County.

Washington's first military experience came with his appointment as a major in the Virginia colonial militia. In 1754, when he had turned twenty-two, he led a small expedition into the Ohio River Valley on behalf of the governor of Virginia to demand that French settlers withdraw from the British-claimed territory. He had his first taste of combat when the French attacked his column, forced its surrender, and sent the "English" back to eastern Virginia.

As a result of the unsuccessful mission, Washington resigned his commission but soon rejoined the militia as a lieutenant colonel and aide to British General Edward Braddock in 1755. He returned with the British force to the Ohio River Valley where the French and Indians ambushed the unit and killed Braddock. Washington assumed command and led the survivors to safety. As a result he was promoted to colonel and continued in that rank to command the defenses of western Virginia in

the early years of the Seven Years' War between Britain and France that began in May 1756.

During the conflict, also known as the French and Indian War, Washington became disillusioned with the British because of the way they ruled the colonies. He resented the superior attitude British officers displayed toward the colonial militia and found their lack of knowledge of the American terrain and people during their fights against the French and their Indian allies despicable. Despite his reservations, he sought a commission in the regular British Army. The refusal of his request furthered his resentment. At the end of the war, Washington again resigned his militia commission and returned to his estate at Mount Vernon.

In 1758 his fellow colonists elected him to the Virginia House of Burgesses, where he served for the next seventeen years. During this time he actively opposed the increasing British repression of the American colonies and the escalating taxation on life and commerce.

In 1759 Washington married Martha Dandridge Custis, the widow of Daniel Parke Custis. The substantial properties from her inheritance, combined with those left to Washington by his family, made them one of the wealthiest couples in Virginia, if not all the colonies. Although their marriage was childless, there is no evidence that their union was based on anything other than mutual love and respect. Washington also took on the role of a loving stepfather to Martha's son and daughter from her marriage to the late Daniel Custis. While she preferred him to remain with her at their Mount Vernon estate, she later wrote, "I cannot blame him for acting according to his ideas of duty in obeying the voice of his country."

When the First Continental Congress met in 1774, Washington represented Virginia. Shortly after the American Revolution began in 1775 with the Battles of Lexington and Concord (43) in Massachusetts, Washington appeared before the Congress in his old militia uniform offering his service. By unanimous vote, the Congress authorized the formation of the Continental Army and appointed Washington as its commander in chief. This selection was not so much based on the Virginian's military qualifications and experience as on his diplomatic and unifying skills. With the American colonies experiencing distinct and often hostile divisions, particularly between North and South, Washington appeared to the Congress to be the leader most capable of uniting the Americans to successfully fight one of the world's strongest armed forces.

Forty-three-year-old George Washington took command of the Continental Army at the Boston Siege (50) in July 1775. He immediately reorganized the force, dealt with Loyalists who still supported Britain, and attempted to form a navy. Familiar with the advantages of terrain from his experience as a surveyor, Washington occupied the unguarded Dorchester Heights and placed cannons captured at Fort Ticonderoga (52) on the high ground overlooking Boston. He shelled the occupied city, forcing the British to flee Boston by ship in March 1776.

Correctly anticipating that the British would next target New York City as a base to split the colonies along the Hudson River, Washington arrived in the area with adequate time to prepare defenses. He was forced to evacuate New York, however, when his soldiers—inferior in both numbers and training—failed in several battles with the British Army (11) in November.

By the time Washington withdrew from New York into Pennsylvania, his demoralized army numbered a mere 3,000 soldiers. The British force of more than 34,000 seemed to be waiting only for spring to finish off the American rebels and end the Rebellion. Washington knew that desperate times called for desperate measures. On Christmas night, 1776, he made his most daring attack by crossing the ice-filled Delaware River to engage the British-hired Hessian mercenaries (37) at their winter garrison in Trenton, New Jersey. With few losses, the rebels captured 900 of the enemy and then a week later defeated another British unit at nearby Princeton.

Neither Trenton (8) nor Princeton was a decisive victory, but together they did provide the first positive news for the Rebellion since Boston. Recruiting became easier, morale within the army rose, and, most importantly, the series of losses had ended. Despite his success, Washington recognized that he could not defeat the larger and better supplied British army in open combat. He also realized that he did not have to do so. Time was on his side. The longer the war lasted, the more likely it was that the British would tire of the expenditures on the distant conflict and that some other, more threatening enemy would go to war against them.

Quite simply, Washington understood that as long as he had an army in the field, victorious or not, the newly declared United States of America existed. In 1777, Washington made only a perfunctory effort to defend the capital at Philadelphia and sent part of his army to upstate New York to block a British invasion from Canada. Although he did not directly participate at Saratoga (3), the rebels won the battle because of Washington's selection of excellent subordinate commanders and his willingness to give them the authority and the available assets to achieve victory.

During the long winter of 1777–1778 at Valley Forge (39), Washington accepted support from American as well as foreign sources. Rebel representatives in Europe recruited experienced leaders to come to Washington's aid. Prussian Friedrich von Steuben (62) proved particularly useful in drilling and training the American army.

By the spring of 1778, neither side could amass enough strength in the North to achieve victory, so the British decided to move against the Southern colonies that provided many of the supplies for the rebel army. Washington elected not to follow but rather to maintain his presence near British-occupied New York. He remained confident that the mere existence of his army assured the continuance of the Rebellion. Nonetheless, he recognized the importance of the Southern colonies and dispatched his most able general, Nathanael Greene (4), to assume command in the South.

During the summer of 1778, France declared war against their longtime foe Great Britain and began openly supporting the rebellious Americans. Meanwhile, Washington remained patient, maintaining a stalemate in the North while Greene fought a series of battles in the Carolinas. After two years Greene forced the British under Lord Cornwallis (22) to withdraw to the Yorktown peninsula of Virginia. Washington, leaving a small detachment to block the British force in the north, then moved south. There, with the support of a 7,000-man French army and a thirty-six ship French fleet offshore to block reinforcements or evacuation, he moved against Yorktown (2). He accepted the surrender of the British army on October 10, 1781.

Yorktown was Washington's only decisive victory of the Revolution, but it proved adequate because it was the victory that mattered most, for it assured America its independence. Although the war did not formally conclude until 1783, for all practical purposes the American Revolution ended at Yorktown. Washington, now a national hero and man renowned around the world, became the first president of the United States of America in February 1789. During two terms, he presided over the formation and initial operations of a democratic government and established many of the procedures and traditions that prevail even today. As a strong supporter of a democratic government, Washington had no desire to become the "King of the Union" and refused to run for a third term. He retired to Mount Vernon, where he died on December 14, 1799, at age sixty-seven.

While his lasting stature results more from his role as president than as general, Washington was nevertheless an accomplished military leader. He simultaneously maintained an army in the field against a far superior force, kept a divisive Congress and population satisfied, and solicited military support from other countries.

Military leaders such as Greene and Horatio Gates (31), significant battles including Yorktown and Saratoga, and momentous events including signing of the *Declaration of Independence* (14) greatly impacted the outcome of the Revolution. Yet none left a legacy of influence that matches that of George Washington. Without Washington, there would have been no lasting Continental Army; without the Continental Army, there would have been no United States. The American colonies would have remained a part of the British Empire and faced a powerless fate similar to that of other colonies. Leaders of the Revolution would have been executed or otherwise punished.

Washington basically ensured the existence of a country that is today the world's longest-surviving democracy and its single most influential and powerful nation. George Washington more than earned the honored title of "Father of His Country."

2

YORKTOWN, VIRGINIA

May–October, 1781

The Battle of Yorktown was the climax of the American Revolution and its outcome resulted in the independence of the United States of America. The battle pitted the best of the American and French military leaders against the largest British force in North America. It was at Yorktown that Generals George Washington (1) and Jean Baptiste de Rochambeau (24) joined to surround the retreating army of General Charles Cornwallis (22) along the Virginia coast. Admiral François de Grasse (27) awaited offshore with his fleet of thirty-six warships to both block British reinforcements and prevent British evacuation.

The idea that a group of poorly armed, loosely organized colonists would have the audacity to challenge the well-equipped, experienced army and navy of King George III (20) seemed preposterous when the Revolution's first shots rang out at Lexington and Concord (43) in 1775. The rebels' chances of success appeared even more far-fetched when the American colonies formally declared their independence from Great Britain on July 4, 1776 (14).

Washington lost a series of battles around New York City during the first year of the Revolution and withdrew the bulk of his army to fight another day. In the interim, several British commanders had unintentionally aided the American efforts with their military ineptness and their arrogant belief that the rebels would agree to a diplomatic end of their revolt.

The Revolution held little promise of success until the American victory at Saratoga (3) in October 1777. The poorly executed British plan to divide New England from the other states by occupying New York's Hudson River Valley had resulted not only in the surrender of nearly 6,000 Redcoats but also in the French recognition of the United States as an independent nation. With the momentum finally working for them, the Americans found support from Spain and the Netherlands as well. Admittedly, the Europeans were more interested in an excuse to war against Britain than in the fate of the colonies, but the Americans benefited nevertheless.

However, by 1778, the war in the Northern states had come to a stalemate, neither side able to gain the upper hand. The British occupied New York, but they were too weak to crush the rebel army while Washington, who remained in the field, similarly lacked the strength to attack the main Redcoat army.

In late 1778, the British commander General Henry Clinton (17) used his superior sea mobility to transfer much of his army under General Charles Cornwallis to the Southern states, where they occupied Savannah (80) and then Charleston (47) in May 1780. Clinton planned for Cornwallis to neutralize and further isolate the Southern states in order to cut off supplies and man power to Washington.

Washington countered by dispatching Nathanael Greene (4), one of his ablest generals, to command the American troops in the South. From 1779 to 1781, Greene and other American commanders fought a series of hit-and-run maneuvers that depleted and exhausted the British. In the spring of 1781—after the battles of Kings Mountain (36), Cowpens (18), and Guilford Courthouse (26)—Cornwallis decided his best course of action was to march to the Virginia coast via North Carolina, there to await supplies and reinforcements from England or to evacuate his army by sea if necessary. At the village of Yorktown, near where the York River empties into Chesapeake Bay, Cornwallis established his defenses in early August. He also fortified an outpost across the river at Gloucester.

Meanwhile, more than 7,000 French soldiers, commanded by Jean Baptiste de Rochambeau, joined Washington's army outside New York City, and a French fleet, led by Admiral François de Grasse, waited in the Caribbean, prepared to sail northward. Washington initially wanted de Grasse to blockade the New York harbor while the combined Franco-American armies attacked Clinton's force. The two French

leaders, learning of the British retreat to Yorktown, proposed instead that they attack Cornwallis. Washington agreed, and on August 21, 1781, he and his main army joined Rochambeau to cover the 200 miles to Yorktown in only fifteen days. Clinton, still convinced New York was the primary rebel target, failed to assist the British army in the South.

While the allied infantry was on its way south, the French navy drove away the British ships in the area at the Battle of Chesapeake Capes (13) in early September. De Grasse then blockaded the entrance to Chesapeake Bay and landed 3,000 additional soldiers to reinforce the growing allied army around Yorktown.

By October 6, Washington had the 9,500-man British force surrounded with its back to the York River while his 20,000-man allied army occupied positions to the river's east, south, and west. De Grasse's navy blocked withdrawal down the river into Chesapeake Bay and to the Atlantic. Three days later Washington's fifty-two siege guns began pounding the British positions while his men dug trenches toward the primary enemy defensive redoubts. The Americans and French captured the forward British fortifications on October 14 and positioned their artillery so they could fire directly into the remaining British defenses. Two days later a British counterattack failed. On October 17, Cornwallis, with casualties mounting from the artillery barrages and no means of escape, asked for a cease-fire. On October 19 he agreed to unconditional surrender.

The British command lost 600 dead or wounded; nearly 8,000 became prisoners. Captured arms included 214 pieces of artillery and more than 7,000 small arms. American losses numbered only 20 dead and 56 wounded. French casualties included 52 killed and 134 wounded.

Cornwallis, claiming illness, sent his deputy Charles O'Hara to surrender in his place. While the British band played "The World Upside Down," O'Hara approached Rochambeau to surrender his sword to his European peer rather than the rebel colonist. The French officer recognized the ploy and deferred to Washington. The American commander turned to his own deputy, Benjamin Lincoln (76), who accepted O'Hara's sword—deputy to deputy—and the British surrender.

Several skirmishes occurred after Yorktown, but for all practical purposes, the Revolution was over. The upheaval and embarrassment over the defeat at Yorktown further turned the British people against the war and brought down the sitting government. The new officials ratified the Treaty of Paris (69) on September 1, 1783, bringing an official end to the conflict and acknowledging the independence of the United States.

Yorktown's influence on the Revolutionary War and the future of the United States is exceeded on this list only by George Washington. Saratoga, which opened the way to final victory, and the leadership of Nathanael Greene in the Southern Campaign are the only battle and leader that even challenge its place in these rankings.

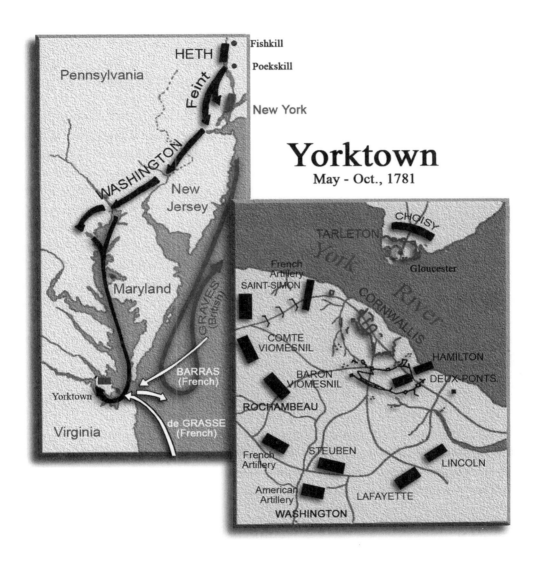

3

SARATOGA, NEW YORK

October 7, 1777

The Battle of Saratoga was the turning point in the American Revolution. The American victory thwarted the British plan to divide the New England colonies from the Southern ones along the Hudson River Valley. More importantly, the battle proved that the Americans could defeat the British in a conventional battle, which greatly boosted morale and confidence of the Revolutionaries. Furthermore, it brought much needed support from France and other European counties (5) that now recognized the Americans might very well be successful in their struggle for independence.

From the first days of the Revolution at Lexington and Concord (43), the rebel Americans had suffered a lack of arms and supplies, the absence of a navy, and the weak and wavering commitment of many of the colonists themselves. Outmanned and outgunned, the Continental Army (7) under General George Washington (1) had still been able to force the British out of Boston before losing a series of battles that led to the Redcoat capture and occupation of New York in late 1776. Perpetually short of soldiers, arms, gunpowder, ammunition, rations, and other equipment while opposing one of the world's strongest and best-equipped armies, Washington decided to follow a protracted defensive war rather than risk traditional offenses on the battlefields.

Washington did, however, need the occasional victory to maintain the morale of his troops and to encourage the enlistment of replacements. He achieved this with the surprise attacks against British winter garrisons at Trenton (8) and Princeton, New Jersey, in December 1776 and January 1777.

Meanwhile, British leaders, tired of the lack of decisive action, developed plans to crush the Rebellion. General William Howe (15), commander in chief of British forces in America with his headquarters in New York City, lobbied London for permission to march against the rebel capital of Philadelphia with an offensive in the summer of 1777. With their seat of government destroyed, the rebels, Howe surmised, would surrender. In Canada, General John Burgoyne (33) proposed a move down the Hudson River Valley in two columns while Howe moved north from New York. The two armies meeting in the vicinity of Albany would separate the New

England states, where the Rebellion had the most support of the people, from the other colonies, which provided much of the supplies for the army. Of the two plans, Burgoyne's made the most sense. However, officials in London approved both plans, which called for more offensive operations than the British army in North America could properly conduct or support.

Howe further complicated the British plans when he took a circuitous route by sea through Maryland instead of marching directly over land from New York to Philadelphia. Although Washington attempted to defend the American capital, he refused to risk his army in sustained combat. By October the British occupied Philadelphia when Washington left the city to the invaders and withdrew to winter quarters.

Burgoyne had his setbacks as well. Howe's slow advance against Philadelphia prevented his movement north to support the invasion from Canada. Then the British column supporting Burgoyne in the east, commanded by Colonel Barry St. Leger (64), had the opposite effect than intended. St. Leger's force, consisting of 800 regulars and irregulars and about 1,000 Native American (99) allies, was supposed to elicit support from Americans wavering between Revolutionaries and Loyalists (34). But the colonists, veterans of more than a century of bloody warfare with the Indians,

were outraged to see the British allied with their traditional enemies and united to oppose them.

St. Leger assembled his army on the southeastern shore of Lake Ontario at Oswego and then marched 45 miles east to Fort Stanwix where the Americans had gathered sufficient troops to block his advance. When many of his Native Americans deserted because they believed they were suffering the bulk of the casualties, St. Leger retreated back to Canada without offering a significant fight.

Burgoyne's column initially had more success when on July 1 the British captured Fort Ticonderoga with little resistance. The route onward to Albany, however, was heavily wooded, infested with summer insects, and filled with challenges. The American commander, General Horatio Gates (31), destroyed bridges, felled trees across roads, and even rerouted streams to create a series of obstacles to delay the British march.

By the time Burgoyne reached the area of Saratoga, Gates had gathered a force of 10,000 Americans who had dug in on Bemis Heights about 10 miles south of town. They outnumbered the British force of 6,500. On September 19, Burgoyne attempted to flank the American defenses by sending General Simon Fraser and 2,000 men to seize the high ground near Freeman's Farm.

Gates countered with a force led by General Benedict Arnold (85) and a unit of expert marksmen commanded by General Daniel Morgan (35). Although Morgan's sharpshooters killed or wounded many of the British officers, the Redcoat artillery finally broke the American ranks and forced the rebels to withdraw back to Bemis Heights. Gates's losses numbered about 300, less than half the British casualties.

Over the next two weeks, an additional 1,000 militiamen joined Gates's defenses. Burgoyne, confronted with supply shortages and demoralized troops, finally decided he had to attack. On October 7, he once again ordered Fraser and 1,600 men against the rebel left flank. Gates deployed Morgan and others to meet the advance in the vicinity of Freeman's Farm. In a brief battle, the Americans repelled the British, inflicting 600 casualties—including Fraser—as opposed to 150 rebel losses.

The British withdrew to Saratoga where more and more Americans arrived to surround the town. On October 17, Burgoyne surrendered the remnants of his exhausted army to Gates.

Burgoyne's surrender had both an immediate and long-range impact on the Revolution. His failure to cut the colonies in half revived the rebel's determination to continue to fight. The huge supply of British small arms and artillery pieces that fell into the hands of the Americans strengthened the army and the will of the rebels. Furthermore, the effects of the battle's outcome also extended far beyond the Hudson

River Valley and North America. The French, sympathetic with the Americans because they hated the British, now saw that supporting the rebels would gain them a new ally against their long-term English enemies. Three months after the Battle of Saratoga, France and the United States signed a treaty of alliance. A month later the French declared war against Great Britain. Encouraged by the actions of France, the Spanish and the Dutch joined the conflict against the British over the next two years.

French backing brought much-needed weapons and supplies to support the Continental Army. More importantly, the powerful French navy protected rebel ports while also slowing the movement of men and equipment from England to the United States. Instead of a Rebellion confined to North America, the British now faced a multifaceted war of international proportions.

Saratoga was the turning point of the American Revolution that led to the final victory at Yorktown (2) and the assured independence of the United States. Only Washington and Yorktown exceed its influence on this list. Washington and his fellow rebels might have very well gone on to victory even if Burgoyne had won at Saratoga, but their fight would have been longer and much more costly. Saratoga truly marked the beginning of the end of the British occupation of its former American colonies.

4

NATHANAEL GREENE

American General

1742–1786

Nathanael Greene ranks second only to George Washington (1) as the most influential individual of the Revolutionary War. After being present during almost every major battle in the North, Greene then took command in the South in 1780. There he led the campaigns that resulted in the ultimate victory at Yorktown (2). In addition to bringing his battlefield leadership to the war, Greene served more than two years as the quartermaster general of the Continental Army (7) where he standardized and streamlined the army's supply system.

Greene rose from an unusual background for a military man. Born in the summer of 1742 in Potowomut, Rhode Island, into a family of wealthy merchant Quakers, Greene received only a basic education when a boy; however, he watched a parade of local militia and became interested in things military, which led to him studying history. Ultimately in his quest to learn more about tactics and warfare, Greene became well read even though he later said, "I lament the want of a liberal education."

This focus on military matters led him first into trouble. His warlike interests evoked the ire of Quaker leaders to the extent that they dismissed him from the Society of Friends.

Then in August 1774, Greene helped organize a militia company known as the East Greenwich Kentish Guards. Despite his being a founding member of the unit, some other members questioned Greene's physical abilities because of a stiff knee that resulted from a childhood injury. Influential friends stood up for Greene, however, and he remained in the militia. The Rhode Island Loyalist (34) governor, supporting King George III (20), refused to allow his militias to join the other rebels at Lexington and Concord (43) in April 1775, but the following month the colony's pro-rebel legislature authorized three regiments to join the Boston Siege (50) with Greene in command as a brigadier general.

Greene fought through the siege but missed the Battle of Bunker Hill (23) because he had returned to Rhode Island for supplies for his regiments. Upon rejoining his unit, he met Washington, who was impressed with the young officer. Washington awarded Greene a commission as brigadier general in the Continental Army and considered him a close confidant. Greene admired his new commander and named his first-born son in honor of Washington.

After the British evacuated Boston, Greene briefly commanded the city's occupation before joining Washington in the New York campaign. Greene missed the Battle of Long Island (32) because of illness but was in the midst of the action at Harlem Heights on September 16, 1776. He then took charge of the rebel defenses at Fort Lee, New Jersey, and Fort Washington (86) across the river on Manhattan Island where he made his only major mistake of the war. In an effort to stage another Bunker Hill, Greene ordered Fort Washington to hold against an attack by a superior British force. The defense failed. Nearly the entire garrison of 3,000 was taken prisoner by the British. Greene then wisely withdrew from Fort Lee and rejoined Washington further south in New Jersey.

During the next year Greene performed superbly at Trenton (8) and Princeton. He then met with the Continental Congress (10) as Washington's representative in March 1777 to convince the assembly how desperately the army needed supplies. At Brandywine (72) on September 11, Greene marched his division 4 miles in less than an hour to cover the retreat of the main army. On October 4, 1777 his command led the army's left wing at Germantown, Pennsylvania (48).

The long winter of 1777–1778 proved extremely difficult for the Continental Army at Valley Forge (39), making clear Washington had to improve the supply system. Washington called upon Greene, now a major general, to assume the new rank of quartermaster general on March 2, 1778. Greene accepted but confessed that neither he nor anyone else had ever heard of such a position. Nevertheless, he immediately improved the transportation system and established forward depots near the fighting regiments. He also lobbied the Continental Congress for additional funds and signed promissory notes on his own accounts when he lacked sufficient government funds to procure what Washington needed.

During the next two years, Greene remained a close confidant of Washington. In addition to his quartermaster duties, he continued to command forces in the field and participated in the Battle of Monmouth (59) in June 1778 and returned to his native Rhode Island to fight in the Battle of Newport (82) the following July and August. He was at West Point, New York (30), when it was revealed that Benedict Arnold (85) was a traitor and headed the court of thirteen generals that tried British Major John Andre as a spy.

While in New York, Greene quarreled with the Continental Congress over its plan to requisition supplies from the individual states and resigned as quartermaster general on July 25. Washington supported Greene's decision and with the defeat of General Horatio Gates (31) at Camden, South Carolina (65), dispatched Greene to command the army in the South to oppose Charles Cornwallis (22).

Greene arrived in South Carolina and reorganized the supply system using the model of field depots and an improved transportation system he had established in the North. He increased the training levels and morale of the army and

then made the daring move of dividing his force. Half his army, led by General Daniel Morgan (35), marched to defeat the British at Cowpens, South Carolina (18), on January 17, 1781. Greene took the other half and fortified Guilford Courthouse, North Carolina (26). In the battle that followed on March 15, Greene did not defeat Cornwallis but so weakened his force that the British general decided to quit his quest for victory in the South and to march northward to rejoin other forces. Greene often said and wrote during this period, "We fight, get beat, rise, and fight again."

While Washington and his French allies (5) made plans to block Cornwallis at Yorktown, Greene continued his offensive to defeat the remaining British in South Carolina. On September 8 he crippled the British forces occupying the interior of South Carolina at the Battle of Eutaw Springs (63) and then moved to besiege the Redcoat stronghold at Charleston. Little further fighting occurred after Cornwallis surrendered, but the British held out for another year before evacuating the port city.

After the war Greene experienced severe financial difficulties as he attempted to settle personal notes and promises he had made to supply the rebel army. In 1785 he sold his remaining property in the North and moved to an estate near Savannah, Georgia, that had been confiscated from a Loyalist. A year later, on June 19, 1786, Greene died at the age of forty-four, apparently from complications of sunstroke. He was buried in the cemetery of Christ Episcopal Church in Savannah, but his remains were moved to a monument erected for him in the city's Johnston Square in 1902. The first great hero of the American South was oddly a Quaker Yankee from Rhode Island.

Throughout the war Washington made it clear that were he to be killed or captured, he wanted Greene to take command of the army. Greene's abilities as quartermaster general maintained the army during its most difficult years and his leadership in the South led to the final success of the Revolution. Thomas Jefferson (87) praised Greene as "second to no one in enterprise, in resource, in sound judgment, promptitude of decision, and every other military talent."

Nathanael Greene does not share the spotlight with George Washington, but the "Father of His Country" might very well not have survived had it not been for his trusted subordinate. Greene is one of the few individuals whose role in the Revolution was truly crucial and without whose help the effort might well have failed. For this reason he ranks below only Washington, Yorktown, and Saratoga (3) in influence.

5

AMERICAN ALLIES

1775–1783

The Americans did not stand alone in their fight against Great Britain. France, Spain, and the Netherlands joined the rebellious colonies in the war against their nemesis while a half-dozen other European countries united in an Armed Neutrality to challenge Britain's naval superiority that dominated trade on the seas. These allies supported the Americans to increase their own land claims around the world and to generate profit for their merchants. While a few Europeans shared the American beliefs in liberty and individual rights, the overwhelming reason behind the cohesiveness of the allies was a shared hatred of the British. The allies could also see future advantage for themselves if the American Revolution succeeded. While in the end, each country was involved for its own gain, the Americans benefited the most.

Great Britain's victory in the Seven Years' War (1756–1763) established the British Empire as the leading military power of the time. The defeated French and Spanish, in particular, suffered under the terms of the Treaty of Paris in 1763 that gave much of their territory in North America and the West Indies (45) to the British. The American colonists, who fought alongside the British in what was known as the French and Indian War, benefited little from the English victory. Instead of granting additional rights to the colonies, the British taxed the Americans to pay for the war debts, creating unrest that eventually led to the opening of the Revolution at Lexington and Concord (43) in April 1775.

Europe, particularly France, observed the increase in tensions between Britain and the American colonists with interest. For the French, any opposition to King George III (20) could only help them in their own efforts to regain lost territory and prestige. Liberal French thinkers admired the idea of American liberty and encouraged their country to support the rebels. Americans were wary of the French, and some still strongly resented France for its use of Native Americans (99) against them in the recent hostilities. The binding force behind any relationship between the French and Americans, however, was neither ideological nor economic. Rather they joined together to do battle against a common enemy.

As much as France wanted to help the Americans against the British at the beginning of the Revolution, the French were not yet strong enough militarily or sufficiently confident that the rebels might not negotiate some kind of agreement to remain in the English fold. So, instead of open support, they clandestinely provided economic and military aid to the Americans. In May 1776, the French established paperwork for the fictitious firm of Hortalez and Cie, led by Pierre de Beaumarchais (29), to funnel supplies into North America. In early 1777 the first shipments of 200 cannons, gunpowder, and other supplies—including blankets, shoes, and clothing to outfit 25,000 soldiers—arrived. Encouraged by the *Declaration of Independence* (14) on July 4, 1776, the French government led by King Louis XVI increased their support. Over the next two years, Hortalez and Cie supplied fully 90 percent of all the gunpowder used by the rebels.

The American victory at Saratoga (3) in October 1777 inspired the British to consider giving the Americans home rule within the Empire. France—fearful of a reconciliation between the King and the colonies and now convinced by Saratoga that the Americans just might win—offered a treaty of alliance to recognize the independence of the United States and officially provide support to defeat the British. On May 4, 1778, the Continental Congress (10) ratified the treaty, joining the Americans and French against the British.

Early military efforts by the French did not go well. At Newport, Rhode Island (82), in late summer 1778, the French fleet withdrew from the harbor in the middle of a battle and sailed to the Caribbean, causing doubts among some Americans about

the benefits of the alliance. When France sent additional supplies and then deployed another fleet and field army over the ensuing months, support for the alliance grew. By the time the French flotilla held off the British at Chesapeake Capes (13) and the French infantry helped storm the enemy redoubts at Yorktown (2) in 1781, the Americans and French were united both at sea and on land.

Spain had also suffered from the Seven Years' War and wanted to retaliate against the British. Like the French, they, too, supplied war materials to the rebels either directly or through the French front company Hortalez and Cie in Paris. Once the Spanish were also convinced that the Americans had a chance of success, they declared war on Great Britain on June 21, 1779. Besides contributing their fleet to oppose the British, the Spanish also ordered their governor of Louisiana, Bernardo de Galvez (40), to recapture territory along the Gulf Coast, lost to the English in the Seven Years' War. By the end of the Revolution, Galvez had taken the major British forts in Mississippi, Alabama, and West Florida.

Holland joined France and Spain by declaring war against Great Britain in 1780, dispatching its fleet against the British and providing monetary loans to the Americans. Over the next three years Russia, Denmark, Norway, the Holy Roman Empire, Prussia, Portugal, and Sicily all joined the Armed Neutrality that united European countries in a "passive hostility" against England. The Armed Neutrality freed neutral-flagged merchant vessels to sail into and deliver supplies to foreign ports regardless of their status of war with other countries. These efforts weakened British control of the seas and increased the amount of non-British supplies reaching the Americans.

In the end, the Americans benefited far more than their allies from their joint efforts. While the rebels accomplished much with little in the war's early years, the clandestine support from France had its influence. If France and Spain, and to a lesser degree Holland, had not declared war on Great Britain, the ultimate end to the American Revolution might have been different. The French gained some prestige and territory, but the seeds of liberty from the Americans had been planted in its own people, and this would soon lead to France's own revolution to oust their king. Spain secured vast land on the Gulf Coast and west of the Mississippi River from the war's aftermath. The Spanish later transferred much of the territory to the French who, in turn, sold it for a few cents per acre to the United States as part of the Louisiana Purchase when France needed funds for other wars.

It is simply not correct to state that the American rebels won their independence from Great Britain. They did so only with the enormous direct assistance of money, supplies, men, and naval assets from their allies. While the intentions of these contrived varied—and were always self-serving—their assistance led to Yorktown and final victory. The influence of America's allies is exceeded in the Revolution only by the rebel leaders George Washington (1) and Nathanael Greene (4), the final victory at Yorktown, and the battle at Saratoga that encouraged the European countries to recognize the United States.

6

ROBERT MORRIS

American Financier

1734–1806

While the best-known heroes of the American Revolution emerged from the halls of the Continental Congress (10) and championed the battlefields from Boston to Charleston, victory for the Americans would not have been possible without Robert Morris, the Financier of the Revolution. Morris was solely responsible for securing money to pay the troops and to purchase the arms, ammunition, and other supplies. When sufficient funds were not available, he drew upon his own personal fortune to finance the Revolution.

Robert Morris began life on January 31, 1734, near Liverpool, England, born into a family headed by a tobacco merchant. At age thirteen, Morris and his father emigrated to Oxford, Maryland, where the boy studied under a series of tutors. Quickly exceeding the knowledge of his teachers, he went to Philadelphia where he became a clerk in a shipping and banking firm owned by Charles Willing. By the time Morris reached age sixteen, he had become an apprentice in the company and four years later, on the death of his employer, joined Willing's son as a full partner in the firm.

Over the next decade, Morris built the import, export, and banking business, and he became a wealthy and influential member of Philadelphia society. The Stamp Act of 1765 (19) significantly impacted his firm's profits, causing Morris to join the protest movement against British control. On September 18, 1775, the Continental Congress established a committee to secure arms and ammunition for the army, and that committee contracted with Morris's company. The first ship in the newly established U.S. Navy, the *Alfred,* came from the Morris fleet of cargo vessels.

On November 3, 1775, Morris joined the Congress as a delegate from Pennsylvania. Initially he opposed independence in hopes of a peaceful reconciliation with King George III (20), but by the summer of 1776, he saw that was not possible and signed the *Declaration of Independence* (14). Morris's fellow members of Congress recognized his expertise in finance and shipping and looked to him for advice as well as direct action. He initiated lotteries to raise cash and dispatched his own fleet as privateers to capture English shipping goods. When there were insufficient funds to pay soldiers returning from the disastrous Canada Invasion (84), Morris lent $10,000 of his own money to cover the debts.

George Washington (1) came to personally rely on Morris to pay and supply his soldiers. Desperate to hold his army together after their retreat from New York, Washington promised each soldier a $10 bonus—money he did not have. Washington turned to Morris who approached a wealthy Quaker merchant for a loan of $50,000. When the Quaker asked what would be provided to secure the loan, Morris replied, "My word and my honor." The merchant responded, "Thou shall have it."

In March 1778, Morris signed the *Articles of Confederation* (16) and in August assumed the chairmanship of the Congressional Committee on Finance. Because of the Pennsylvania state limits on terms, Morris left the Continental Congress the following November and within days took a seat in his state's assembly. Morris continued to use his firm and his personal influence to provide money and supplies for the army and navy. He also helped enact taxes and land sales in Pennsylvania to produce additional funding.

In 1779, Washington again called on Morris, telling him about the shortage of lead to make musket balls. Morris immediately gathered lead spouting from houses, lead pipes, and any other lead available. In the midst of the scrounging, one of Morris's ships arrived in port carrying tons of lead as ballast. Morris consolidated the metal, employed a hundred men to make bullets, and within days had filled the musket ball bags of the Continental Army (7).

During this period Morris also became a center of controversy when detractors accused him of increasing his personal wealth while supplying the Revolution. His supporters, who outnumbered his opponents, knew that Morris, a merchant and businessman, was also contributing much more to the Revolution than he was personally profiting.

Morris had what he considered more pressing problems. He had always opposed the Continental Congress issuing paper currency with no gold or silver backing. In 1781 the currency system collapsed, making the paper bills worth more as wallpaper than as money. When Morris assumed the position of superintendent of finances for the United States, the term "as worthless as a Continental" was not a figurative term. One of his first actions was to establish a national financial institution to centralize the finances of the Revolution and country. In founding the Bank of North America, he not only coordinated the contributions from the states but also, more importantly, opened the way for hard currency loans from European countries.

When Charles Cornwallis (22) retreated toward Yorktown (2) in 1781, the Americans moved to unite their northern and southern armies to defeat the British. Once again their major obstacle was money—to pay the troops and purchase supplies. Washington wrote Morris that many of his troops were reluctant to march south but that "a little hard money would put them in a proper temper." Once again Morris solved the problem. He approached French officers, now allied with the Americans, for a loan of $200,000—which they approved on Morris's personal promise of repayment. Morris forwarded the money to Washington.

Morris, who is attributed with creating the dollar sign ($), continued in the war's final days to rely on his own fortune when other funds were not available. On September 20, 1781, he wrote to the governor of Pennsylvania, stating, "The late movements of the army have so entirely drained me of money that I have been obliged to pledge my personal credit very deeply in a variety of instances, besides borrowing money from my friends and advancing to promote to public service every shilling of my own."

The end of the war left both Morris and the United States deeply in debt. For his country he attempted to levy various taxes to pay off the national debt but received little cooperation from the states. By renegotiating loans, he barely managed to keep the country's finances afloat.

Morris left government to return to private business in 1783. One of his ships, the *Empress of China*, is believed to have been the first to cross the Pacific to begin trade with Asia. In 1787, he served as a delegate to the Constitutional Convention and supported ratification of the resulting Constitution.

Back in Pennsylvania he speculated in land but fell deeper in debt from taxes and interest on loans he had secured during the Revolution. In 1798 his creditors had him arrested, and he spent three years in debtor's prison. His release was finally gained through the Bankruptcy Laws passed by Congress in part to free the financier.

Morris spent the remainder of his days in poor health and broke. He died on May 8, 1806, and is buried at Christ Church in Philadelphia.

The orators of Congress and the generals on the battlefields led the Rebellion, but it was the financial genius of Robert Morris that provided the "beans and bullets" that meant the difference between success and failure. John Adams (51) wrote of him, "I think he has a masterly understanding, an open temper, and an honest heart."

CONTINENTAL ARMY

1775–1783

The Continental Army unified the soldiers of the thirteen states for the first time and bore the brunt of the fighting required to secure independence for the United States. These "regulars," described in their early years by friend and foe alike as "uncoordinated amateurs," went through a series of organizations and reorganizations before they emerged with enough training, skills, and leadership to be victorious.

From the time the English settled in North America, each colony organized its own militia to defend itself against Native American attacks. These militia units, formed from villages and surrounding farms, elected their own leaders and only loosely followed any military discipline. Some of the colonial militias joined the British during the French and Indian War from 1754 to 1763, but at no time was there any real desire by the colonies to form a united military force.

After the local militias fought the British at Lexington and Concord (43) on April 19, 1775, however, they joined other New England militia units—from Massachusetts, Connecticut, Rhode Island, and New Hampshire—to besiege the Redcoat garrison at Boston (50). Prior to this siege, delegates of the Continental Congress (10) had had an aversion to a standing army, fearing loss of powers for the individual states. They now realized, however, that the numerous militia units from many states could not operate without central command and control. On June 14, Congress created the Continental Army composed of the state militias surrounding Boston. The next day, by a unanimous vote, they selected George Washington (1) as the army's commander. Congress also selected four major generals and eight brigadier generals from the state militias to serve as Washington's subordinates.

Washington arrived at Boston on July 3 to take command of 17,000 Continental soldiers, all former militiamen and all of whom were nearing the expiration of their year of service commitment. Representatives of the New England colonies met with Washington and determined that the army should be increased in size to 20,370 infantrymen organized into 26 battalions (also called regiments at the time) of eight companies each. Numbers for artillery and cavalry were not yet determined.

Over the next six months, Washington recruited vigorously as he converted militia companies and regiments into regular units. Fewer than 6,000 men volunteered, so Washington had to ask the former militiamen to remain on active duty after their discharge dates. On January 1, 1776, the old militia units from the four states sent to surround Boston reorganized into the regiments under numerical designations from the 1st through the 22nd. Their commanders and internal organizations remained mostly unchanged.

Washington continued to raise the level of leadership and discipline in the regular army while making it clear to Congress that he thought the militias that had not been inducted into the Continental Army did more harm than good to the war effort. He also saw short-term enlistments as one of his biggest problems. In a letter to his military secretary, John Reed, on February 1, 1776, he wrote, "It takes you two or three months to bring new men in any tolerable degree acquainted with their duty. It takes a longer time to bring a people of the temper and genius of these into such a subordinate way of thinking as is necessary for a soldier. Before this is accomplished, the time approaches for their dismissal."

On September 16, 1776, Congress responded to Washington by ordering the thirteen states to contribute eighty-eight regiments based on their proportional populations. They also authorized enlistment bounties and set the terms of enlistment to be "the length of the war." A reorganization on March 29, 1779, reduced the number of regular regiments to eighty, and in the latter years there was another reduction down to fifty-eight. Independent state militias remained on duty, used mostly for local defense and occasionally to support operations of the regular army.

Total enlistments during the entire war numbered 231,771. Multiple re-enlistments by the same soldiers, battle casualties, disease, and desertion meant that nowhere near this number served at any one time. In fact, the greatest strength the Continental Army ever amassed was in late 1778 when its ranks numbered 35,000. At no time did Washington have more than 17,000 soldiers in the field, and that count includes local militiamen as well as regulars. During the Trenton (8) and Princeton campaign, Washington's army totaled a mere 4,000 soldiers.

As with armies past and future, the enlisted men of the Continental Army came from among the poorest. Many joined for regular pay and rations, which they later found to be not so regular; some joined out of a spirit of adventure that has always prompted young men to leave home and take up arms; few signed up out of any sense of patriotism, this sentiment being foreign to men who had little exposure to life beyond their families and villages.

Officers generally came from the more affluent, better-educated colonists, but their petty bickering over rank and privilege often interfered with their leadership. More pressing than patriotism for many of these land- and business-owners was the fight for opportunity to create their own wealth and to avoid being tried for treason if the Revolution failed.

After the British signed the Treaty of Paris (69) and finally evacuated New York, neither Congress nor the newly independent American people wanted a peacetime military force. On September 3, 1783, Congress reduced the army to 700 men and then the following year to 80 "with a proportional number of officers, no officers above the rank of captain."

The success of the Continental Army, like that of the Revolution itself, defied logic. From inception to victory, it was leaders like Washington and his subordinates who made the army into a force capable of defeating the world's most powerful empire. While the American people learned and relearned that liberty and independence cannot exist without a large standing military to defend them, the Continental Army evolved into the United States Army of today that is now the world's most powerful military. Without those soldiers who endured the struggle for freedom, there could not have been a victory. The Continental Army ranks near the top of this list—exceeded only by its primary leaders and the battles the army itself won.

8

TRENTON, NEW JERSEY

December 26, 1776

George Washington (1) and his Continental Army (7) gained their first victory over the Hessian mercenaries (37) at the Battle of Trenton on the morning after Christmas in 1776. The battle served as a rallying point for the American people, who had become disillusioned with the failures of the Revolution. After Trenton, and the subsequent victory at Princeton a week later, volunteers for the militias came forward and the civilian population renewed their support in providing supplies and provisions for the rebel army.

After losses on Long Island (32) in August, at White Plains (77) in October, and at Fort Washington (86) in November, the Continental Army had been forced to retreat into New Jersey with the British army in pursuit. Washington withdrew the main body of the army southward with General Charles Lee (79) responsible for the rear guard. Along the way many of the enlistment contracts of the Continental Army and state militia soldiers expired, and they left the ranks to return home. Other soldiers simply deserted. Civilians, who had generally supported the army prior to the defeats in New York, now feared the Revolution was a lost cause and ceased providing food and even shelter during the severe winter weather.

Felling trees across roads and destroying bridges in his rear to slow the pursuing British under General William Howe (15) as he retreated southward from New York, Washington reached the Delaware River in early December and gathered all available boats to cross into Pennsylvania. By the time the Continental Army reached Pennsylvania, it consisted of only 3,000 men, many of whom suffered from illness or wounds.

Howe reached the Delaware on December 8 to be met by a feeble rebel artillery barrage from across the river. Although he substantially outnumbered the demoralized and poorly equipped rebels, the British general decided to take up winter quarters in New Jersey and New York rather than pursue the Americans. His subordinates recommend that they "finish off the rebels," but neither their pleas nor the news that one of his cavalry patrols had captured Lee, Washington's second in command, on December 13, changed his mind.

Well aware that support for his army and the Revolution might not last the winter, Washington assumed the offensive. One thousand Pennsylvanian militiamen and a few hundred from New Jersey answered his call for reinforcements, increasing his troop strength to about 4,700. Using information from a civilian informant on the numbers and dispositions of Hessian troops occupying Trenton, Washington selected that New Jersey town as his objective. To add to his chances of success, the American general decided to attack in the early morning hours after Christmas Day when he hoped the Hessians would be sleeping off their holiday celebrations.

After dark on December 25, Washington ferried his men across the Delaware. Winds and an icy snowstorm allowed the rebels to get only about two-thirds of their attack force across the river, but as daylight neared, Washington had 2,400 soldiers and 18 cannons prepared for the attack.

Meanwhile in Trenton, the 1,400-man garrison of Hessians slept in their warm quarters, the approaches of the town guarded only by a few pickets. Despite subsequent stories to the contrary, few suffered hangovers from celebrating. They simply believed they had little to fear in the way of attacks from the disorganized rebels in the terrible weather.

In fact, their commander, Colonel Johann Rall, had called off his regular night patrols because of the snowstorm. Rall had also delayed the building of fortifications at the town's primary approaches, declaring, "Let them come. We need no trenches. We will go at them with the bayonet."

Rall had been correct about using the bayonet, but it was rebel blade rather than Hessian that shed the most blood over the next few hours. Washington's troops, delayed by the storm, did not reach Trenton until about 8:00 a.m., but they quickly swept past the Hessian sentries and advanced down the town's two main streets—King (now Warren) and Queen (now Broad). The harsh weather prevented the fire of most muskets on both sides, but the Americans were able to get their cannons in action to sweep the streets. Hessian soldiers charged from their barracks only to be met by cannon fire and rebel bayonets. Their four senior-most officers, including Rall, were killed or mortally wounded immediately. Never able to organize their units or defenses, the surviving Hessians surrendered after a one-hour fight.

At least 23 Hessians lay dead on Trenton's streets, another 90 suffered wounds, and 918 became captives of the Americans. The remainder escaped into the countryside. Washington's losses totaled 2 dead and 5 wounded in the battle and several more causalities from the cold during their march.

Washington gathered the captured Hessians, along with their weapons and stores, and recrossed the Delaware back into Pennsylvania. The much-needed supplies went to feed and arm his men while the Hessians captives ended up at Carlisle where they spent the remainder of the war building powder magazines and other structures, some of which survive today.

Within a few days, Washington again crossed the Delaware River to prepare defenses in Trenton. Howe dispatched General Charles Cornwallis (22) to retake the town, but when he approached the rebel army on January 2, 1777, Washington used campfires as a ruse for his real location and slipped past the British in the night to attack nearby Princeton the next morning. Again he gained surprise and drove the British and the Hessians from the town at the cost of 40 American dead and wounded to the enemy's losses of more than 300. Following Princeton, Washington withdrew his army into winter quarters at Morristown while Howe called off further operations until the arrival of warmer weather.

The victory at Trenton, reinforced by that at Princeton, reenergized the support for the Rebellion. Volunteers came forward to join the army and previously reluctant civilians added their moral and physical support. After a series of disastrous losses earlier in the year that had left New York and New Jersey in the hands of the British, Washington had taken the initiative and recaptured much of the territory east of the Delaware. The British, previously contemptuous of the American army, now had to admit the rebels were formidable opponents. A Hessian officer, noting the lack of trenches and breastworks at Trenton, wrote, "We must now give them the honor of fortifications."

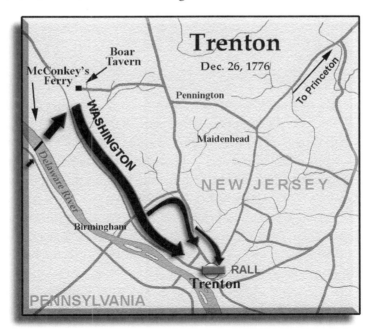

During the final preparations for the advance against Trenton, Washington explained the reasons for the attack, stating, "Necessity, dire necessity, will, nay must, justify my attack."

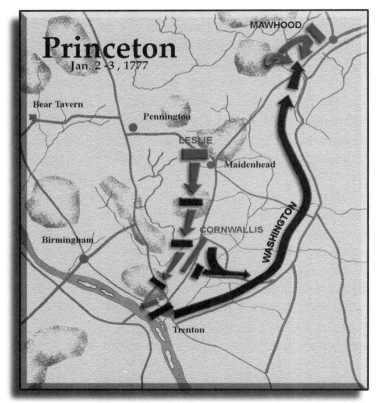

British Secretary of State George Germain (9) summarized the battle's impact in a speech to the House of Lords a few weeks after the defeat when he said, "All our hopes were blasted by the unhappy affair at Trenton."

Trenton served as a major turning point in the war, becoming "the battle that saved the Revolution." In New York the Hessians had defeated or stood against the Continental Army in every engagement. The rebel army, the Continental Congress, and the American people were tired of the war and fearful that the chances of victory were past. Trenton changed all that, giving hope to the army and the newly declared United States of America. The war was far from over, but it was Trenton that provided a beginning to the end and the promise of lasting independence. Only the battles of Saratoga (3) and Yorktown (2) had greater influence on the outcome of the American Revolutionary War.

9

GEORGE SACKVILLE GERMAIN

British Secretary of State

1716–1785

George Germain, once cashiered from the British army as "unfit to serve in any military capacity whatever," nurtured a series of political alliances during his career in Parliament to be appointed the secretary of state for American Colonies on November 10, 1775. In this position, which he held for the remainder of the war, Germain was the primary government official responsible for the colonial administration of North America and for the military operations to counter the Revolution. The secretary directed the war from London rather than in America and maintained grudges against many of his officers that dated back to his own time in uniform. In the conflict that cost the British their American colonies, many government and military officials were responsible for their defeat. But none was more responsible than George Germain.

Born as George Sackville on January 26, 1716, to a British dragoon officer in London, the future secretary of state spent much of his youth with his father in Ireland. After graduation from Dublin's Trinity University in 1734, he joined the army as an infantry officer. Over the next decade, he advanced in rank while also returning home to become a member of Parliament. Sackville saw his first combat at the Battle of Fontenoy in 1745 in the War of Austrian Succession. In a charge against enemy lines Sackville's troops penetrated so deeply that he nearly captured the French king before being severely wounded.

Recovered from his injuries, Sackville continued his military career, rising to the rank of major general over the next decade. Despite his violent temper and unpleasant personality, Sackville maintained the reputation as a competent military commander until the Battle of Minden on August 1, 1759, during the Seven Years' War. In an assault against French lines that had already killed the father of future American general Marquis de Lafayette (46), Sackville received orders to bring his cavalry reserve forward to deliver the decisive blow. Sackville, claiming his orders were not clear, failed to do so.

Accused of cowardice and deliberate disobedience that kept his fellow generals from gaining glory, Sackville faced court-martial. Sackville's influential family and friends successfully rallied behind him to prevent the court from finding him guilty of cowardice, but he was convicted of disobeying orders. The court dismissed him from the service, and King George II ordered that the judgment against Sackville as "unfit for service in any military capacity whatever" be entered in the order book of every British regiment. The king also removed Sackville from the list of personal advisors known as the Privy Councilors.

Sackville nevertheless remained popular with the British public, and he maintained important friendships with many in high positions. Meanwhile George II died and the Seven Years' War ended, events that helped bury Sackville's record.

In 1770, Sackville's wife, Lady Betty Germain, died and he became, through rights of inheritance, Lord George Germain. Rehabilitated by both time and a new title, Germain, back on the rolls of Privy Councilors since 1763, became the secretary of state for American Colonies in 1775. This position made him the primary British official in charge of ending the American Rebellion. He participated in military planning and assumed responsibility for the provision of man power and supplies. Germain also held the power to promote and relieve his subordinate generals—many of whom he still harbored ill will against. These included Guy Carleton (49), the governor of Canada, who had testified against Germain at his trial. He also held grudges against William Howe (15) and Henry Clinton (17), both of whom would become commanders of British troops fighting the rebels.

One would presume that Germain, with such a past, must have possessed brilliant leadership and administrative abilities to garner such an important position. This was simply not the case. Germain considered the Americans "country clowns" who were little more than a rabble of an army. He incorrectly assumed that he could use tactics proven on European battlefields to fight in North America and that the Loyalist (34) numbers would swell to help quell the Rebellion.

Germain also had the propensity to issue confusing and, at times, conflicting orders. His separate and differing orders to John Burgoyne (33) and Howe prior to the Battle of Saratoga (3) in October 1777 led to the pivotal American victory. The confusing orders sent to Clinton and Charles Cornwallis (22) contributed to the British surrender at Yorktown (2) in October 1781. All the while, Germain continued to guide the war from his London office from where he never developed an appreciation for the vastness of the colonies or the resolve of the rebel leaders. Except for a few officers who benefited from their close friendship with Germain, most of the British commanders remembered him for his performance at Minden and held him in low esteem.

After Yorktown even Germain realized the war was lost, and he resigned his position on February 11, 1782. Ignoring the failures that made him the individual most responsible for the loss of the American colonies and motions by members of Parliament to block his nomination, George III (20) elevated Germain from lord to viscount on the same day of his resignation.

Germain, now the Viscount Sackville, still faced opposition in Parliament but did not continue the fight. In failing health he retired to his country estate in Sussex where he died on August 26, 1785.

Throughout his military and civil career, Germain never displayed even an adequate level of competence. He is the classic example of politics trumping performance. His mistakes rarely stayed with him for long and, despite his contemptible personality, he managed to maintain a degree of popularity outside the military—especially with those royal and political leaders who really counted. Whether the British could have won the American Revolution with any other secretary of state is, of course, unknowable, but there is little doubt that the British would have had difficulty finding anyone more inept or in more constant conflict with his senior subordinates. Germain's entire career is a study of personal vendettas over patriotism.

Today Germain rarely merits attention in American history books, but he should be hailed as one of the most influential individuals in the British failure to quash the Rebellion. Without his ineptitude, short-sightedness, and petty quarrels, the war might have ended differently. Germain merits inclusion near the top of this list as the most influential British officer or official of the war.

10

CONTINENTAL CONGRESS

September 5, 1774–March 1, 1781

The Continental Congress was the primary organization that unified the colonies against Great Britain. Initially formed to counter British acts that restricted westward growth and trade, the First Continental Congress met initially on September 5, 1774. The Second Continental Congress first met on May 10, 1775, then served as the de facto national government for directing and managing the American Revolutionary War.

At the close of the French and Indian War in 1763, the victorious British took control of captured French territory in Canada and increased colonial tariffs in the colonies to pay for the conflict, taxes that provoked protests such as the Boston Tea Party. The Quebec Act of May 20, 1774 (19), recognized former land ownership by French Canadians and allowed them to continue to freely practice their Catholic religion. Another provision of the Act extended Canada's southern boundary to the Ohio River, eliminating westward claims of several colonies that included Massachusetts and Virginia.

In late May and early June 1774, the British also passed legislation, known in America as the Intolerable Acts, to punish the colonies for the Boston Tea Party protests and to raise more revenue for America's expenses. The Intolerable Acts prohibited further imports or exports from Boston Harbor until the colonists paid for the destroyed tea. The British also enacted measures to quarter soldiers in civilian houses and restricted the powers of the colonial government.

In response to these punitive measures, the Committees of Correspondence, already secretly organized in each colony, called for a meeting of colonial delegates for the First Continental Congress to begin on September 5, 1774, in Philadelphia. Fifty-five delegates came from twelve colonies. Georgia, Canada, and Florida did not participate. The First Continental Congress had no legislative authority, more resembling a consultative body than a Congress.

The delegates to the Congress greatly differed in purpose and outlook. Some supported the status quo; some proposed American home rule under British control; still others, led by John Adams (51), favored complete independence. After seven weeks of intense debate, the Congress agreed to seek a peaceful resolution. On October 20,

1774, the First Continental Congress drafted the Articles of Association that stated the colonies would boycott all British imports and cease exports to Britain until the British government repealed the Intolerable Acts. The Congress then agreed to meet again on May 10, 1775, if their demands had not been met.

By the time the Second Continental Congress convened in the spring of 1775—again without Georgia in attendance—hostilities at Lexington and Concord (43) and the beginning of the Boston Siege (50) had overcome the Articles of Association as an issue. Despite the fighting in Massachusetts, many of the delegates still supported only enough military action to force Britain to remove the Intolerable Acts. Nevertheless they agreed to raise funds for a postal department and an army and navy. The most important early action of the SCC was to appoint George Washington (1) the commander in chief of the new force.

The Second Continental Congress adjourned on August 2, 1775, but reconvened on September 12. This time Georgia sent delegates, finally bringing all thirteen colonies under the same convention. During the first year, the delegates of the Second Continental Congress remained divided. Each colony maintained its own autonomy over militias, currency, and tariffs. The failure of King George III (20) to redress their grievances and the maneuvers by the British army, however, unified the delegates for independence. By now it was evident that there would be no peaceful resolution and that each man attending the Congress as a delegate was a traitor in the eyes of the British.

On July 2, 1776, the Congress passed the *Declaration of Independence* (14) without a single dissenting vote. Two days later the delegates authenticated, printed, and distributed the document. "Victory or death" now seemed the only possible outcomes. Benjamin Franklin (25) stated, "We must all hang together, or assuredly we shall all hang separately."

Not only was the Revolution now official, but also the *Declaration of Independence* opened the way for the newly declared United States to seek foreign aid. Congress still had difficulties gathering the funds and exercising authority to conduct the war, but the representatives did the best they could under the dire circumstances. When British military action forced the Congress to flee Philadelphia, the members met in Baltimore in December 1776. They returned in March 1777 only to again be chased from the city the following September. After meeting one day in Lancaster, Pennsylvania, they moved on to nearby York where they met until June 1778. The military situation finally allowed them to return to Philadelphia on July 2, 1778, where they stayed for the remainder of the war.

While they frequently fled before the advancing British, many members of the Second Continental Congress exhibited personal bravery in support of the Revolution. Even though most of the delegates were over forty years of age, 134 of the 342 delegates elected during the tenure of the Congress served either in the Continental Army or in their states' militias. One died in combat, twelve suffered serious wounds, and twenty-three became prisoners of the British.

On November 15, 1777, the Second Continental Congress adopted the *Articles of Confederation* (16), the country's first Constitution. Key to the Articles was the provision for each state to fund the Revolution in proportion to its land mass. Debate over state boundaries delayed ratification of the Articles by all the colonies until March 1, 1781. On that same day the Second Continental Congress adjourned for the last time. The next day the delegates met again as the Congress of the Confederation. In that capacity they supervised the remainder of the Revolution.

Throughout their tenure, the First and Second Continental Congresses struggled. Created in a time of emergency with delegates either unsure or in conflict about their purpose, the Congresses still managed to issue the Articles of Association that contributed to starting the Revolution, the *Declaration of Independence* that established the United States of America, and the *Articles of Confederation* that formed the new country's first constitution.

For these accomplishments the Continental Congress merits a ranking near the top of this list and higher than the documents they produced. The two Congresses also rank so high because of their wisdom in selecting George Washington to head the Continental Army they authorized and in their diligent efforts, even though not always successful, to supply and support the soldiers in the field.

BRITISH ARMY

1775–1783

In the latter half of the eighteenth century, the British reigned invincible. Great Britain had defeated its European enemies into submission at home and turned its attention to conquering the world. Behind its status and power stood its proud, experienced, and well-equipped military. It is not surprising then that the leadership of such prowess had difficulty taking seriously a threat of revolt from a group of disorganized, inexperienced, and ill-equipped colonists living in North America. When the Rebellion became official, the British expected their army to quell the fuss quickly; they never expected their navy even to have to get overly involved. When the Americans defeated the British, they brought the world's most powerful empire to its knees. While the Redcoats fought with discipline and bravery that had marked the British army throughout history, in the Revolutionary War they lost their footing.

At the start of the Revolutionary War in 1775, the regular army of Great Britain worldwide contained more than 48,000 soldiers—39,000 infantrymen; 7,000 cavalrymen; and 2,500 artillerymen. Of this number, 8,500 were serving in North America at outposts from Canada to Florida with the majority stationed in Boston. After the first battles at Lexington and Concord (43), the British dispatched additional regiments to America and actively recruited for more in England. By 1778 the American rebels faced 50,000 British regulars plus their Hessian mercenaries (37) and Loyalist supporters (34).

These numbers are not impressive by twenty - first century standards and, in fact, were not large for their time either. Single battles on the European continent earlier in the century had boasted armies in the hundreds of thousands. Frederick the Great led an army of 77,000 against the French force of 85,000 in 1745 in the Battle of Hohenfriedeberg. In 1809 a French army of 167,000 fought against 130,000 Austrians. In contrast, the battle with the most participants in the American Revolution pitted 15,000 Redcoats against 9,500 rebels at New York City in August 1776.

The reduced size of the British force in America was the result of London's two-fold problem. First, the British people, distrustful of a large standing army, did not support compulsory military service through conscription. Second, the middle and

upper classes did not want to pay the taxes necessary to support such an army; they wanted to put down the Rebellion as cheaply as possible.

Fortunately for British army recruiters, the population of Great Britain had been booming for the past several generations, increasing 3 to 8 percent per year. Widespread poverty and unemployment encouraged many men to seek food and shelter in the military. In peacetime, volunteers signed on for lifelong commitments, but when it became more difficult to find recruits during the American Revolution, British officials lowered the enlistment commitment to three years to encourage volunteers. Most who responded to the enticements and the free liquor provided by recruiters joined for job security and for the age-old goal of leaving home to see the world. There is little evidence of men enlisting in the British army out of any sense of civil duty.

The criteria for recruits included the following: those joining the army had to be between the ages of seventeen and forty-five years old, appear in good health, and stand at least five feet six and a half inches tall. While the British army, like armies throughout history, included criminals, those from all other walks of life far eclipsed the number of felons. Nearly all British recruits shared the characteristic that they were poor. Some had been born economically deprived, while others, such as weavers, had recently lost their jobs to mechanization.

When a soldier reported to the active army, he found his pay, food, uniforms, and medical care (67) barely adequate. He also discovered that his fellow countrymen had little respect for his profession. Except for agricultural laborers, men in uniform occupied the lowest position of British workers. A popular saying of the time proclaimed, "A friend before a neighbor, a neighbor before a stranger, a stranger before a dog, and a dog before a soldier." Part of this contempt reflected the soldier's social status before he volunteered, while even more resentment came from the British practice of quartering its men in the homes of civilians rather than their own barracks.

When the majority of their regiments arrived in North America, the British army had fought no major land battles since the last days of the French and Indian War in 1763, thirteen years before. Even though few veterans remained in the ranks, the regiments were well-trained through repetitive drills before leaving England, and the men were well-disciplined by threat and use of the lash and other physical punishments. How these soldiers performed in battle varied by regiment and engagement—conflicting evaluations often emerged from the same encounter. After the Battle of Bunker Hill (23) in June 1775, British Lieutenant William Fielding wrote that his few veterans claimed that it was "the hottest fire they ever saw" and that the younger soldiers "who had never seen a ball fired" performed "with the greatest courage." Captain Francis Rawdon (73) saw the battle differently, writing that while some men fought with "infinite courage," others "behaved remarkably ill."

Most of the senior British commanders, all appointed by the king, were veterans of the Seven Years' War in Europe or the French and Indian War in North America, but few officers below the rank of colonel had ever heard a hostile shot fired. At the beginning of the American Revolution, the British officer corps contained 3,700 infantry officers and 400 cavalry officers, 60 percent of whom had purchased their commissions and gained their epaulets of rank with money rather than skill. Colonels and above were appointed by the king; ranks below could be bought from officers departing the service. However, when an officer was killed, retired, or otherwise left the army, his rank was first offered for sale to the next junior officer. This, in turn, created a chain of "promotions by purchase."

Usually only the lower commissions of ensign and lieutenant were available to men desiring military service as an officer. With this system favoring those with money, volunteers for the officer corps generally came from distinguished families whose second and later sons were not in line to inherit their fathers' wealth and titles. Their "well born" backgrounds, combined with the traditions and training of the officer corps provided mostly good leaders. In a profession where honor and bravery were expected, most British officers led from the front and shared equally in the dangers of the battlefield with their men. Generals and colonels died or suffered wounds in all the major battles; captains and lieutenants filled the casualty lists in numbers far exceeding their percentage of the total force.

After the British defeat in a minor skirmish in South Carolina in April 1781, Colonel Otho Williams wrote, "Many of our officers are mortally mortified at our late inglorious retreat. I say mortally because I cannot doubt but some of us must fall in endeavoring the next opportunity to reestablish our reputation. Dear reputation! What trouble do you occasion, what dangers do you expose us to."

In the end, the simplest evaluation of the regular British army in the American Revolution is that they lost. That is not to say, however, that they did not influence the war by fighting well, bravely, and even honorably for most of the conflict. Their final defeat was not so much the product of their performance on the battlefield as it was the failure of the British government and people to support the war. The loss of the American colonies was not the first, nor would it be the last, instance where the lack of national will undermined the prowess of the military. As the losers, the British army ranks below the Continental Army (7), but the Redcoats rank above the American militias (53) whom they out-performed and above their own Hessian mercenary and Loyalist allies as well.

12

HENRY KNOX

American General

1750–1806

Henry Knox advanced from Boston bookseller to chief of artillery of the Continental Army (7). His personal leadership in first acquiring and then moving artillery pieces and ammunition directly influenced the American victory at the Boston Siege (50) and forced the evacuation of the British. Knox became a trusted advisor and friend of General George Washington (1). He accompanied Washington in every major battle in the Northern theater, and his artillery played an important role in the final victory at Yorktown (2).

Born in Boston on July 25, 1750, to Scots-Irish immigrants, Knox terminated his formal schooling at age twelve to support his mother after his father died. He went to work for a bookseller, and at age twenty-one opened his own shop. During this period he read voraciously, especially on military history, tactics, and artillery. In 1772 he joined a local militia unit and upon the outbreak of the Revolution, left his bookstore to become a full-time soldier.

Knox performed bravely at the Battle of Bunker Hill (23) on June 17, 1775, and first met Washington the following month. The commander of the Continental Army was most impressed with the young Knox, and they immediately established a close working relationship as well as a personal and professional friendship.

On November 17, Washington appointed Knox as the army's chief of artillery with the rank of colonel despite the fact that all Knox's knowledge about artillery came only from books. Knox had no actual experience with cannon warfare, but that was hardly relevant because artillery pieces were nearly nonexistent in the Continental Army.

Colonel Knox proposed that the solution to the problem lay in the recently captured British artillery at Fort Ticonderoga (52) and requested permission to move the pieces to Boston. This was no small task, as it was the middle of winter and the travel distance was more than 300 miles. With Washington's approval Knox departed Cambridge outside Boston with a small escort and reached Ticonderoga on December 5. There he built forty-two sleds and acquired eighty yokes of oxen and a sufficient number of teamsters to move about fifty-five (the exact figure is unknown, with estimates varying from fifty to sixty) cannons.

The cannon column moved to the south end of Lake Champlain down the western side of the Hudson River to Albany. There they crossed the river and journeyed east through the rugged Berkshire Mountains. Despite heavy snows, miserable cold, and poor roads, the lead ox teams reached Cambridge on January 24, 1776. Knox, with Washington's approval, then positioned the artillery on Dorchester Heights, which commanded high ground over Boston and its harbor, forcing the British to evacuate the city in March.

For the remainder of the war, Knox was never far from Washington's side. He maneuvered the general's artillery in the battles around New York City in the fall and winter of 1776, and he was responsible for the movement of the men, horses, and artillery across the Delaware River for the attack on Trenton (8) in December, earning a promotion to brigadier general. Knox remained at Washington's side at Princeton, Valley Forge (39), Brandywine (72), Germantown (48), and Monmouth (59). While the army was in winter quarters at Morristown, New Jersey, in 1777, Knox returned to Boston to establish the Springfield Armory, which provided much-needed weapons and ammunition for the remainder of the war. In 1779, Knox founded a military academy at Morristown for the education of future officers that was a predecessor to the later U.S. Military Academy at West Point.

At Yorktown in the fall of 1781, Henry Knox's artillery performed so well that Washington later reported to Congress about Knox, saying, "The resources of his genius supplied the deficit of means." On March 22, 1782, the Continental Congress (10) promoted Knox to the rank of major general, back-dated to November 15, 1781. Knox assumed command of the defenses of West Point, New York (30), on August 29, 1782, and succeeded Washington as commander in chief on December 23, 1783. When Washington left the army on December 4, 1783, after addressing his officers at New York's Fraunces Tavern, the first hand he shook was that of his former artillery commander. Knox resigned from the army on June 20, 1784, to return to private life as a businessman in Boston.

On March 8, 1785, the former artillery commander became the secretary of war under the *Articles of Confederation* (16) and then remained in that position under the Constitution and election of Washington as the president of the United States.

Secretary Knox provided for a national militia, helped create the regular navy, formed national Indian policies, and established a series of defenses along the Atlantic coast.

Knox finally left public service on December 31, 1794, and lived out the remainder of his life on a large estate, inherited by his wife from her maternal grandfather, near Thomaston, Maine (at that time still a part of Massachusetts), near the head of the St. George's River. He died there at the age of fifty-six on October 25, 1806, of an intestinal infection from a chicken bone he had swallowed a few days previously.

Knox was known for his loyalty, military knowledge, and cheerful optimism. His critics—few that they were—noted his profanity, his pompous attitudes, and his 300-pound girth.

Knox's achievement in moving the guns from Ticonderoga to Boston alone merits his inclusion on this list. His participation in the major battles in the North and at Yorktown as well as his foresight in establishing armories and training academies earn him a ranking exceeded only by the American military leaders Washington and Nathanael Greene (4). He is truly a hero of the Revolution and an excellent example of a patriot who with little military experience, used his guile, intelligence, and leadership to influence the outcome of the war.

13

CHESAPEAKE CAPES, VIRGINIA

September 5, 1781

The naval battle between the British and French fleets just outside Chesapeake Bay on September 5, 1781, was within itself a minor, inconclusive fight that produced few casualties or damaged warships. However, the engagement left the French in control of the entrance to Chesapeake Bay, allowing the landing of reinforcements for the army of George Washington's (1) army and preventing the arrival of assistance or a means of escape for the command of Charles Cornwallis (22). The Battle of the Chesapeake Capes led directly to the Franco-American victory at Yorktown (2), a battle that ended serious British resistance to the Revolutionary War and assured the independence of the United States.

After their initial successes in the Southern theater, the British lost a series of battles to the Americans commanded by Nathanael Greene (4). With the arrival of an army led by Jean Baptiste de Rochambeau (24) in New England in July 1781, the British feared that the French and Americans would unite to threaten their headquarters and primary defenses in New York City. Cornwallis moved northward toward his British commander Henry Clinton (17) but then decided to shorten his march by deploying to the mouth of the York River in Virginia. There he and his troops could receive reinforcements or evacuate on the West Indian fleet vessels that would be sailing up the Atlantic Coast to avoid the Caribbean hurricane season.

Washington and Rochambeau saw that this maneuver offered the perfect opportunity to defeat Cornwallis and end the war. The combined Franco-American army bypassed New York City and moved southward. Meanwhile, in a close coordination between the navy and army, the French fleet in the West Indies also sailed northward.

The British fleet of fourteen vessels, commanded by Admiral Samuel Hood, arrived off Chesapeake Bay on August 25, 1781, to find no French ships in the vicinity. Hood decided to sail on to New York where he anticipated joining the larger fleet of Admiral Thomas Graves before engaging the French. In New York, Hood discovered that the northern fleet had only five seaworthy warships, but the two commanders nevertheless united their fleets under the command of the senior Graves and sailed back south.

Meanwhile the French fleet of twenty-four ships, commanded by Admiral François de Grasse (27), sailed into Chesapeake Bay on August 30. De Grasse immediately sealed off any sea escape routes that might be used by Cornwallis and prepared plans to receive more ships that were en route from Rhode Island with Rochambeau's siege supplies and cannons.

Graves arrived off Chesapeake Bay on the morning of September 5, surprised to find the French already inside the Bay and holding a numerical advantage in ships and guns. De Grasse, with his twenty-four ships mounting 1,788 cannons, preferred to fight in the open ocean rather than the confines of the bay, so he waited for a favorable tide and at noon sailed out to meet the British. Graves, with his nineteen vessels armed with 1,410 guns, maneuvered to meet them.

It took several hours for the sailing ships to close to within firing range. A two-and-a-half-hour battle followed in a area known as Chesapeake Capes before darkness brought an end to the fighting. Because of the winds and tides, only fifteen French and eight British vessels actually maneuvered near enough to engage in sustained combat. Neither side gained a significant advantage over the other in the direct battle. The French lost 221 sailors; the English casualties totaled about 336 men and one vessel, the *Terrible,* which was the only ship damaged beyond repair.

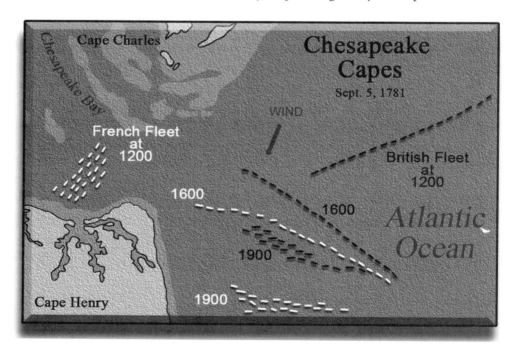

Over the next two days, the two fleets drifted southward but never again closed near enough to resume the fight. On September 8, de Grasse turned back northward so he could resume his blocking of Chesapeake Bay and protect the other vessels that arrived from Rhode Island on September 9. Graves, now even more outnumbered, returned to New York, leaving Cornwallis with no naval support or avenue of escape. During the following week, de Grasse supervised the unloading of the siege supplies and transported Washington's army down Chesapeake Bay and up the James River to Williamsburg. From here the rebels could close around Yorktown from the south and west. Within six weeks, Cornwallis surrendered and the Revolution was as good as over.

Graves underestimated the size of the French fleet and the importance of controlling Chesapeake Bay. His desire to protect his own fleet and return to secure New York City meant that he left Cornwallis in an untenable position. Graves saved his ships and crews, but his departure ultimately forced the surrender of the British army in the South and loss of the war and the American colonies.

The Battle of Chesapeake Capes is easily the most influential naval engagement of the American Revolution. It also stands as the most successful cooperation and coordination between sea and land forces during the entire conflict. Without de Grasse gaining control of the Bay, Cornwallis might have escaped the rebel army and rejoined Clinton in the North to continue the war. Instead, with all avenues of escape closed, Cornwallis surrendered, making Yorktown the most influential battle of the war. That ranking would not have been possible without Chesapeake Capes, and as a result the sea battle ranks only behind the land victory it produced and the pivotal battles of Saratoga (3) and Trenton (8) on this list.

14

DECLARATION OF INDEPENDENCE

July 4, 1776

By formally executing the *Declaration of Independence*, the Second Continental Congress (10) officially separated the American colonies from Great Britain. The document's fifty-six signers represented all thirteen colonies when they announced, "The Unanimous Declaration of the thirteen united states of America." Its issuance ended any chance of reconciliation between the rebels and British and July 4, 1776, became the birth date of the United States.

During the decades leading up to that fateful day, the American colonies had protested against increasing "taxation without representation" and other controls mandated by King George III (20). However, as late as the mid-1760s most colonial leaders were content enough with Britain. It was not until the post-French and Indian War restrictions of trade, quartering acts, and additional taxes forced them to rethink their situation that the colonies formed their own unofficial governments and communicated via Committees of Correspondence. When the British showed that they would take military action to prevent colonial militias from stockpiling weapons and ammunition at the battles of Lexington and Concord (43) in April 1775, these shadow governments ousted the royal officials and took control of the colonial governments. Thomas Paine in the pamphlet *Common Sense* (21) further outlined the need for, and indeed the right of, independence.

By the spring of 1776, the Americans were committed to the Revolution. They had forced the British to evacuate Boston and had fought the battles that led to the British occupation of New York. On April 12, 1776, the government of North Carolina authorized its delegates to the Continental Congress to officially sanction independence. Virginia joined their North Carolinian neighbors on May 7, and on June 7 their delegate Richard Henry Lee offered a resolution "that these United Colonies are, and of right ought to be, free and independent states." John Adams (51) of Massachusetts seconded the motion.

On June 11, Congress selected Adams, Thomas Jefferson (87), Benjamin Franklin (25), Roger Sherman, and Robert R. Livingston as committeemen to draw up a resolution to that effect. Jefferson, known for his skills in political writing, took the lead in drafting the document. Franklin made forty or more corrections or changes while

the other committee members contributed to a much lesser extent. One of the most debated sections concerned condemning King George for interfering with colonial law prohibiting the continued importation of slaves, but Southern delegates objected, and the subject was eliminated. Jefferson rewrote the final document and submitted it to the entire Congress. John Adams led the debate for its adoption, securing first the approval for Lee's June 7 Resolution and then support for the *Declaration of Independence* on July 4. Although issued on July 4, the document did not actually have signatures until August 2.

The Declaration began with the thirteen United States of American unanimously declaring, "When, in the course of human events, it becomes necessary for one people to dissolve the political bands which have connected them with another, and to assume, among the powers of the earth, the separate and equal station to which the laws of nature and of nature's God entitle them, a decent respect to the opinions of mankind requires that they should declare the causes which impel them to separation."

It continued with a preamble outlining the justification of the Revolution, including, "We hold these truths to be self evident: That all men are created equal: that they are endowed by their Creator with certain unalienable rights; that among these are life, liberty, and the pursuit of happiness." It continued by asserting that government powers can only be derived from the consent of the governed and that abuses should not be allowed.

Subsequent paragraphs indicted the king for abusing taxation, limiting trade and commerce, dispensing of jury trials, establishing a military dictatorship, quartering soldiers in time of peace, employing mercenaries, encouraging slave insurrections, and committing other crimes and injuries. The Declaration ended this list of accusations with the firm statement, "We must, therefore, acquiesce in the necessity which denounces our separation, and hold them, as we hold the rest of mankind, enemies in war, and in peace friends."

The final paragraph absolved the colonies from "all allegiance to the British Crown" and again summarized necessity of declaring their independence. The bottom of the document provided ample space for the signature of the delegates. At the top, in large bold script, was the signature of John Hancock, the president of the Congress. Over the following weeks, fifty-six men representing each of the newly declared thirteen independent states added their signatures. Their signatures alone marked these men as traitors to the Crown and candidates for possible execution for treason if their Revolution failed. Because this outcome seemed very possible, early copies of the Declaration were issued without signatures, and only after the American victories at Trenton (8) and Princeton were copies complete with signatures distributed to the states and abroad.

The *Declaration of Independence* had its intended impact. The Founding Fathers wrote, "We mutually pledge to each other our lives, our fortunes, and our sacred honor." No longer would anyone on either side of the Atlantic Ocean view the revolt as a method for the colonies to gain additional rights as a British possession. Their clear objective was now independence. The Americans could now solicit assistance from France and other countries.

Other resolutions, including the *Articles of Confederation* (16) adopted by Congress in late 1777 that provided the structure to govern the new country, were important to the Revolution, but the *Declaration of Independence* was the birth certificate of the United States of America. It founded the country, motivated citizens, and articulated the necessity for revolution. Over the years since, it has served as an inspiration and guideline to revolutions large and small around the world.

The only entry on this list comparable to the Declaration is the *Articles of Confederation*, but the latter would not have existed without the former. The *Declaration of Independence* merits a higher ranking for its influence and the fact that the Articles lasted only until their replacement by the Constitution in 1787. The Declaration and the Fourth of July have become lasting symbols of the Revolution and of the independent nation it produced.

15

WILLIAM HOWE

British General

1729–1814

William Howe commanded the British forces in the American colonies for most of the first three years of the Revolution. He won the costly battle of Bunker Hill (23), bested George Washington at Long Island (32) and Brandywine Creek (72), forced the Americans from the field at White Plains (77), and gained still another victory because of rebel errors at Germantown (48). Howe captured and occupied the rebel commerce center of New York and its capital at Philadelphia, yet in neither instance did he exploit his advantages. Although a competent field commander, Howe failed to grasp the strategic opportunities to win the war, being more reluctant than aggressive by nature.

Born in England into an aristocratic family with a grandmother who had been a mistress to King George I, Howe was an illegitimate uncle of King George III (20). After attending Eaton, Howe joined the army at age seventeen and in 1746 saw his first combat during the War of Austrian Succession. After the war he befriended General James Wolfe, whom he joined in America during the French and Indian War. There he led the assault up the cliffs to secure the Plains of Abraham in the Battle of Quebec in 1759. In this and several following battles, Howe exhibited competent leadership and a high degree of personal bravery as he advanced to the rank of brigadier general.

In the Parliamentary election of 1761, the residents of Nottingham elected William Howe to the House of Commons. This was not unusual, as the British people rewarded sixty other veterans with similar positions in the same election. Howe agreed with those who were generally sympathetic to the American colonies and opposed several of the acts that limited their trade and commerce. He claimed that he would do his best to avoid returning to active duty in the event of military actions in America, but after the initial fighting at Lexington and Concord (43), he had little choice but to don his uniform when King George asked him to do so.

America, it seemed, was to be the fate of the family. Howe's eldest brother George became a British hero in America when he died fighting at Ticonderoga in 1758.

Their middle brother Richard (90) served the British Empire as a naval officer, eventually joining William in America during the Revolution.

Major General Howe arrived in Boston on May 15, 1775, along with 4,000 reinforcements for the army of General Thomas Gage. A month later, Howe commanded the frontal attack against the rebels occupying Breed's Hill in what became known as the Battle of Bunker Hill. Howe again performed bravely in personally leading the attack, but, while the assault was successful, the bloodshed of officer and soldier alike made a lasting impression on the general.

King George III rewarded Howe with knighthood and then on October 10, 1775, made him commander in chief of all British forces in America. Howe's first action was to evacuate Boston in March 1776 (50) when the Americans dominated the city by positioning artillery on Dorchester Heights. He headed for Canada where he stayed only briefly before setting sail southward in the summer of 1776 to capture the important commerce and shipping center of New York. Howe handily defeated Washington at the Battle of Long Island in August and forced the Americans from White Plains in October. All of the New York City area was under his control by the end of the following month.

The British wintered in New York City, where they made plans to split the rebel colonies in two halves along the Hudson River. They would attack southward from Canada and northward from Manhattan. Howe planned to send 10,000 men up the Hudson but in the late summer of 1777 decided instead to first capture the rebel capital in Philadelphia. Sailing from New York, Howe landed his army at Head of Elk, Maryland, and then marched inland. Washington attempted to block him at Brandywine Creek on September 11, but Howe used superior intelligence to out-maneuver the American general and then to occupy Philadelphia. On October 4, Washington counterattacked at Germantown, but the complexity of his plan—combined with the bravery of a few British defenders—once again scored a victory for Howe.

Even though Howe had gained the upper hand after each of the major battles of the New York and Philadelphia campaigns, he never exploited his advantages. His aggressiveness had been lost along with the lives of many of his subordinates on the bloody slope of Breed's Hill. Also Howe enjoyed the comforts and pleasures of a mistress along with other benefits provided by American cities more than the rough life of pursuing rebels in the countryside.

Howe's choice to capture Philadelphia rather than support the column advancing southward from Canada was a pivotal decision and a major contribution to General John Burgoyne's (33) defeat at Saratoga (3) on October 7, 1777. The occupation of

Philadelphia made little impression upon European observers watching the Rebellion unfold, but the American victory at Saratoga convinced several of them that the Revolution against their common British enemy had a good chance of success. Soon France, then Spain, and then the Netherlands joined the war against Britain.

As the overall British commander in the newly declared United States, Howe took much of the blame for the failure at Saratoga and the expansion of the conflict. This,  along with the departure from office of several of his most vocal supporters in the British government, forced Howe to resign and return to England in May 1778. The following year Parliament investigated Howe's performance but judged him not responsible for the situation in America because of their own failure to provide sufficient man power and supplies. In 1782 he advanced in rank to lieutenant general and, four years later, to full general. He served in several administrative positions before assuming the governorship of Plymouth, where he died on July 12, 1814. Howe is buried in the Holly Road Cemetery of Twickenham, England.

Described as six feet tall with bad teeth and a swarthy complexion, Howe was known to be lax in administrative matters, often not bothering to read documents placed before him for signature. Nevertheless he was popular, and he was respected by his officers and men alike despite criticism of his being too soft on the Americans. While he appeared reluctant, Howe can be ranked the most efficient and influential of the British senior officers. Because he did not exploit his advantages and thereby more substantially influence the war in his own favor, Howe ranks below the American commanders, major battles, and events that led to the independence of the United States.

16

ARTICLES OF CONFEDERATION AND PERPETUAL UNION

1776–1788

*T*he *Articles of Confederation and Perpetual Union* was the first governing document of the United States of America. The Articles vested all the power of the new government in a Congress, ignoring any need for either judicial or executive branches. While not officially ratified by all thirteen states until the war was nearly over, the agreement served as the de facto system of government for the Continental Congress (10) to wage the Revolutionary War. As flawed as it was, this document served as a guide for the creation of the U.S. Constitution in 1789.

The Revolution broke out at Lexington and Concord (43) and spread to Boston and then New York. All the while the rebellious Americans had no central government. The Continental Congress, little more than a conference composed of ambassadors of the thirteen states, had no authority and little concurrence. The representatives from the states agreed on the fact that they all wanted independence from Great Britain but on little else, including how to accomplish this objective or how the states should interact.

When Richard Henry Lee presented his resolution for a formal *Declaration of Independence* to the Congress on June 7, 1776, he also suggested creating a confederation of states. On July 12, John Dickinson of Pennsylvania presented his committee's recommendations for the *Articles of Confederation and Perpetual Union* to the Continental Congress. For the next year, while the war continued in the field with little guidance or support, Congress debated the Articles before formally adopting them on November 15, 1777. Two days later copies were dispatched to each state for ratification.

The thirteen articles officially established the confederation of "The United States of America," declaring them a "perpetual Union." The document explained that this union of states was "for the common defense, the security of their liberties, and their mutual and general welfare, binding themselves to assist each other, against all force offered to, or attacks made upon them." Individuals were granted freedom of movement between the states, and criminals were to be extradited to the state in which the crime was committed.

Each state would have only one vote in Congress but could send between two and seven delegates appointed by their legislatures, depending on their population. No state could establish an alliance with another nor could they form their own army or navy or engage in war without permission from the Congress; however, the Articles encouraged state militias and granted state legislatures authority to appoint officers in the rank of colonel and below. Further, state legislatures were responsible for raising funds to support the national government based on their real estate property values.

Under provisions of the Articles, the Continental Congress claimed the sole right to declare war, to conduct foreign relations, to establish a postal system, and to set weights and measures, including coins. Congress would be the final court for disputes between the states, and the Confederation would assume the debt for the war's expenditures to date. Nine of the thirteen members would have to agree to the admission of any new state but, still hoping for assistance from the North, preapproved Canada's admission to the Union if it chose to join the Rebellion.

These provisions were a good start but were not sufficiently comprehensive to govern a new nation—for a good reason. The states had rebelled against Great Britain out of their displeasure over an all-powerful central government, and their delegates had no desire to leave one abusive power only to create another. As a result, the *Articles of Confederation* ensured that the states preserved many of their own individual powers and required agreement from all states for any change to the document. However, nothing in the Articles provided Congress the authority or the means to levy taxes, to regulate foreign commerce, or to enforce laws.

Delaware ratified the Articles on February 5, 1778, but the approval process by other states took several years. The larger states complained that they bore the brunt of the burden in supporting the Rebellion with men and supplies while the smaller states, which contributed less, maintained an equal vote in Congress. Also in dispute were unclaimed lands to the west. Congress ultimately disposed of the vast western region "for the common good" of the present states but agreed to admit future states from the frontier with approval of the states that existed then. Virginia finally ratified the Articles on January 2, 1781, and Maryland signed as the final state on February 27. On March 1, 1781, the Continental Congress formally ratified the Articles and the next day changed their name to "The United States in Congress Assembled."

Both before and after ratification, the *Articles of Confederation* depended on the willingness of the states to cooperate. If the Revolution failed, states would revert to British colonies and rebel leaders would face the loss of their property at best and the gallows as traitors at worst. To paraphrase Benjamin Franklin (25), it was better to hang together than hang separately.

The Articles served other purposes as well as unifying the states. After learning of the American victory at Saratoga (3) in October 1777, Congress had the Articles translated and sent to France as evidence that the United States would survive. This ploy was to seek French military and commercial support.

After the Battle of Yorktown (2) in 1781 and the Treaty of Paris (69) in 1783 brought an end to the war and the guaranteed independence of the United States, the *Articles of Confederation* remained the country's only governing document. Congress tried several times to amend the Articles, but none of the alterations received the unanimous vote required to make them law. Finally, on September 28, 1787, Congress agreed on a new Constitution and sent it to the states for their approval. Ratification was completed on November 21, 1788, providing for the legislative, judicial, and executive branches that still govern the United States today. The last Congress under the *Articles of Confederation* met on March 4, 1789.

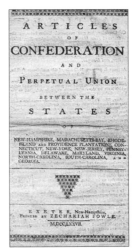

The *Articles of Confederation*, based on its content and authority, was by no means a "great" document. It was, however, the document that fit the needs and requirements of its times. During a period when the country and the Rebellion were in danger of being crushed and the states were far from united, the Articles patched together a confederation that yielded eventual victory and brought reality to its *Declaration of Independence*. While not as important as the Declaration of July 4, the Articles still rank in the top third of this list for the structure they provided the American rebels.

17

HENRY CLINTON

British General

1738–1795

Henry Clinton held the rank of commander in chief of the British army in the rebellious colonies for the longest period of any officer during the Revolutionary War. Although he performed well in battles in both the Northern and Southern theaters, he was not present at the pivotal Battle of Yorktown (2), a fact that led the British to hold him responsible for the loss of the conflict and their American territories.

Born in 1738 in the British colony of Newfoundland where his father was governor, Clinton had a privileged upbringing. The elder Clinton became the governor of New York in 1743, and Henry briefly served in the colony's militia there before sailing for England in 1751. Through family position and monetary purchase, he secured an officer's commission in the Coldstream Guards. By 1758 he had advanced in rank to lieutenant colonel and two years later saw his first combat against Prince Ferdinand of Brunswick in the Seven Years' War. By 1762 he had survived battle wounds and gained promotion to full colonel.

After his return to England, Clinton assumed command of an infantry regiment. Through his leadership abilities, greatly enhanced by his political connections, Clinton achieved the rank of major general and a seat in Parliament in 1772. He retained this government position for the next twelve years, even though he was often absent performing his military duties.

In 1775, Clinton returned to his native North America along with fellow major generals William Howe (15) and John Burgoyne (33) in response to unrest in Boston. Although subordinate to Howe, Clinton was the one who led the bloody assaults against the rebel defenses at Bunker Hill (23) in June 1775. After the battle, Clinton encouraged Howe to occupy and prepare defenses on Dorchester Heights that offered high ground dominating the city and harbor. Howe disagreed, and in January 1776 dispatched Clinton, now a lieutenant general, and 1,500 men on a reconnaissance expedition to determine rebel strength in the Carolinas. Despite substantial naval support, Clinton failed in his effort to capture Charleston in June. He then returned northward.

During Clinton's absence, George Washington (1) and the Continental Army (7) had occupied Dorchester Heights and forced Howe to evacuate to Nova Scotia. Clinton arrived back in time to join Howe in the offensive to capture New York City. Clinton's plan for the envelopment attack on Long Island (32) proved successful, but he and Howe differed on strategy for the remainder of the New York campaign and the subsequent New Jersey operation. Clinton favored bold offensives to destroy Washington and his army while Howe held steadfast in occupying territory rather than engaging in direct combat. Howe, of course, as the senior commander, had his way. In December 1776, Howe dispatched Clinton and 6,000 men to capture Newport, Rhode Island, for use as a naval base—a convenient way to remove the troublesome Clinton from his headquarters.

Clinton accomplished his mission, but news of Washington's successful attacks against Trenton (8) and Princeton eroded his confidence in Howe. Further disillusioned by reports that British officials at home held him responsible for the failure at Charleston, Clinton returned to England on leave with the intention, or at least the threat, of resigning his commission. British Secretary of State George Germain (9) and King George III (20) placated the general with knighthood and convinced him to return to America.

On his arrival in the war zone in July 1777, Clinton was angered to find that Howe, still his superior, had not yet left his winter quarters in New York. He was then aghast when Howe sailed away to attack Philadelphia instead of marching a column north to meet Burgoyne, who was headed south from Canada. Although Howe eventually occupied the rebel capitol, Burgoyne—without Howe's reinforcements—failed miserably. British officials blamed Burgoyne for the loss of Saratoga (3) and Howe for the subsequent entrance of France on the side of the rebels. As a result Germain relieved Howe from command and promoted Clinton to commander in chief on May 7, 1778.

Faced with France's entry into the war and what he felt were overextended British supply lines, Clinton consolidated the army back in New York after a difficult retreat across New Jersey in the Monmouth Campaign (59). For the next year the British did little more than conduct raids, attempting to attrite the Continental Army and its supplies. During this period Clinton received reinforcements and strategized taking the war into the Southern colonies where he was convinced the support for the revolution was weak. General Charles Cornwallis (22) joined him as his second in command, and Admiral Marriot Arbuthnot provided a fleet of warships and transports.

Clinton and 14,000 men sailed from New York at the end of 1779 and, in what is considered one of the most brilliant campaigns of the war, captured Charleston, South Carolina (47) in May 1780. Even though victorious, Clinton and his naval commander developed an animosity toward each other that lasted for the remainder of their acquaintance.

Shortly after occupying Charleston, Clinton learned of an approaching French fleet that might threaten his base in New York. Leaving half the army under Cornwallis in Charleston, Clinton sailed northward with 8,000 men. From his re-occupied headquarters in New York, Clinton supervised the subsequent Southern operations of Cornwallis, but the two generally disagreed on how to conduct the campaign. When Cornwallis became entrapped at Yorktown, Clinton did little to come to his rescue.

After Cornwallis's surrender at Yorktown in October 1781, Clinton remained in New York until May 1782, when he was recalled to England and replaced as commander in chief in America by Guy Carleton (49). Upon his return home Clinton found he was held responsible for Cornwallis's defeat at Yorktown and the eventual loss of the American colonies. Parliament denied his request for an inquest, and in 1784 he lost his seat in that governing body. During the following years, Clinton wrote a lengthy narrative on the American Revolution, but he made no attempt to publish it. The manuscript languished with his other papers until purchased and published by an American collector in 1925.

In spite of the ill will toward him, Clinton won reelection to Parliament in 1793. The following year he resumed his rank of general and became the governor of Gibraltar. He died on December 23, 1795.

Two words dominate any accounts of Clinton in the American Revolution—*unlucky* and *scapegoat*. He was unlucky in his initial appointment as subordinate to Howe and unluckier still to suffer the poor performances of Cornwallis and Arbuthnot. Luck evaded him further when his political supporters back home, crucial to any British general's career at the time, were either out of favor or out of office at the time Clinton needed them most. The label of scapegoat is even simpler to explain. As one of the strongest military powers in the world, the British had to blame their defeat by a "rabble of rebels" on someone other than themselves. Clinton, as commander in chief, had to assume the responsibility.

Described as a short, somewhat overweight man with little charisma, Clinton was a much better general than his legacy reflects. He was right about the need to defend

Dorchester Heights; he did, in fact, devise the plan for the victory at Long Island; and he led the campaign that captured Charleston. His strategy to take the war to the rebels to defeat Washington's army was sound and much better than Howe's land-occupation tactic. Still, he was in charge when the British lost their most significant battle, and he had been the British commander in America longer than anyone else. Had Clinton's ideas on how to conduct the war in the early years been followed, the British might have crushed the revolt. But by the time he assumed overall command, the French had already allied with the Americans, ending any real chance of success.

Howe and Cornwallis are the only British military officers to rival Clinton for influence in the conflict and these rankings. For his early successes, Howe merits a slightly higher ranking, while Cornwallis ranks just below his commander in chief.

18

COWPENS, SOUTH CAROLINA

January 17, 1781

The Battle of Cowpens in northwest South Carolina was the turning point for the American rebels in the Southern theater, opening the way for their final victory at Yorktown (2) ten months later. Daniel Morgan (35), the rebel commander, combined his personal leadership with an excellent tactical plan that integrated terrain and weapons to deliver an overwhelming defeat to the British. The battle raised morale and renewed confidence in the Rebellion in the Southern states while elevating Morgan to the status of hero of the Revolution and greatly tainting the reputation of the British "boy colonel" Banastre Tarleton (44).

An invasion force led by Henry Clinton (17) defeated and occupied Charleston, South Carolina, in May 1780, soon after the British refocused their efforts to the South. Clinton then returned to New York, leaving Charles Cornwallis (22) in charge with orders to further neutralize the Rebellion in the Southern states. Cornwallis crushed the American army under Horatio Gates (31) at Camden (65) the following August. The British commander then crossed into North Carolina, stopping at Charlotte, before the defeat of one of his detachments at Kings Mountain, South Carolina (36), on October 7 halted his offensive.

General Nathanael Greene (4) arrived in the Carolinas to assume command of all American troops on December 3, 1780. Despite the rebel victory at Kings Mountain, Greene found an army and civilian population with low morale and declining confidence in the success of the Revolution. Going against the military wisdom of never dividing one's forces, Greene took the bold action of dispatching Daniel Morgan and about 1,900 regulars and militiamen to the British rear to harass and interrupt their lines of supply and communications.

Cornwallis realized that he must eliminate the threat before he could continue his offensive northward. He also saw an opportunity to cut off and destroy Morgan's force while it was separated from the remainder of the American army. Cornwallis ordered Lieutenant Colonel Banastre Tarleton and a well-trained detachment of British regulars and Loyalists (34) to pursue Morgan. Tarleton planned to destroy Morgan's army or keep him from returning to American lines until the main Redcoat army could arrive. Tarleton, at the age of only twenty-six, had performed

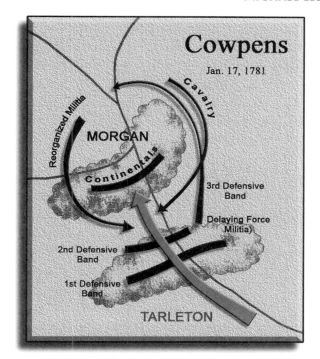

well at Charleston and Camden. His most impressive action, however, had been in overwhelming the retreating Americans at Waxhaw Creek (74) the previous May. In this latter battle he had garnered the hatred of the rebels for his alleged orders of "no quarter" for prisoners or the wounded. Most of the senior officers, except Cornwallis, resented the popularity and quick rise of the youthful Tarleton.

Morgan was aware that half his contingent was inexperienced and poorly motivated and that Tarleton was a bold officer with a veteran force. With ample time to prepare, Morgan appropriately selected an area northwest of Spartanburg, South Carolina, among rolling hills called the Cowpens. The spot, familiar to several of Morgan's officers, was just as its name indicated—a series of wooden enclosures in which to gather cattle. Morgan liked the fact that the nearby Broad River blocked any ready retreat if his militiamen decided to desert the battlefield.

Morgan strengthened his risky position with a brilliant deployment of his forces that he organized into three defensive bands. About 300 meters to the front of his main force and situated on a small elevation, he positioned 150 of his best marksmen armed with rifles. Although slower to load, these rifled-barrel weapons were much more accurate than the ordinary smooth-bore infantry muskets. In a second rank halfway between the forward position and the main force, Morgan placed 300 inexperienced militiamen. All Morgan asked of these men was that each fire three shots at the British after the first line withdrew. Morgan ordered the rest of his regulars to form the center of his third line while he put more militiamen on his flanks. A mounted unit of about 125 men constituted his only reserve. To make clear his objective and to encourage his men, Morgan announced, "On this ground I will defeat the British or lay down my bones." He also let it be known that Tarleton was not in the habit of offering quarter to those who surrendered and that prisoners could expect to be executed.

Meanwhile, Tarleton was pushing his pursuing troops hard, fearing that the Americans would escape back to the main body. By the time he reached the Cowpens on the early morning of January 17, 1781, his soldiers were exhausted and hungry. Nonetheless, Tarleton, who had little respect for the Americans—having easily defeated them in earlier fights—ordered an immediate attack. On the clear, bitterly cold morning his advance troops encountered the outer band of American marksmen who, following Morgan's orders to "shoot at the epaulettes," struck down several officers.

The first rank fell back through the second line of militia, who then followed orders to fire three volleys. The second line then retreated through the third rank. By the time the British reached the third and primary defensive line, their numbers were depleted, but Tarleton believed they had the rebels on the run. The battle intensified with the Americans holding against the repeated British charges. After about thirty minutes of fighting, the militiamen who had retreated past the lines joined the rebel cavalry in a counterattack against the British right flank and rear. Within minutes the bulk of the British survivors began surrendering and begging for mercy. Tarleton, along with several hundred mounted troops, escaped.

On the battlefield lay 110 British dead and about twice that number wounded. Americans captured either 524 or 767 prisoners, depending on the report. Rebel losses totaled 12 dead and 61 wounded.

Cornwallis did not hold Tarleton responsible for the debacle at Cowpens, but his fellow officers relished the young colonel's failure. Cowpens ended Cornwallis's plans for an offensive to neutralize the Carolinas and take the entire South out of the war. Instead, Cornwallis, who kept Tarleton with him, was soon himself in retreat and on his way to surrender in Virginia. Soon after the battle, Morgan marched to the northeast to rejoin Greene and the main army. Although he had won the most tactically brilliant battle of the war, it would be his last major action. Already ill, he would not recover sufficiently to resume command in the field.

If Tarleton had destroyed Morgan's force at Cowpens, then he and Cornwallis would likely have defeated Greene and possibly ended the Revolution. Instead,

Morgan's victory renewed the fervor of revolution, and encouraged those already engaged and rallying new followers to the cause. Cowpens does not equate in influence with Yorktown (2), Saratoga (3), or Trenton (8), but it was the only other land battle to play such a significant role in the outcome of the American War for Independence. Before Cowpens, the South—if not the entire war—appeared lost; afterward the road to victory stood open.

19

NAVIGATION, STAMP, TOWNSHEND, BOSTON PORT, QUEBEC, AND QUARTERING ACTS

1763–1774

The British imposed a series of taxes and laws that the American colonists found intolerable—and the colonists let their displeasure be known. The colonists believed that they, as British subjects, deserved full democratic and economic rights assured all Englishman at home. When Britain ignored their demands, they took up the cry, "No taxation without representation." War became inevitable.

In the centuries before the settlement of North America, England evolved from feudalism to economic nationalism known as mercantilism. Under this system, the government regulated trade and commerce while establishing colonies to enrich the mother country. Colonies existed to provide raw materials and to act as consumers of manufactured goods from the homeland. To enforce mercantilism, the English enacted a series of Navigation Acts.

The first Navigation Act in 1645 evolved over the next century to require that all goods to and from their colonies be carried by British-flagged ships. In essence, this meant English colonies could sell to and buy from only Britain itself. Since exported raw materials sold for less than imported manufactured goods, the colonists stayed in a constant state of indebtedness.

During their early years, the Americans were at worst inconvenienced by the Navigation Acts. The British were lax in their enforcement, and the Americans were ingenious in circumventing the rules—or in out-and-out smuggling when necessary. By the mid-eighteenth century, American colonial merchants were becoming wealthy with their illegal trade.

It was the Seven Years' War in 1763 and the great debt that it imposed that caused the British to tighten their control over the American colonies. Premier George Grenville insisted that the Americans be partially responsible for the war debt since they themselves had been saved from the French and their Indian allies. He proposed that not only should the colonists pay part of the cost of the war, but also they should pay part of the cost of maintaining British garrisons in North America.

Grenville ordered the British navy to rigidly enforce the Navigation Acts. He secured Parliamentary approval of the Stamp Act of 1765 that placed a tax, by way of a stamp that had to be purchased, on all printed matter, including newspapers, pamphlets, and even playing cards. While the Stamp Act tax was not overly severe in and of itself, the Americans protested due to a postwar financial depression of their own. Many colonists worried that the small tax might lead to larger taxation, and groups such as the Sons of Liberty formed to harass stamp agents into resigning their posts while the general public took up the cry, "Taxation without representation is tyranny."

British officials capitulated in 1766, deciding it was easier to appease the colonists than to enforce the regulations. They repealed the Stamp Act. Parliament, to save face, passed the Declaratory Act that stated the British still held the right "to bind" the colonies in all matters of taxation or any other matter whatsoever.

The "whatsoever" arrived when Charles Townshend took control of the British ministry in 1767. He lobbied for acts to place import levies on glass, lead, paper, and tea for the colonists. The revenue generated would pay the salaries of royal colonial judges and governors. Although the taxes were again not severe, the Americans once more protested. They did so by increasing their smuggling and directly confronting tax agents. British officials stationed two regiments of troops in Boston in 1768 to enforce the tax and keep order. The Redcoats became the targets of colonial hostilities. After months of protest, British soldiers fired on rioting colonists in what became known as the Boston Massacre (93).

Angry colonists organized Committees of Correspondence to communicate and unify themselves. King George III (20), under pressure from the colonies as well as British merchants, finally convinced Parliament to repeal the Townshend Act. To prove they still held the power, Parliament left the tax on tea in place. The Americans, in turn, showed their resolve by dumping an entire shipload of tea in the harbor on December 16, 1773, in what became known as the Boston Tea Party.

Parliament, outraged at the insolent Americans, passed a series of punitive acts. The Boston Port Act closed the city's harbor until colonists paid for the lost tea, another ordered colonists be tried in England rather than in colonial courts, and yet another diminished the power authorized in the Massachusetts colonial charter. Parliament also expanded the Quartering Act, which had originally allowed only

public and unoccupied houses to be used for housing British soldiers, to include quartering them in homes of colonists throughout North America. Collectively the colonists referred to these measures as the Intolerable Acts. More and more Americans encouraged each other to resist.

Although supposedly unrelated to the Boston Tea Party, the British also passed the Quebec Act. The real purpose of the act was to appease the Canadians so they would not join the rebellious Americans. Parliament extended Canada's borders south to the Ohio River and agreed that the French-Canadians could continue to practice their Catholic religion instead of requiring that they join the Church of England. The Americans were furious about this loss of territories they claimed in the west.

The First Continental Congress (10) attempted to solve American differences with the British government to no avail. King George and Parliament, confident and arrogant, believed the colonies were their possessions to be used to increase the wealth of the crown and empire. They had spent more than twenty years passing acts that damaged their own economy just to try to control the colonies, which they could never envision as anything other than their property. When the American militia rose up in arms at Lexington and Concord (43) in 1775, the British thought that they could easily squash any rebellion in the colonies and reinstate order.

There would be no peace again. While there were other causes of the American Revolution—including religious freedom and concepts of personal liberty—what really elevated the differences between colonists and mother country was the opportunity for wealth. The various acts restricted or prevented monetary gain of many of the colonists, and those laws, combined with increasing British control over their day-to-day lives, led to the battlefield and eventually to independence. These acts by the British Parliament between 1763 and 1774 provided the spark that ignited the American Revolution, earning them a place near the top of this list.

20

GEORGE III

King of Great Britain

1738–1820

In his efforts to exert the power of the British crown in America, King George III endorsed measures that fanned resentment in the colonies into a full revolution. Although many of the colonial issues that eventually led to the war were more the result of oppression by his subordinates, King George became the symbol of all that the rebellious colonists opposed.

Born George William Frederick in London on June 4, 1738, the son of Frederick, the Prince of Wales, and the grandson of King George II, the future king of Great Britain was a dull, apathetic child who did not learn to read until age eleven. Upon the death of his father in 1751, George III assumed his father's title and became the heir to the throne. Upon the death of his grandfather, George III became king on October 25, 1760.

As the third British ruler from the Hanoverian line, George III was the first to be born in England and to speak English as his primary language. Despite his uninspiring persona, the British Empire, including the American colonies, welcomed their new ruler. Most, however, believed that George III would be like his two predecessors, who took little direct interest or control over their kingdom other than to enjoy the benefits of their position.

For the previous two generations, Parliament, under the control of a few wealthy Whig families, had ruled the Empire. Although only twenty-two years old, George III was determined to follow the constant advice of this mother—"George, be king!"—and to take back control of the government. Fortunately for George III, times were ripe for a change. Many of the Whigs were advancing in age; representation had become disproportioned because of emerging population centers. Unfortunately for the Empire, George III lacked characteristics of leadership and statesmanship.

Despite these weaknesses, George had the strength of position and wealth. Through the selling of titles and the conferring of new ones, George III quickly gained a Tory majority in Parliament. As the self-declared leader of the Tory opposition party, one of his first moves was also one of his worst when he forced the resignation of

William Pitt, the Whig prime minister. Pitt had led the British government during the Seven Years' War, known as the French and Indian War in North America, and had been instrumental in the British capture of Canada and India.

Soon after gaining control of the Parliament, the Tories legislated a series of taxes to force the American colonies to pay for their own current expenses of government and to repay the debts incurred in the recent French and Indian War that protected them. Many of the early actions, including various trade and navigation acts in the early 1760s, came at the initiation of Parliament rather than George III, but the king received blame for the new taxes.

In 1770, after a succession of prime ministers who did not please him, George III appointed Lord Frederick North to the position. North, neither overly intelligent nor otherwise qualified, nevertheless was loyal to his king. That single characteristic sufficed for him to remain prime minister during the next dozen years—some of the most critical in the history of the empire and the very period in which the empire lost its American colonies.

Upon his appointment, Lord North and George III looked to the colonies for even more revenue than they had been producing. Parliament and the Royal Family expected their colonies worldwide to provide income to support their government and fund the royal households even though British citizens at home had no such levies.

Taxes on items ranging from lead to paper to tea soon had American colonists talking of revolution and independence. "Committees of Correspondence" formed in each of the colonies to discuss possible courses of action. Some American colonists struck back by covertly smuggling goods through other counties and by harassing— and on occasion even tarring and feathering—customs agents. The protests came to a head with the Boston Tea Party in 1773, when angry colonists threw a boatload of tea into Boston Harbor rather than pay the assigned tax on it.

Meanwhile George III had already taken other measures to punish the colonies and to drain them of revenue. Parliament passed acts allowing quartering of soldiers in colonists' homes, placed further restricts on ports, and curtailed the growth of colonies into the western frontier.

By 1775 opposition to George III and his "taxation without representation" pushed the colonists into open warfare against the British. Despite the advice of his subordinates that Great Britain did not have the assets to fight a rebellion across the Atlantic, George III unwisely chose war over appeasement.

When the Americans formally declared their intentions in their *Declaration of Independence* (14) on July 4, 1776, they made it clear whom they held responsible for their action. At the head of a long list of grievances was the statement, "The history of the present King of Great Britain is a history of repeated injuries and usurpations, all having in direct object the absolute tyranny over these states." Then followed a long series of "He has… " complaints.

George III had the loyalty of the Parliament he had created and the general backing of the British people early in the war. However, after the loss at Saratoga (3) in late 1777 and the alliance between the Americans and the French in 1778, even the king's most ardent supporters began to lose their enthusiasm for the war. North encouraged George III to bring back William Pitt as prime minister, but the stubborn king refused. George III even attempted to continue the war after the British defeat at Yorktown (2) in 1781, but ultimately he had to agree to the Treaty of Paris (69) in 1783 that called for the evacuation of his remaining troops from the now United States of America.

Regardless of their lack of qualifications or their failures, men who become kings based on nothing other than their birthright remain on the throne for life. George III continued to rule over the next decades with no more apparent abilities than before.

Forever "the king who lost the American colonies," George III was also the king who went mad. Victim of various mental problems, George suffered his first major symptoms of insanity in 1765. By 1810 his mental facilities had so eroded that he was locked away in Windsor Castle. Parliament then passed the Regency Act of 1811, appointing George's eldest son, the prince of Wales, as the king's regent. The prince of Wales performed those duties until he became King George IV on the death of his father on January 29, 1820.

Historians have debated the responsibility of George III for the American Revolution since 1776. Some blame Lord North or Secretary of State George Germain (9), many point at Parliament, and others place responsibility directly on the shoulders of the king. All of these are correct. Parliament became what King George made it. Neither he nor his appointees had the foresight to appease the colonists to keep them in the fold or the will and resources to battle them into submission. As a result, the United States became independent and evolved into today's single world superpower rather than remain in the empire.

For these reasons George III stands in the top quarter of these rankings. He would rank even higher except for the fact that the American colonies were settled and led by a people who respected hard work, independence, and self-worth rather than birthright and royalty. In all probability, the colonists would have demanded their independence eventually despite appeasement. George III just happened to provide motive, opportunity, and symbolism.

21

COMMON SENSE AND *THE CRISIS*

1776

*C*ommon Sense, a brief, forty-seven-page pamphlet, outlined the reasons for American independence from Great Britain. Basically, its author, Thomas Paine, wrote that efforts by the colonists to appease King George III (20) were against "common sense" and that the Americans had a moral obligation to form an independent, democratic republic separate from the British monarchy. After the colonists had followed this advice only to find their revolution in danger of failing, Paine issued another series of pamphlets named *The Crisis* that rallied the rebels during their most trying times.

The author of *Common Sense* and *The Crisis* lived humbly before his monumental pamphlets. Born on January 29, 1737, in Thetford, England, to a Quaker family, Thomas Paine dropped out of school at age twelve to join his father as a corset maker. At age nineteen, Paine went to sea but found the sailor's life was not for him. For the next sixteen years, he worked intermittently as a personal servant, school teacher, grocer, and excise collector. In this latter occupation his supervisors suspended him for more than a year for his claiming to have inspected goods when he had only seen paper inventories.

During this suspension period, Paine spent most of his time making up for his lack of education by reading and studying natural and political sciences. In 1772 Paine published his first political article in a lengthy paper to Parliament asking for better pay and working conditions for himself and his fellow excisemen. His paper was not well received, resulting in Paine's dismissal.

The bankrupt and jobless Paine met the visiting American colonist Benjamin Franklin (25) in London in 1774. Franklin encouraged Paine to emigrate to America and provided him letters of introduction, describing him as an "ingenious, worthy young man." Paine arrived in Philadelphia on November 30, 1774, where he worked as a freelance journalist and met many of the town's leading citizens.

By 1775 the various acts of taxation and other measures forced upon the colonies had many Americans advocating civil disobedience and others outright revolution. Those who supported revolt knew there were many like-minded colonists, but their views had not yet been recorded or distributed. One of the leading proponents of revolt, Doctor Benjamin Rush, encouraged Paine to write and publish his ideas and views.

He explained to the young writer that he wanted to write the paper himself but that it would be safer, at least for the doctor, if it came from a less well-known individual.

On January 19, 1776, *Common Sense* appeared as an anonymous pamphlet. It contained few original ideas; instead it recorded the words many dissatisfied colonists were thinking and talking about. Unlike earlier articles on the subject, Paine did not write for the highly educated but rather for the common man.

Paine wrote that the indecision on the part of the colonists on whether to break away from Great Britain simply defied common sense. He called King George III "the Royal Brute of Great Britain" and questioned why the tiny island of England should have the right to exercise control over the much larger American continent. "Everything that is right or reasonable pleads for separation. The blood of the slain, the weeping voice of nature cries 'Tis time to part,'" wrote Paine. He concluded, "O ye that love mankind! Ye that dare oppose not only the tyranny but the tyrant, stand forth! Every spot of the old world is overrun with oppression. Freedom hath been hunted round the globe. Asia and Africa have long expelled her. Europe regards her like a stranger, and England hath given her warning to depart. O receive the fugitive, and prepare in time an asylum for mankind."

The English looked at *Common Sense* as treason, while many colonists saw it as the plain truth. It was in reality both good journalism and excellent propaganda. More importantly, it reinforced the beliefs of those who favored independence and rallied thousands to the cause who had previously wavered or been undecided. Within weeks 120,000 copies of the pamphlet were distributed throughout the colonies among a total population of 2.5 million. It quickly became the bestselling publication of eighteenth-century North America.

Paine showed that his support of the cause was not just rhetoric by enlisting in the militia. Inspired by *Common Sense,* many other Americans also joined the Rebellion. In March 1776, they forced the British out of Boston and on July 4 formally declared their independence. The rebels soon discovered, however, that printed pamphlets did not stop the British infantry regiments and cannon batteries. By October the rebel invasion of Canada was in full retreat, and the Redcoats defeated George Washington's army at New York in December.

Once again rebel leaders called upon the pen of Paine to energize the Rebellion and raise the morale of the rebels. On December 19, 1776, Paine began publishing a series of articles in the *Pennsylvania Journal* titled "The Crisis." The first of these, republished as a pamphlet on December 23, began, "These are the times that try men's souls. The summer soldiers and the sunshine patriots will, in this crisis, shrink from the service of their country; but he that stands it now, deserves the love and thanks of man and woman. Tyranny, like hell, is not easily conquered; yet we have this consolation with us, that the harder the conflict, the more glorious the triumph."

The Crisis so impressed Washington that he had it read to all his soldiers prior to the crossing of the Delaware River on December 25. With the words of *The Crisis* on

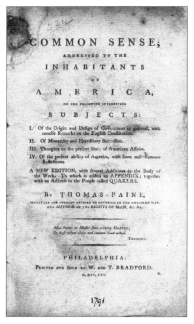

their minds, the troops proved themselves to be neither "summer soldiers" nor "sunshine patriots" when they swept the Hessians (37) from Trenton (8) and then marched to do the same at Princeton—critical turning points in the future of the Revolution.

As a reward, the Continental Congress (10) appointed Paine as secretary to the Committee on Foreign Affairs in 1777 and as the clerk of the Pennsylvania Assembly in 1779. He continued to publish an additional eleven articles under the title of *The Crisis* and in 1781 accompanied American representatives seeking additional supplies and funds from France. After the war Paine settled in New Rochelle, New York, on a former Loyalist's (34) estate presented to him by Congress. Pennsylvania added a pension, allowing Paine to bask in his fame as the "author of the Revolution" and to work on inventions, including an iron bridge.

In 1787, Paine sailed for England seeking financial backing for his invention. There he published the aptly titled *Rights of Man* in response to criticism of the French Revolution. The British did not appreciate the writings, but the French hailed Paine as a hero and granted him citizenship. Paine reportedly met with Napoleon Bonaparte in 1800 and the "Little Emperor" informed the American writer that he slept every night with a copy of *Rights of Man* under his pillow.

In 1802, Paine returned to America but found no welcome. While in France between 1794 and 1796, Paine had written a series of tracts titled *The Age of Reason* that proclaimed religion to be every bit as much a tyrant as kings. He had said, "All national institutions of churches, whether Jewish, Christian, or Turkish, appear to me no other than human inventions, set up to terrify and enslave mankind, and monopolize power and profit."

Such words did not resonate with the same level of approval in America as had admonishment of King George and of summer patriots. As a result, Paine lived out the remainder of his life in poverty and obscurity. He died on June 8, 1809, with only six mourners in attendance at his funeral. A few years later, his remains were removed by land-reform radical William Corbett who said he intended to return them to Paine's native England. When Corbett died twenty years later, the bones were still on his estate—unburied. They later disappeared. Today there are several people who claim to possess Paine's skull and other skeletal parts.

Common Sense and *The Crisis* remain two of the most famous and influential documents of the American Revolution, outranked only by the *Declaration of Independence* (14) and the *Articles of Confederation* (16). The public could easily comprehend *Common Sense*, which made clear the rationale for revolt. When the revolution was at it lowest point, Paine again took up the pen to clarify the purpose and to rekindle the spark of revolution with *The Crisis*.

22

CHARLES CORNWALLIS

British General

1738–1805

Charles Cornwallis is most remembered as the British officer who surrendered the bulk of the Redcoat army at Yorktown (2) in 1781, an act which brought an end to major fighting in the American Revolution. Despite his failure in Virginia, Cornwallis was a capable commander known for his humanity and for his loyalty to the crown. He continued to distinguish himself in postwar civil and military service in India and Ireland.

Cornwallis, born in London on December 31, 1738, did not seek the life of the idle rich despite being a member of a wealthy, titled, and aristocratic family. After schooling at Eaton College, he joined the British army as an ensign at age eighteen. He briefly attended the Prussian military school at Turin before rejoining his regiment to spend the bulk of the Seven Years' War fighting throughout the German provinces. By the end of the conflict, he had advanced in rank to lieutenant colonel, gained command of an infantry regiment, and become known for his valor in battle.

Between tours on the continent, Cornwallis returned home to earn election to the House of Commons in 1760, and in 1762 inherited his father's earldom. From that time on, Cornwallis carried the titles of both his military and civilian ranks.

During the years after the conclusion of the Seven Years' War, Cornwallis focused more on his political than military duties. During the late 1760s and early 1770s, he frequently spoke out and voted against the harsh British tax policies imposed on the American colonies.

Cornwallis's loyalty to his king and country, however, far exceeded his sympathies for the Americans, and he readily accepted a promotion to major general and orders to sail to North America. He arrived in the colonies in time to join William Howe's (15) offensive against Long Island (32) and New York City in the late summer of 1776. Cornwallis then participated in the pursuit of George Washington (1) across New Jersey, commanding the Hessians (37) at the outposts in Trenton and Princeton that fell to the rebels in late December 1776 and early January 1777.

Many of his fellow officers placed the blame for the American victories in New Jersey directly on the shoulders of Cornwallis. Henry Clinton (17) condemned Cornwallis's actions as "the most consummate ignorance I have ever heard of in any officer above a corporal." Most realized, however, that the Hessians had been defeated by a brilliant maneuver by the rebels—supported by horrible weather—rather than any failure on the part of Cornwallis.

After a brief return to London, Cornwallis resumed his command and participated in the Philadelphia campaign. He fought particularly well at Brandywine Creek (72) and at Germantown (48) in the fall of 1777. During this period Cornwallis criticized both Howe and Clinton for their lack of initiative but continued to serve loyally in the field.

Cornwallis again briefly returned to England in January 1778 to accept a promotion to lieutenant general. Upon his arrival back in America three months later, he assumed the position as second in command under Clinton, who had replaced Howe as commander of British forces in North America. Cornwallis had previously offered his resignation to Clinton because of their earlier disputes, but Clinton had rejected it, recognizing the abilities of his subordinate.

Never one to suppress his opinions, Cornwallis opposed Clinton's plan to evacuate Philadelphia and withdraw to New York in the spring of 1778. When Clinton made it clear he would not change his plan, Cornwallis accepted the orders and became instrumental in repulsing an American attack led by Charles Lee (79) at Monmouth Court House (59) on June 28. Cornwallis again sailed to London when he received news that his wife had become ill. When she died in early 1779, he returned to America where he rejoined Clinton for the successful siege of Charleston, South Carolina (47) that ended on May 12, 1780.

When Clinton sailed back to New York, Cornwallis assumed command of British forces in the South. On August 16, 1780, he soundly defeated the rebels led by Horatio Gates (31) at the Battle of Camden (65) and then pursued the Americans, now led by Nathanael Greene (4). Extended supply lines and the growing numbers of rebels caused Cornwallis's soldiers to lose battles at South Carolina's Kings Mountain (36) in October 1780 and at Cowpens (18) in January 1781. Short of troops and supplies, Cornwallis marched toward Yorktown where he hoped to be met by the British fleet. Instead of his own navy, he found a French flotilla offshore blocking reinforcements and a large combined army of French and Americans besieging his land routes.

Aware that any more fighting would only result in the dissemination of his remaining army, Cornwallis surrendered. Although the war dragged on for several more years, for all purposes it ended at Yorktown. Neither the British officials nor public held Cornwallis wholly responsible "for losing the colonies," because the conflict had spread so widely that the British were now fighting a world war. While Cornwallis might have defeated the rebels alone, he could not defeat the combined forces of the Americans, the French, and their other allies (5).

Cornwallis, after a prisoner exchange, returned to England in May 1782 and four years later accepted an appointment as the governor-general of India. There he initiated land and government reforms while also leading successful military campaigns against rebellious natives. In 1798 Cornwallis became the viceroy and commander in chief of Ireland. During his tenure, he was one of the few British officials in the long history of Ireland to gain the respect of Irish Catholics and Protestants for his fair treatment of both. In 1805 he returned to India as governor-general and died there at Ghazipur on October 5 at the age of sixty-six.

Descriptions of Cornwallis comment on his good manners and his lack of pretentiousness. He was tolerant of comrades and opponents alike and appeared to care little about wealth in his zeal to serve his country and king. Although best known for his surrender at Yorktown, he served Britain with distinction throughout the war and then sustained a brilliant civil and military career in both India and Ireland in the postwar period.

Because he served on the side of the losers and surrendered at Yorktown, Cornwallis cannot rank at the top of the list or above Howe or Clinton. As controversial as he still is, Cornwallis was the type of commander whom soldiers want as their leader and who remains worthy of a ranking in the top half of this list.

23

BUNKER HILL, MASSACHUSETTS

June 17, 1775

Bunker Hill, the first major engagement of the American Revolution, became the most famous contest of the war and one of its most influential battles because it unified the rebels in their cause and obliterated any chance of reconciliation between Great Britain and the colonies. In the fight, both sides exhibited tremendous bravery as well as drastic tactical errors.

After the colonial militiamen had repulsed the British raiding expeditions at Lexington and Concord (43) on April 19, 1775, the rebel Americans pursued the Redcoats back toward Boston. Other colonial militias joined them there to lay a loose siege along the landward approaches to city. For the next two months neither side took much action, as no one was convinced that the American colonies were ready for a full-scale revolution against the crown.

In June, General Thomas Gage, the British commander in Boston, planned to occupy Dorchester Heights to the southeast of the city in order to strengthen his defenses. The Americans learned of the plan and countered the British move. During the night of June 16–17, about 1,600 militiamen—organized into various units commanded by Colonels William Prescott, John Stark (68), and Israel Putnam—moved down Charlestown Neck to occupy the high ground outside the village of Charlestown. Officially none of the three commanders was in charge of the others, but the circumstance of the battle that followed clearly revealed that it was "Colonel Prescott's battle."

The original plan called for the militiamen to occupy the peninsula's highest elevation on a 110-foot rise known as Bunker Hill. For reasons never made clear, Prescott and Putnam decided to move the majority of the force 600 yards further southeast and to prepare positions on ground that rose only 75 feet. Little known at the time, this knoll was Breed's Hill. A few men remained on Bunker Hill while Stark, the third commander, and a hundred men took up defenses to the northeast along the Mystic River to defend the flank.

Prescott's choice of Breed's rather than Bunker Hill for his primary position was a poor use of the terrain. However, along with other senior American leaders, he was

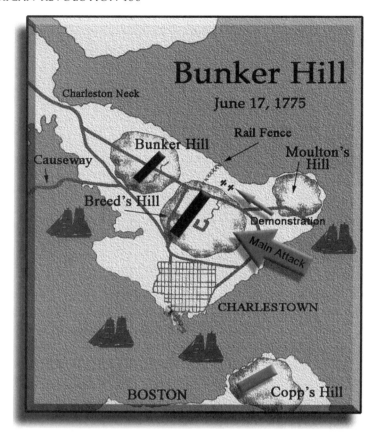

a veteran of the French and Indian War who knew how to build fortifications and to inspire his soldiers.

By daybreak the rebels on Breed's Hill had built a 45-yard square redoubt with sufficient mounds of dirt to protect them from cannon fire. In their respective locations, Putnam and Stark were also dug into defensive trenches. The British in Boston had heard the digging during the night but were unaware of the magnitude of the rebel defenses until daybreak. Gage and his generals immediately planned to push the rebels back. Initial plans called for diversionary attacks on both the front and the flank while a larger force landed in the rear on Charlestown Neck. This would effectively cut off the rebels from the mainland, and the British could then starve them into submission.

This plan, although sound, met with little support. Gage's subordinates had no respect for the military abilities of the colonists, and clamored for a direct, frontal attack. Just after noon the first British units, led by General William Howe (15) and supported by naval gunfire, landed on the southeastern shore of the peninsula and moved up the beach only to be stopped by a hail of musket fire from Stark's detachment. Howe turned his main attack against Breed's Hill.

About this time Putnam left the defenses at Breed's Hill in an attempt to rally reinforcements from Bunker Hill and Charlestown Neck. He failed but fully shared in its later glory despite the fact he had not returned to the battle.

Prescott, aware of a shortage of ammunition and powder as well as the inaccuracy of smoothbore muskets, has received credit for issuing the most famous single order of the Revolution. As Howe's redcoats approached, Prescott shouted to his men, "Don't fire until you see the whites of their eyes!" The militiamen did indeed hold their fire until the first British soldiers closed to less than fifty yards. Their fire shredded the British ranks, but the disciplined survivors and following units continued the advance only to again meet volleys of rebel gunfire.

Howe withdrew for fifteen minutes and then attacked a second time only to suffer the same results. Again he withdrew, this time back to the beach landing site to integrate 400 reinforcements into his ranks. Prescott's militiamen were now nearly out of ammunition. They attempted to repel the third British attack with bayonets and clubs but were finally forced to retreat back over Bunker Hill and across Charlestown Neck. Howe pursed only as far as Bunker Hill where he began preparing defenses of his own.

The two-and-a-half-hour battle took its toll on both sides. Of the 1,600 American militiamen who fought on and around Breed's Hill, 140 were dead, 271 wounded, and 30 captured. The British had committed about 2,500 men to the fight, and 226 of them lay dead on the field. Another 800 were wounded. British officer casualties showed the fury of the rebel infantrymen. Of their officers, 19 were dead and 70 were among the wounded. This totaled about 20 percent of the British officer casualties of the entire war.

After the battle, the Boston Siege (50) returned to a stalemate. A few weeks later George Washington (1) arrived to assume command of the new Continental Army (7). Because Bunker Hill was better known than Breed's Hill, the first major engagement of the Revolution took its name. The battle outside Charlestown shed so much blood that the chance of reconciliation between America and the Motherland was forever lost. The colonists now knew that the famed British army was not invincible. The British would eventually be forced out of Boston, but neither King George III (20) nor his commanders would give up the colonies without a fight.

The Battle of Bunker Hill was a collision of errors. The Americans had chosen the wrong terrain, and then the British had attacked with a flawed plan. The battle's immediate notoriety resulted from a profusion of bloodshed not heretofore seen in the American colonies. The long-term result was a protracted war and ultimately the independence of the United States. Bunker Hill was less influential than Yorktown (2), Saratoga (3), Trenton (8), or Cowpens (18), yet the battle was significant for its ferocity and for solidifying each side into its own resolution to fight the war.

24

JEAN BAPTISTE DE ROCHAMBEAU

French General

1725–1807

As the commander of the French army in America, Jean Baptiste de Rochambeau significantly influenced the Battle of Yorktown (2) and the end of the Revolutionary War. His leadership and administrative skills allowed him to maintain an efficient, well-trained army, while his diplomacy and goodwill produced an effective partnership with his American allies. Rochambeau and his French army were the final ingredients needed by George Washington (1) and the Americans to achieve their independence from Great Britain.

Rochambeau began life on July 1, 1725, in a well-established family in Vendome, southwest of Paris. As a youth he studied for the clergy, but when his older brother died, he switched to a military career. He experienced his first combat in 1742 during the Austrian War of Succession where he participated in the Bohemian, Bavarian, and Rhine campaigns. By 1747 he had advanced in rank to colonel and became the military aide to the Duke of Orleans. The following year Rochambeau participated in the siege and capture of the Dutch city of Maestricht before returning home in 1749 to succeed his father as governor of Vendome.

At the outbreak of the Seven Years' War in 1756, Rochambeau returned to the battlefield to distinguish himself in the capture of the British island of Minorca in the Mediterranean Sea. For the next three years, he fought in Germany, where he suffered several wounds as he advanced in rank to brigadier general. In the postwar years Rochambeau improved cavalry tactics, overall discipline, living conditions, and personal welfare of his soldiers. During this time he also advised the French ministers on military matters.

On March 1, 1780, King Louis XVI promoted Rochambeau to lieutenant general and to command of 5,000 troops committed to sail to America to support the rebels in their fight against the British. Rochambeau persuaded the king to increase his numbers by another 1,000 soldiers before embarking from Brest in the first week of May. The French army went ashore July 10 at Newport, Rhode Island, where Rochambeau faced several difficult problems. Less than two decades had passed since

France had fought in the Seven Years' War against these same Americans who were now their allies. Two years earlier Rochambeau's predecessor in North America, Charles d'Estaing (92), had performed poorly and left few friends of France among the rebels. On top of everything else, Rochambeau also did not particularly care for the Marquis de Lafayette (46) whom the Americans appointed as their liaison to the French army.

For the next year the French remained in Rhode Island, George Washington (1) stood fast in New York, and Nathanael Greene (4) fought the war in the South. Rochambeau rejected proposals to attack the British at New York City, remaining instead cautious while strengthening his supply lines from France and waiting for a French war fleet to arrive.

In the spring of 1781, Rochambeau learned that a sea expedition led by Admiral François de Grasse (27) was on the way to the West Indies with orders to assist the French army in North America. Rochambeau marched over land through Connecticut to the Hudson River where he joined Washington in July. The two generals moved southward, encouraged by news from Virginia that Greene had British General Charles Cornwallis (22) on the run and that de Grasse's fleet was sailing toward Chesapeake Bay. On September 22 the Franco-American army from the north besieged Cornwallis at Yorktown (2). After several gallant charges by the French and Americans, the British surrendered.

At the final victory at Yorktown, the Americans under Washington and the French led by Rochambeau were both present to accept the surrender of Cornwallis. When the British general attempted to have a subordinate surrender to the French commander rather than the rebel leader, Rochambeau refused and turned to the Americans. This act is symbolic of the French officer's service to the Revolution. From the time of his arrival in Rhode Island, he never wavered in regarding Washington as his superior officer. He ensured that his own subordinates responded likewise.

Washington and Rochambeau considered an attack on New York City to neutralize the last major British stronghold in the United States, but they correctly agreed that the war would soon end in their favor without more bloodshed. Rochambeau returned to Rhode Island where he made plans to transport his army to France. After a brief final visit with Washington, he sailed home on January 14, 1783. Upon his arrival in March, King Louis XVI recognized his accomplishments in North America with commendations and rewards.

Over the next decade Rochambeau served in both civil and military positions. Although he was an aristocrat, he joined the rebels in the French Revolution, assuming command of their Northern Army in 1790 and advancing in rank to Marshal of France the following year. His differences with some of the commanders of the French Revolution led to his resignation in 1792 and almost resulted in his execution before his release and retirement with a military pension. Rochambeau died on May 10, 1807, at Thore-la-Rochette.

Rochambeau, along with Lafayette, did much to overcome resentments from previous conflicts between the French and Americans to make the Franco-American army a united force that ultimately defeated the British. Although Rochambeau did not speak English, he knew how to work with the Americans to achieve final victory. His remarkable diplomacy enabled him to survive the French Revolution and remain a hero on both sides of the Atlantic Ocean.

Without France, it is doubtful the Revolution would have been successful. Rochambeau, who was key to the partnership that worked so well, is well-deserving of a high ranking on this list.

25

BENJAMIN FRANKLIN

American Diplomat

1706–1790

Not all the influential leaders of the Revolutionary War served on the battle-field or at sea. Benjamin Franklin—already an internationally famous writer, publisher, scientist, and inventor—was almost seventy years old when the war started. Even so, he persuaded France to lend its unofficial support to the war effort even before the Battle of Saratoga (3) convinced the French that the Americans could win. Franklin also worked to unify the colonies, helped draft and signed the *Declaration of Independence* (14), negotiated the Treaty of Paris (69), and endorsed the U.S. Constitution.

Franklin began life as the son of a Boston tallow-shop owner on January 17, 1706. He received only two years of formal schooling before joining his father's business, but he continued to educate himself by reading any printed material he could acquire. At age sixteen he wrote several articles for a local newspaper in which he satirized Boston authorities and society. A year later he departed for Pennsylvania, probably because of sibling rivalry with his older brother. Although he arrived almost penniless in Philadelphia in 1723, he soon became part owner of the city's *Gazette* and at age twenty-four bought the newspaper, which he continued to edit for the next two decades.

In 1732, Franklin began publishing *Poor Richard's Almanac,* a magazine of current interests, and continued producing it until 1757. During these years he also established a debating society, a library, a fire company, and a school that later became the University of Pennsylvania. In 1742 he invented his Franklin stove, and in 1752 he confirmed his theories about lightning and electricity with his kite experiments.

Franklin joined the Pennsylvania Assembly as a clerk in 1736 and remained in that position until he became a member of that body in 1751. In 1754 he represented Pennsylvania at the Albany Congress that had been called to unite the colonies in the French and Indian War. During the proceedings Franklin proposed that the colonies join to form a central authority. The Congress adopted his plan, but the colonial legislatures later rejected the idea because they believed it encroached on their separate authorities.

In 1757, Franklin sailed to London to represent the interests of Pennsylvania and through the following years became the agent for Massachusetts, New Jersey, and Georgia as well. Except for a two-year return to America in 1762–1764, he remained in London until 1775. Franklin arrived a loyal supporter of the Crown, but over the ensuing years he came to believe that the British did not have the authority to tax the colonies. Becoming a most vocal spokesman on rights for the Americans, he helped secure the repeal of the Stamp Act of 1765 and protested the subsequent acts that limited colonial trade and commerce.

The former newspaper editor both anticipated and dreaded the possibility of the colonies and Great Britain going to war. On May 5, 1775, he wrote, "I cannot but lament the impending calamities Britain and her colonies are about to suffer. Passion governs and she never governs well."

Franklin returned to North America on May 5, 1775, after the first shots of the Revolution had already been fired. Despite his age, he accepted the positions of Pennsylvania delegate to the Second Continental Congress (10) and postmaster general. He helped draft the *Declaration of Independence* and then became its oldest signer. On September 26, 1776, Congress selected Franklin as its commissioner to France with instruction to secure assistance and an alliance.

The French welcomed Franklin as a well-known writer and inventor but did not officially receive him as a representative of the United States because they had not yet recognized his country as an independent nation. Behind the scenes Franklin charmed the French with his wit and personality as he secured the help of Pierre de Beaumarchais (29) and his front company of Hortalez and Cie to provide arms, ammunition, and other supplies to the Continental Army (7). His unrelenting efforts and the American victory at Saratoga brought about the alliance in May 1778 in which France officially recognized the United States and offered its military assistance in the war against Great Britain.

On June 8, 1781, Congress named Franklin a representative to the peace negotiations that would end the war. It was Franklin's proposals and his force of will that secured for the United States the official recognition of independence from Great Britain, the evacuation of all British forces from occupied areas, fishing rights in the

Atlantic Ocean off Newfoundland, and western boundaries that stretched all the way to the Mississippi River. Franklin returned to Philadelphia in 1785 to become a member of the Constitutional Convention three years later. Often too weak to stand, Franklin opposed some of the basic ideas in the initial document, but he later joined the majority in approving the draft and used his humor and wit to help win its final approval.

Serving as the first president of the Pennsylvania Society for the Abolition of Slavery and signing a letter to Congress encouraging them to end the practice of bondage were among Franklin's last acts. He died on April 17, 1790, in Philadelphia and rests in its Christ Church Burial Ground. The nation mourned as more than 20,000 attended his funeral.

During the entire Revolutionary War, Benjamin Franklin never heard a shot fired in anger or visited a field of battle during or after the fight. He is proof that not all wars are won on land or at sea but rather as often in clandestine meeting rooms and in social halls. Franklin, as the American who signed all three of its principal documents—the *Declaration of Independence*, the Treaty of Paris (69), and the Constitution—was one of the first to envision an independent United States and then one of the hardest workers in bringing the concept to fruition.

Any list of American or international leaders of any ilk—or of writers, scientists, or inventors—must include the venerable Franklin. The fact that his most influential and distinguished work came in his seventies and eighties makes him all the more remarkable. All of these factors easily elevate Franklin to the most influential American nonmilitary member of this list and rank him only behind the few field commanders and battles that made the Revolution a success and the United States a reality.

26

GUILFORD COURT HOUSE, NORTH CAROLINA

March 15, 1781

The battle at Guilford Court House, North Carolina, was the last victory for General Charles Cornwallis (22) and the British in the American Revolutionary War, though no one knew it at the time. Although outnumbered more than two to one, Cornwallis attacked American defensive positions and achieved a surprising tactical victory on March 15, 1781. The triumph came at a high price for the British with more than a fourth of their number either killed or wounded. Cornwallis and his depleted army then moved on toward Yorktown (2) and eventual surrender.

The British decision to take the war into the Southern states to cut off rebel supplies and reinforcements to the North initially proved sound. With the capture of Charleston (47) and the decisive defeat of the Americans at Camden (65) in the spring and summer of 1780, the British took control of South Carolina and Georgia. For months the only rebel resistance in the area came from bands of partisans led by Francis Marion (60) and Thomas Sumter (83). It was not until the arrival of General Nathanael Greene (4) from the North that the rebels resumed the initiative and disrupted Cornwallis's drive toward North Carolina. Cornwallis lost parts of his army with Patrick Ferguson's (94) defeat at Kings Mountain (36) in October 1780 and Banastre Tarleton's (44) debacle at Cowpens, South Carolina (18), in January 1781. Still, Cornwallis pushed on, hoping to destroy Greene's main army.

Greene retreated northward, outdistancing the British, to escape across the Dan River into southern Virginia. There he obtained replacement troops and supplies before recrossing the Dan back into North Carolina on February 25. Meanwhile Cornwallis had halted at Hillsboro, North Carolina, and, when he learned that the Americans had begun their march back southward, ordered his army to intercept the rebels. When information reached Cornwallis that the rebels now numbered 4,400, he planned to attack, even though his army now totaled only 1,900. Cornwallis, having great confidence in his well-trained veteran regulars and Hessian mercenaries (37), had nothing but disdain for the fighting abilities of the Americans, particularly their militia units that made up about a third of Greene's army.

Greene believed that Cornwallis would attack despite the odds and prepared defenses when he reached Guilford Court House (within today's Greensboro).

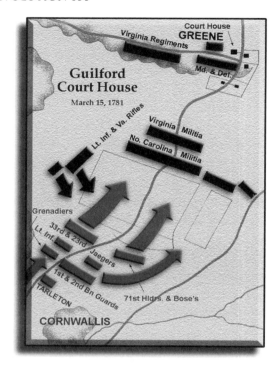

Having previously ridden through the area, the American commander had already formulated a battle plan. When he received a letter from Daniel Morgan (35) suggesting the use of the same defensive alignment that had worked so successfully at Cowpens, Greene made modifications to the plan to complement his own and to fit the terrain and the caliber of his troops.

Along a split-rail fence to his far front, Greene deployed the inexperienced militia from North Carolina with orders for them to fire two volleys before withdrawing. More seasoned militiamen from Virginia occupied the second defensive line 300 yards to the rear while the Continental army regulars stood 500 yards further back in the third defensive band. At Morgan's recommendations, Greene stationed separate parties of regulars to the flanks and rear of the militiamen with orders to shoot any militiaman who abandoned his position before firing the prescribed two volleys. Unlike the battle at Cowpens, because of the terrain the three defensive lines were too far apart to be mutually supporting. Greene also placed all his troops on the line, deciding not to hold back any in reserve.

Cornwallis approached the American defenses on the cold, clear morning of March 15, 1781. The British were tired and hungry from their long march, but Cornwallis ordered them to attack. After a short artillery barrage, the Redcoats moved forward toward the first rebel line. A British infantryman later noted that when he first saw the American militiamen they "had their arms presented and resting on the picket fence, they were taking aim with nice precision."

The militiamen fired their prescribed two volleys and hastily beat an unorganized retreat. Some discarded their equipment as they ran through the next two defensive belts, and many did not stop until they were miles from the battlefield. The second line of militiamen briefly stopped the advancing British and inflicted significant causalities before they withdrew in a fairly orderly fashion. At the third line the now nearly exhausted British charged once again only to meet the musket balls and bayonets of the American regulars. Greene, who wanted to minimize casualties, had his men hold the line until he believed the British were gaining the advantage, and then he ordered a retreat.

Cornwallis, who had his horse shot from beneath him during the battle, occupied the field, but his army was too tired and weak to pursue the Americans. The British commander, in a letter to Secretary of State George Germain (9), wrote, "The conduct and actions of the officers and soldiers that composed this little army will do more justice to their merit than I can by words. Their persevering intrepidity in action, their invincible patience in hardships and fatigues of march of above 600 miles, in which they forded several large rivers and numberless creeks, many of which would be reckoned large rivers in any other country in the world, without tents or covering against the climate, and often without provisions, will sufficiently manifest their ardent zeal for the honor and interest of their Sovereign and their country."

No one doubted the bravery of Cornwallis's army, but many did not think Guilford Court House was a great victory. Charles J. Fox, a member of the House of Commons and a opponent of the war, remarked, "Another such victory would ruin the British army."

Fox was correct in his assessment. British total killed, wounded, and captured numbered 532, more than a third of Cornwallis's army. Officially the Americans lost 1,310, but many of the "casualties" were some of the more than 1,000 militiamen who fired their two volleys and deserted the battlefield.

Guilford Court House would be Cornwallis's last victory. With his depleted army running out of supplies, he marched to Wilmington, North Carolina, and then on to Yorktown, Virginia, in hopes of receiving reinforcements or being evacuated by sea to the Northern theater. Greene did not pursue Cornwallis, deciding instead to continue southward to recapture South Carolina. By October the Americans and French, moving from the North by land and by sea, had Cornwallis surrounded. They forced his surrender and effectively ended the war.

It is difficult to assess whether Cowpens or Guilford Court House is the more influential. In the long run Guilford Court House, while a defeat for the Americans, so depleted the British army that it had to move toward ultimate surrender. Without the rebel victory at Cowpens, however, Guilford Court House might not have occurred at all, so it receives a slightly lower ranking on this list than the battle in South Carolina. Both battles, and to a lesser degree Kings Mountain, substantially influenced the outcome of the war and ensured the independence of the United States.

27

FRANÇOIS JOSEPH PAUL DE GRASSE

French Admiral

1722–1788

French Admiral François Joseph Paul de Grasse, who spent only a brief portion of his long naval career supporting the American Revolution, was the most influential naval officer of the war. His actions against the British fleet at Chesapeake Capes (13) prevented reinforcements or evacuation of the army of General Charles Cornwallis (22), forcing the British surrender at Yorktown (2) in October 1781.

Born in the south of France in September 1722 into one of the oldest families of French nobility, de Grasse began his career at sea at the young age of eleven in the service of the Knights of Malta. After serving in the Turkish and Moorish wars, he entered the French navy in 1739 during the War of Jenkins' Ear where he was captured and held for several months as a prisoner by the English. He returned to sea after his release and over the next decades fought in the War of Austrian Succession and the Seven Years' War, advancing in rank to captain in command of his own vessel. Tall at six feet two inches, described as one of the handsomest men of his times, de Grasse proved to be an efficient and knowledgeable leader.

In June 1775, de Grasse sailed to the West Indies to secure the French claim on Haiti before returning to France a year later to receive a promotion to commodore. When France announced its official alliance with the United States in 1778, de Grasse led a fleet that engaged the British in an indecisive battle near the island of Ushant off the west end of the Brittany Peninsula on July 27. De Grasse then led a squadron under Admiral Charles d'Estaing (92) in operations to capture Savannah, Georgia, in September 1779. After another excursion into the West Indies, de Grasse, now in poor health, sailed home in early January 1781.

Although not fully recovered from his illness and nearly sixty years old, de Grasse accepted a promotion to admiral in command of a new fleet with orders to sail for America the following March. After safely escorting a merchant convoy to the West Indies, de Grasse turned northward. His mission was to support the joint operations of George Washington (1) and Jean Baptiste de Rochambeau (24) to surround the British at Yorktown. De Grasse landed 3,000 troops on the Virginia coast and then

sailed out to confront the British fleet so that they could neither reinforce nor evacuate the British army under Cornwallis.

On September 5 the French and British fleets met at Chesapeake Capes. Winds and tides prevented de Grasse and all his ships from engaging the British vessels, and the afternoon-long battle proved indecisive. Over the next several days de Grasse paralleled the British fleet as they sailed with the southward winds, but de Grasse would never again engage the rival ships. Finally the British turned out to sea and back northward to New York City, leaving Cornwallis surrounded and cut off from any further aid.

Cornwallis, with no hope of reinforcements, surrendered at Yorktown in October 1781. The day after Cornwallis gave up, Washington sent de Grasse a letter praising him and noting, "The surrender of Yorktown, the honor of which belongs to your Excellency." Washington also made arrangements for two of the captured British cannons to be transported to de Grasse's home in France in recognition of his assistance.

De Grasse departed the waters of Chesapeake Bay for the West Indies where he captured St. Kitts on February 12, 1782. Less than a year later, de Grasse's luck expired when he was forced to surrender his battered ship to the British in the major French defeat at the Battle of Les Saintes in the Lesser Antilles on April 12, 1782. Again a captive of the English, de Grasse spent the next year in London, though more as a guest than a prisoner. During this time he met with high-ranking British officials to discuss possible peace negotiations. When paroled a year later, de Grasse worked with French leaders to draft the treaty that finally ended France's role in the American Revolutionary War.

Back home, de Grasse found himself accused of being responsible for the French defeat at Saint's Passage. Even though the French government took no action against the admiral, the aged de Grasse remained out of favor with the king. He retired from naval service to his country home, Chateau de Tilly, 50 miles west of Paris. Four years later, on January 14, 1788, he died at his townhouse in Paris.

Shortly after his death, the French themselves revolted. The rebels viewed the de Grasse family as a part of the aristocracy and destroyed de Grasse's country estate and dragged off his Yorktown cannons to be melted into revolutionary coinage. De Grasse's four daughters and one son fled France and made their way to the United States where Americans welcomed them as children of a Revolutionary hero. The siblings settled in Charleston, South Carolina, and the U.S. Congress voted to give them an annual pension.

American Admiral John Paul Jones (58) and French Admiral d'Estaing are the most famous naval commanders of the Revolution. The most influential, however, is the lesser known de Grasse. His leadership off the shore of Virginia directly contributed to the allied victory at Yorktown and the ultimate success of the American Revolution.

28

VALCOUR ISLAND, NEW YORK

October 11–12, 1776

In the Battle of Valcour Island in Lake Champlain in the fall of 1776, the Americans suffered a tactical defeat but gained a strategic victory. It was here that the rebels delayed the British advance southward by several months, a feat that may very well have "saved the revolution." The battle was the first significant fight by the U.S. Navy and further enhanced the early reputation of Benedict Arnold (85) as one of the ablest American generals.

After repelling the rebel Canada Invasion (84) at Quebec on January 1, 1776, the British planned a counterattack that called for them to push southward to join General William Howe (15) who would be moving north from New York. The unification of the two offensives would effectively split the colonies in two, preventing New England from receiving support from the South. Because few roads existed between Canada and New York, the British intended to use Lake Champlain and the Hudson River waterways as easy routes for the movement of troops and supplies.

General Guy Carleton (49) gathered ships and boats that had sufficient draft to navigate inland waterways at St. Jean on the Richelieu River just south of Montreal. Prefabricated gunboats also arrived from England and were reassembled to join the fleet. Carleton had no problem mustering sufficient arms for his men and cannons for his boats. By early October 1776, Carleton had amassed 13,000 men—1,500 who manned his twenty-nine vessels equipped with eighty-seven guns.

Commanders in the American army understood the importance of preventing the two British forces from linking up. George Washington (1) moved his army from Boston shortly after the British evacuation to begin fortifying New York City. In the north General Philip Schuyler convened his subordinates at Crown Point to determine their best course of action, given the few they had. They had too few soldiers to block the larger British infantry units on land or to even defend Crown Point. Finally, the Americans decided to abandon Crown Point and rely on a flotilla of lake boats to counter the British movement down Lake Champlain.

The American boats, commanded by Commodore Jacobus Wynkoop, were ill-prepared and too few to conduct a successful defense. Schuyler took the rare step of placing a soldier in charge of the navy when he appointed the recently promoted

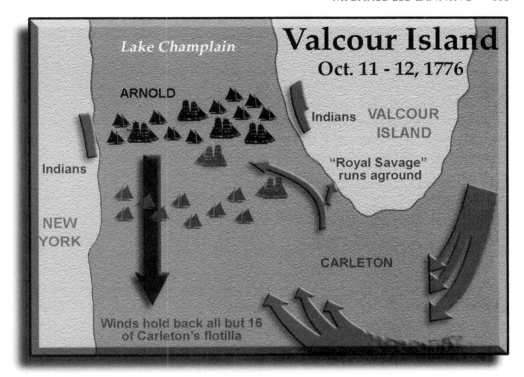

Brigadier General Benedict Arnold to be in charge of the lake flotilla on August 7, 1776. Despite being an army rather than a naval officer, Arnold had had much experience with ships and the sea. Before the war, he had earned his living shipping goods to the Caribbean from New England.

Although he had the experience, Arnold had little else. Greatly hampered by a shortage of men and supplies, including nails and other ironwork for his boats, Arnold built additional vessels and repaired those already in the fleet at Skenesborough. Unlike the efficient British supply system, Arnold had to rely on his own guile in gathering planks from sawmills, near and far away, and using blacksmiths to adapt any and all iron objects into nails, brackets, and needed works. Sailors to man his ships were also in short supply, forcing Arnold to recruit men from infantry regiments, mostly from New Hampshire, and make them into seamen.

Despite the difficulties, Arnold assembled sixteen vessels armed with eighty-three guns and carrying 800 crewmembers and soldiers. Fully half of the fleet were small, lightly armed gondolas that could be powered by both sail and oars. Arnold, whose spies kept him abreast of Carleton's preparation, fully understood the British superiority in men and ships. Knowing he did not have the strength to conduct an attack, he planned on forcing the British to attack him.

Arnold proceeded about two thirds of the way up the lake and arrayed his flotilla between the New York mainland and Valcour Island. As he hoped, when the British navy sailed down the lake on the morning of October 11, they kept to the east of the island in the main channel and did not spot the Americans until they were well past Valcour. They turned, but now the wind was against them, slowing their progress. Over the next seven hours the two fleets traded cannon shot, with the stronger British ships severely crippling the Americans.

Nightfall brought an end to the fighting. The British planned to finish off the Americans the next morning, but Arnold used the darkness and cloth-muffled oar locks on his gondolas to ease past the enemy fleet during the night. At daybreak the surprised British searched around Valcour Island before beginning a pursuit down the lake. At Split Rock they caught up with Arnold, who fought a delaying action before sailing his few remaining boats into the shallow Buttonmould Bay. The deeper draft British boats were unable to follow, allowing Arnold to remove guns and anything else of value before scuttling his surviving vessels. Arnold and his men marched overland to Crown Point and then on to Fort Ticonderoga, carrying their wounded in litters made from the tattered sails of their doomed vessels.

Carleton arrived at Crown Point on October 20 to find the fort destroyed and a winter snow already falling. Delayed by Arnold and with his force weakened by the fight at and beyond Valcour Island, the British general decided to postpone his offensive down the Hudson River until spring.

The British defeat of the Americans at Valcour Island was complete. All of the rebel vessels were either sunk by British fire or scuttled during Arnold's retreat. Eighty Americans lay dead or wounded; another 120 were British prisoners. Carleton's losses totaled three gunboats and 40 killed or wounded.

Short-term tactical victories do not, however, always produce long-range strategic accomplishments. The Battle of Valcour Island sufficiently weakened and delayed the British offensive so that it had to be put off until the following spring. By the time the British renewed their efforts to cut the colonies in two along the Hudson River in the 1777, the Continental Army (7) was much improved. This time a tactical, as well as strategic, victory came for the rebels at Saratoga (3), a victory that ended most British aggression in the North and transferred the war to the South. It also encouraged European allies (5) to rally to the side of the Americans. Noted naval theorist Alfred Thayer Mahan later wrote, "The little American navy was wiped out, but never had any force, big or small, lived to better purpose or died more gloriously."

Valcour Island merits but a footnote in today's history books, but it was one the most influential battles of the American Revolution. Perhaps Arnold's later treason took much of the attention away from the important engagement, but if his small navy of Americans had not delayed the British on Lake Champlain, they might very well have advanced down the Hudson to join Howe in New York and bring the Rebellion to a conclusion. Bunker Hill (23), Saratoga, Yorktown (2), and the pivotal fights in the Southern theater are the only battles that outrank its influence in the ultimate independence of the United States. It also ranks as the second most influential navy battle of the war, exceeded only by Chesapeake Capes (13).

29

PIERRE AUGUSTIN CARON DE BEAUMARCHAIS

French Merchant

1732–1799

As the director of the French-and-Spanish-subsidized company called Roderigue Hortalez and Cie, Pierre Augustin Caron de Beaumarchais transported large stores of weapons, gunpowder, and other supplies from Europe to the American colonies. During the early years of the Revolutionary War, Hortalez and Cie became the principal source of munitions and funds for the American rebels. It is estimated that de Beaumarchais supplied up to 90 percent of the weapons and equipment used to defeat the British at the pivotal Battle of Saratoga (3) in October 1777.

Born Pierre Augustin Caron on January 24, 1732, in Paris, as the son of a watchmaker, the future weapons merchant left school at age thirteen to apprentice under his father. In his early twenties, Caron invented a mechanism that made watches much more accurate and compact but despite his mechanical aptitude soon left the business to pursue a career in music. In 1756 he assumed the surname of de Beaumarchais derived from the land holdings of his first wife. By 1758 he had become the harp teacher for the daughters of King Louis XV, only to resign to pursue still another career as a businessman and merchant.

His new path was to be neither smooth nor straight. De Beaumarchais maintained an interest in music as a hobby and, during his business travels in Spain, developed the ideas and characters for the opera *The Barber of Seville,* produced on the stage in 1775. Turmoil and court cases, however, marked much of de Beaumarchais's early business career after he quarreled with his partner and later his partner's heirs. During this period de Beaumarchais published a pamphlet expounding on his personal interests that coincided with the support for the individual liberties and social justice.

His writings made him a hero of the people but brought him trouble in the courts. In 1773 the former watchmaker served several months in jail and had to pay fines and forfeitures that ruined him financially. To regain favor with the French crown, de Beaumarchais volunteered to travel to London, Amsterdam, and Vienna on various clandestine missions, including an effort to suppress an unfavorable pamphlet about one of King Louis XV's mistresses.

At the outbreak of the American Revolution, the French, still suffering from their losses in the Seven Years' War, wanted to assist the rebels against the British. Under the concept of "the enemy of our enemy is our friend," King Louis XVI sought ways to aid the Americans without openly joining the war. Spain shared the king's views of opposing Great Britain and agreed to a partnership. Because of his background as a businessman, spy, and now friend of the court, de Beaumarchais was the obvious man to put in charge.

In June 1776 de Beaumarchais established a front company called Roderigue Hortalez and Cie under an agreement that he, the French, and the Spanish would each contribute $200,000. After this initial infusion of cash, Hortalez and Cie would become self-supporting, with all profits or losses going to its director.

The concept of Hortalez and Cie was rather simple. De Beaumarchais would acquire weapons, gunpowder, and other supplies from European arsenals, ship them from France to the West Indies, and transfer them on to the United States. Upon delivery to the rebels, he would accept monetary payment or raw goods, such as rice and tobacco, ship those products to France, and then sell them to buy more weapons and munitions.

A merchant fleet commissioned by Hortalez and Cie made its first delivery to the American rebels at Portsmouth, New Hampshire, in early 1777. The twelve vessels landed 200 field pieces; several thousand muskets; a large store of gunpowder; and supplies that included blankets, shoes, and uniforms—enough to arm and clothe an army of 25,000. Over the next months de Beaumarchais increased his fleet to forty vessels as he continued to deliver supplies to the American army. By September 1777 the ships of Hortalez and Cie had delivered more than $1 million (more than $12.5 million in today's dollars) of weapons and equipment to the rebels.

In return the Americans paid nothing—no money, no rice, no tobacco, no form of reimbursement. According to some reports, U.S. representatives to France claimed that the French had agreed to provide the shipments as grants with no intention of receiving payment. It is noteworthy that American farmers were unwilling to provide their goods for shipment back to France without money up-front—and the new American government had no funds to pay anyone for anything.

Despite the lack of payment, de Beaumarchais continued to send aid to the Americans. When France officially allied with the rebels in February 1778, the Hortalez and Cie fleets sailed under the protection of the French navy, making their deliveries safer and more reliable. De Beaumarchais, always the good businessman, accepted that the Americans were not going to pay, so he diverted his vessels after their deliveries to the rebels back through the West Indies on their return trips. At Martinique and San Domingo, they took on cargos of sugar and other products for sale in Europe. By the time Hortalez and Cie dissolved in 1783, the company showed a small profit for their six years of existence, notwithstanding the more than $62 million of arms and supplies delivered to the Americans.

De Beaumarchais continued his interest in music even while supplying the American Revolution. In 1778, he wrote *The Marriage of Figaro,* but, because its theme involved a servant and his master competing for the favors of a young lady in a personification of the class struggle in pre-Revolutionary France, the opera was not publicly produced until six years later. During the 1780s he also acquired many of the unpublished works of Voltaire and put them in print, preserving much of the philosopher's work that otherwise might have been lost. By the time of the outbreak of the French Revolution, he had acquired a rank in the French nobility and was living comfortably in Paris from funds gained by supplying the city's drinking water. De Beaumarchais, always looking to the future, pledged his services to the new Republic and attempted to acquire 60,000 muskets from Holland to support the Revolution.

Despite his work for the new government, enemies in the regime declared him to be still loyal to the royals. De Beaumarchais spent two and a half years in exile in

Germany before finally returning to Paris in 1796. He died there on May 18, 1799, and is buried in the city's Père-Lachaise Cemetery.

De Beaumarchais devoted his final years to gaining payment for his debts in America. The U.S. Congress investigated its responsibility to repay the Frenchman in 1787, but it was not until thirty-six years later that they finally made some restitution to de Beaumarchais's heirs.

The French and Spanish support of the American Revolution provided through the firm of Roderigue Hortalez and Cie and its administrator de Beaumarchais proved critical to the success of the United States. Without this assistance, Americans might not have even been able to field an army for any substantial period. The role of de Beaumarchais in securing the funds, acquiring the supplies, and delivering them to America is remarkable. He managed to balance the intrigue of the French court, maintain a relationship with the Spanish, and determine how to make it a profitable business when the Americans would and could pay nothing. De Beaumarchais and his company are true heroes of the American Revolution and deserving of a place high on this list.

30

WEST POINT, NEW YORK

1775–1783

General George Washington (1) declared the heights above the Hudson River at West Point to be "the key to America." The topography of the waterway, the cannons on the heights, and a chain across the river prevented the British from sailing north to divide New England from the other colonies. West Point's defenses also limited British supplies and reinforcements from Canada and convinced the Redcoats that the fortress was so impregnable that they never mounted an attack. American possession of West Point even withstood an attempt at treason by its commander, Benedict Arnold (85).

From the beginning of the Revolutionary War, both the Americans and the British realized that controlling the Hudson River was key to conducting the war. Extending from the upper lakes of the state to New York City, the waterway provided easy access to Canadian provinces for food and supplies as well as a ready route for quickly moving large groups of soldiers. The river became even more important when the Redcoats, forced to abandon Boston, occupied New York City after hard-fought battles on Long Island (32) and White Plains (77) in the fall of 1776.

The rebels attempted to block the British from sailing up the Hudson by erecting a chain-and-log-boom mechanism across the river from Fort Washington (86) on upper Manhattan Island to Fort Lee on the western shore. When these forts fell to the British in November 1776, the Americans withdrew north about 40 miles to a point where the river enters a gorge that forms cliffs above the water. There they established another chain-and-log boom at Fort Montgomery.

In the fall of 1777, the British planned a three-column attack to take control of the Hudson River Valley in order to separate the New England states from the others. The strategy called for General John Burgoyne (33) to move south out of Canada with the main column supported by a smaller second column led by Colonel Barry St. Leger (64). Meanwhile, British commander in New York, General Henry Clinton (17), was to maneuver northward up the Hudson. The first two columns started south, but Clinton delayed his part of the attack before finally moving up river to neutralize Fort Montgomery on October 6, 1777. By this time St. Leger had already turned back to Canada, and a day later Burgoyne surrendered at Saratoga (3).

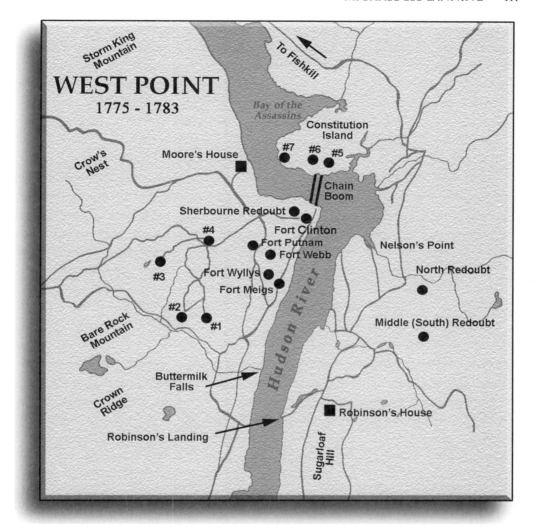

When he learned of Burgoyne's defeat, Clinton returned to New York City, leaving the Hudson River to be reclaimed by the rebels. This time Washington selected a position about 5 miles north of Fort Montgomery and 45 miles north of New York City where the otherwise straight river makes an S-curve. He chose this spot because these two right angles were all but impossible for sailing ships to traverse and the cliffs overlooking the river, known as West Point, dominated the approaches. General Friedrich von Steuben (62), who drilled troops on the plain above the river, declared, "Let us hold West Point, and the end of the campaign will be glorious."

In the winter of 1777–1778, the Americans moved cannons captured at Saratoga to the West Point heights where they established Forts Arnold (later renamed Fort Clinton) and Putnam. With Polish-engineer-turned-American-officer Thaddeus Kosciuszko as the chief planner, they built another fortification across the river on Constitution Island and a series of other outposts to guard the approaches to these primary defenses. The Americans added more and more captured cannons to the fortifications over the following months until it boasted more than 160 pieces of artillery, making it the strongest rebel defensive position in the country.

On January 20, 1778, the rebels assembled an iron chain consisting of 800 two-foot-long links weighing about 125 pounds each. These links, forged at the nearby Sterling Furnace in Warwick, floated atop fifty-foot-long pine log rafts that spanned the 1,500-foot-wide river. General Alexander McDougall, commander of the region, recorded simply in his diary on April 30, "Chain put across." In the winters that followed, the rebels removed the chain so the annual ice flows would not destroy it. Since the British did not conduct operations in the winter months, this was a safe practice. Each spring the rebels labored to replace the chain boom before the arrival of warm weather.

Many inhabitants of the Hudson River Valley favored the British, and these Loyalists (34) kept Clinton in New York abreast of the American activities at West Point. Even so, with the river blocked by the chain and boom and a series of forts preventing a land attack, Clinton decided to refocus his efforts to crush the Rebellion from the North to the South. No more major battles would take place in New York or New England.

Meanwhile, the blocked Hudson River limited Clinton's forces in New York to receiving resupply only from the sea. As a result, his army became an island surrounded by a land of rebels. Clinton's only opportunity to take West Point and control the Hudson came in 1779 when the disgruntled American commander of the region, Benedict Arnold, approached the British. Arnold proposed that he disperse the land defenders, sabotage the river chain, and surrender the fortifications in exchange for money and a commission in the British army.

Clinton's own aide, Major John Andre, served as a go-between with Arnold. The treachery was nearly complete when an American patrol captured Andre along with incriminating papers from Arnold to Clinton on September 23, 1780. Word of the capture reached Arnold in time for him to escape down river to a British warship. Andre, dressed in civilian clothes when captured, died on the gallows as a spy. The Americans quickly reinforced West Point to ensure Clinton would not attack. West Point remained unchallenged for the remainder of the Revolution.

When the war finally ended, newly independent Americans had no desire for a peacetime regular army. They abolished the bulk of the Continental Army on June 2, 1784, leaving West Point garrisoned by only fifty-five men and a captain. During this period George Washington lobbied for a national military school to produce future officers. It was not until July 4, 1804, however, when Thomas Jefferson (87) was president that the U.S. Military Academy at West Point became a reality. West Point today is the oldest U. S. military post over which the stars and stripes have continuously flown. Cadets still drill on the same plain used by von Steuben, and some relics of the Revolution are preserved on campus, including a few remaining links of the great chain that once crossed the Hudson.

Holding West Point was crucial for the Americans, and the fact that they succeeded in that had enormous influence on the outcome of the American Revolution. It anchored the American defenses in the North, isolated New York City, and forced the British to move their primary efforts to the South where they eventually lost. With the Revolutionary War, West Point became a tradition that today is synonymous with military excellence and leadership.

31

HORATIO GATES

American General

1728–1806

Horatio Gates joined the rebellion as one of its most experienced officers to serve as commander of both the Northern and Southern Continental armies. His most influential accomplishment was his victory over John Burgoyne (33) at the Battle of Saratoga (3). Despite this great feat, he is better known for the defeat suffered at Camden (65) and for his overall quarrelsome personality.

Gates began life sometime in 1728, or possibly a year or two earlier, in Maldon, England, as the son of a wealthy family's housekeeper. During his whole life he resented his servant-class upbringing and did his best to rise above this station. Through friendship with the sons of influential families, he secured a lieutenant's commission in the British army in 1745. He then served in Germany during the War of the Austrian Succession before sailing for Canada where he advanced to captain in the provincial ranks of Nova Scotia. During the French and Indian War he fought alongside the American colonial militias in the Ohio Valley, being seriously wounded at Fort Duquesne. During this time he met colonial officers including George Washington (1), Daniel Morgan (35), and Charles Lee (79).

In 1762, Gates participated in the capture of the French island of Martinique. Back in England, where advance in rank depended upon wealth and influence rather than battlefield prowess, Gates became dissatisfied with the military and retired on half pay as a major in 1765. In August 1772, at the encouragement of his old friend Washington, Gates moved to Virginia and settled on a modest plantation.

Upon learning of the outbreak of the Revolution in 1775, Gates rushed to Mount Vernon to offer his services to Washington and the colonies. It is likely he sided with the Americans because of his resentment of the English social system, which continued to exclude him, rather than on any beliefs in liberty and independence. Regardless, Washington and the Continental Congress (10) welcomed the experienced Gates and appointed him the adjutant general of the Continental Army (7).

Gates's administrative skills greatly contributed to the initial organization of the army, but he wanted a command in the field. He joined the army's retreat from

Canada in the fall of 1776, only to be placed subordinate to General Philip Schuyler. Both Schuyler and Gates had their supporters in Congress, each openly opposing the other's advancement. Finally, in August 1777, Gates's politicizing, combined with Schuyler's loss of Fort Ticonderoga, led to Gates's assumption of command of the Northern Army.

In six weeks Gates reorganized and trained his 6,000 regulars, augmented by 17,000 militiamen. He placed his force in defensive positions near Saratoga to block the advance of Burgoyne's British column. Gates's subordinates fought well in the ensuing battle and earned the rebels a major victory. Gates, as well as his friends in Congress, then lobbied for his promotion to replace Washington, who had not fared well in the New York campaign. On October 17, Congress placed Gates at the head of the Board of War, one of the first efforts to establish an executive department to supervise the military.

Washington's successes at Trenton (8) and Princeton two months later ended any hopes Gates had of his assuming the command of the Continental Army. In April 1778, Gates returned to the Northern army and in the fall moved to Boston as the leader of the Eastern Department. During this time he lobbied for a transfer to assume the leadership of the Southern army where most of the combat had shifted. When General Benjamin Lincoln (76) lost Charleston, South Carolina (47), and much of the Southern army in May 1780, Gates got his chance.

By July Gates was in command in North Carolina and initiated tactics similar to those that had been successful at Saratoga. This time, however, the terrain was unfamiliar, the army suffered low morale, and many of the men were sick. He then went against the recommendations of his subordinates and marched toward Camden, South Carolina, where he was routed by the British under General Charles Cornwallis (22). Gates, on the pretext of securing reinforcements and supplies, abandoned his army and fled 180 miles in only three and a half days to the sanctuary of Hillsborough, North Carolina.

Gates still had his supporters, but now he had far more critics. At Washington's urging, Congress dispatched Nathanael Greene (4) to take over command of the Southern army, leaving Gates to lobby Congress from his Virginia home. Gates pressed Congress for an inquiry to clear his name. In 1782, Congress finally did so, and Gates joined Washington's staff at Newburgh. There he supported Washington in settling the discontent among Continental officers that led to the Newburgh

Addresses (89). It is also noteworthy that Gates was originally one of the leaders of the group that instigated the crisis.

Gates retired to his Virginia farm in 1783 and never again served in uniform. His wife died that same year, and in 1786 he remarried a wealthy widow. Four years later, at the urging of his friend John Adams (51), Gates freed his slaves rather than sell them when he relocated to New York. Settling on a farm on Manhattan Island in 1790, Gates and his wife enjoyed the amenities of the New York social scene, but Gates also insisted that some of his wife's fortune go to supporting various causes for veterans' relief.

Gates, always the politician, supported the presidential campaign of Thomas Jefferson (87) in 1786, which in effect ended his friendship with John Adams, who was Jefferson's opponent. In 1800, Gates formally entered the political arena himself and won a single term in the New York legislature. He died on April 10, 1806, and is buried in Trinity Church graveyard on Wall Street.

Most descriptions of Gates, even by his friends, describe him as a ruddy-faced man who wore thick spectacles that made him appear "bug-eyed." Some thought him snobbish; others found him overly pious. Everyone, however, agreed that he was a quarrelsome individual. Still, he could be, if not charming, at least convincing enough to gain the trust of many in Congress and to regain the support of Washington even after trying to replace the general.

Gates journeyed a long way from his common English birth to rise as a leader in the new United States. While far from the influential level of Washington, Greene, and Morgan, his tenure in command at the great victory at Saratoga secures Gates a place in the top third of this list and in the annals of the heroes of the American Revolution.

32

LONG ISLAND, NEW YORK

August 27, 1776

The Battle of Long Island was the first major—and the largest—battle of the American Revolution. British General William Howe (15) executed superior generalship by maneuvering his more experienced and disciplined troops to easily best George Washington (1) and his rebels from the field. Only Howe's failure to exploit his advantage and Washington's ability to use fog and darkness to evacuate his surviving troops saved the Continental Army (7) and possibly the Rebellion from annihilation.

When the long Boston Siege (50) ended in March 1776 with the British evacuation to Nova Scotia, Washington knew the Redcoats would return and that their likely target would be the communications and shipping center of New York City. In April the American commander marched his army of nearly 19,000 to the New York area and ordered General Israel Putnam and his force of 7,000 to prepare defensive positions on the southwestern end of Long Island.

As expected, in July 1776, Howe arrived off the New York shore. He had with him the largest armada of armed forces ever assembled in North America until the Civil War. With an army of 22,000—including 9,000 Hessian mercenaries (37)—aboard 500 war and merchant ships commanded by his brother Admiral Richard Howe (90), the British general established his headquarters on Staten Island. Howe's primary objective was to defeat Washington's army and bring an end to the Rebellion. If not totally successful, then he intended to occupy New York City, which he knew had a large number of Loyalists (34). By occupying New York he could control a main shipping point and also limit communications among the colonies.

Between August 22 and 25, Howe, under the cover of the fleet's guns, landed most of his army at Gravesend's Bay to the south of Putnam's positions that occupied the present Flatbush section of Brooklyn. Just after midnight on August 27, Howe struck the American center with a probing force of only several hundred soldiers. When this probe gained the attention of the American commanders, he attacked with the bulk of his force in a wide circle movement to the east through Jamaica Pass. The following morning the British, led by General Henry Clinton (17), struck the American left flank and quickly collapsed their defenses. Other British columns

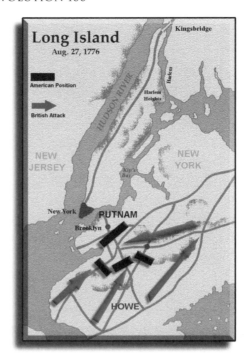

joined the assault that sent most of the ill-trained American militiamen into retreat. Only a desperate stand by a rear guard of Maryland soldiers saved the main American army from death or capture.

The battle had been costly for the rebels. Casualty figures vary greatly, but best estimates are that the Americans sustained 1,500 casualties, including 200 dead. British casualties numbered only about 400.

Following his victory, Howe had the tactical and numerical advantage but not the will to exploit his opportunity. With the Battle of Bunker Hill (23) in his mind, he did not want to directly assault the American defenses on Brooklyn Heights. Instead he decided to besiege the rebels.

Washington arrived on the battlefield shortly after Putnam took up his new positions and observed that the defenses were untenable. With the British army blocking any land route of retreat and their navy securing the waterways, Washington decided to evacuate his army. Fortunately for the Americans, winds and rain hampered British observation. Employing Massachusetts militiamen, who were also experienced sea-going fishermen, to gather and man small transport boats, he used the fog and darkness of the night of August 29–30 to transport the army across the East River onto Manhattan Island. The British were unaware of the move until they awoke the next morning to find the trenches of Brooklyn Heights empty.

The numbers of casualties on Long Island made an impression on both sides. American John Sullivan (71), captured in the fight, met with the Howe brothers to discuss possible peace negotiations. On September 5, Sullivan, with the Howe's permission, approached the Continental Congress (10) to suggest they send a delegation to meet with the British leaders. Six days later Benjamin Franklin (25), John Adams (51) and Edward Rutledge met with Admiral Howe rather than General Howe on Staten Island. General Howe's absence from the meeting was an indication that the field commanders had no real authority to negotiate any agreements with the rebels.

Admiral Howe received his guests amiably but made it clear they would have to revoke their *Declaration of Independence* (14) for any further action to take place. In his later letter to Secretary of State George Germain (9), he wrote that he had told the Americans that "for obvious reasons, we could not enter into any treaty with their Congress, and much less proceed in any conference of negotiations upon the inadmissible ground of independence."

The Americans returned to Philadelphia to make their report while the Howes made further plans to defeat Washington. On September 15, General Howe landed on Manhattan to find the American army firmly entrenched on the north end of the island at Harlem Heights. After a brief unsuccessful probe Howe, again not wanting to risk a frontal assault, withdrew. On October 12, Howe again flanked Washington by sailing up the East River to land at Pell's Point behind the Americans. Washington retreated northward to White Plains (77) where, on October 28, Howe forced the Americans once more to retreat. A month later the British captured Fort Washington (86), allowing them to occupy New York City.

The city remained under British control for the remainder of the war, never being recaptured by the Americans. At the end of the conflict the triumphant Americans allowed the British to sail away from the city with their weapons, Loyalist supporters, and many slaves who had escaped from their rebel owners.

Long Island ranks above White Plains on this list because it was the largest concentration of soldiers on both sides to meet on the battlefield during the Revolution. It was also the last opportunity for a negotiated settlement. These factors merit its being in the top third of this list.

33

JOHN BURGOYNE

British General

1722–1792

John Burgoyne served the British Empire well as a soldier, as a member of Parliament, and as a writer and playwright. His presence on this list, however, is for his defeat in the one of the most important battles of the American Revolution. Burgoyne's loss at Saratoga (3) provided encouragement to the faltering Rebellion and secured much-needed foreign aid for the Americans.

Born in London in 1722, Burgoyne received a gentleman's education at Westminster School before joining the British army as a cornet in 1740. Officer commissions at the time could be purchased, and Burgoyne used family funds to advance to the rank of lieutenant the following year. In 1743 the young officer eloped with the daughter of the wealthy Earl of Derby, but the unhappy father-in-law provided his daughter only a relatively small dowry and declared he would offer no further support.

Burgoyne used his bride's money to purchase a captaincy, and the couple lived well in London for the next three years. The Burgoynes, however, lived beyond their means, and he was forced to sell his commission and move to France. There Burgoyne learned the language and studied literature and writing. In 1756 Burgoyne, now in the good graces of his father-in-law, used Derby's influences to return to the army. At age thirty-six, Captain Burgoyne experienced his first combat in the Seven Years' War. In operations along the French coast, he displayed excellent leadership that advanced him to command of a regiment. His organizational skills became apparent as he introduced the first light cavalry units into the British army.

In 1761 Burgoyne sailed to England to take a seat in Parliament. The following year he returned to the field at the head of his light cavalry regiment in Portugal where he earned high honors in fighting the Spanish. It was also during this period that he acquired the name "Gentleman Johnny" from his troops. In a time when commanders treated their soldiers with brutality and harshness, Burgoyne opposed frequent corporal punishment and declared that the men should be treated as thinking human beings rather than animals. Along with their affection, Burgoyne's ideas earned him the loyal following of his command.

Burgoyne returned to Parliament in 1768 where he became known for his outspoken manner and his investigations into the East India Company. He was a fixture of the London social scene and gambling halls as he continued to work on his writing skills, leading to the production of his first play in 1772.

In response to the unrest in America, Burgoyne—along with Generals William Howe (15) and Henry Clinton (17)—sailed for Boston in May 1775 to join General Thomas Gage. Although now a major general, Burgoyne was the junior of the British officers and quickly became disenchanted with his lack of authority. He witnessed—but did not take part in—the Battle of Bunker Hill (23) on June 17. In November he retuned to England and used his political connections to lead reinforcements back to North America to join General Guy Carleton's (49) defense of Canada against an American invasion.

Burgoyne arrived in Canada in November 1775 and helped turn back the rebels in June 1776 about halfway between Quebec and Montreal at the Trovis River. He then took part in the pursuit of the Americans that halted at Valcour Island (28) on Lake Champlain in October. Burgoyne, unhappy with Carleton's leadership and not looking forward to wintering in Canada, took leave and returned to London. There he spoke out against Carleton and lobbied for his own plan to invade the rebel colonies from Canada.

In the spring of 1777, Burgoyne received approval from King George III (20) to return to Canada to lead the invasion army as he wanted. The force, composed mostly of Carleton's former command, was to recapture Fort Ticonderoga and then push southward down the Hudson River to effectively cut off New England from the rest of the colonies. The plan also called for General William Howe to advance north from New York to meet Burgoyne's army and for Colonel Barry St. Leger (64) to sail across Lake Ontario and move through the Mohawk Valley joining the other two columns near Albany.

Burgoyne's plan was sound; its execution was not. The Americans abandoned Ticonderoga without a fight. Burgoyne, confident after this bloodless victory, moved his column slowly. A large number of supply wagons followed his British army, cutting new roads through the forest, carrying essentials as well as luxuries, and accommodating a number of officers' wives and other camp followers. Burgoyne's column advanced only 20 miles in three weeks.

Unbeknownst to Burgoyne, the Americans had marshaled and reinforced their army along his route and by September had restricted his lines of communication back to Canada. Meanwhile, St. Leger had been turned back by the Continentals in the Mohawk Valley and Howe had never advanced north from New York. Burgoyne was now alone. His slow march allowed General Horatio Gates (31) to assemble an army of 7,000 rebels on Bemis Heights south of Saratoga. Short of supplies and leading a force reduced to about 6,000, Burgoyne attempted twice to break through the American lines to reach Albany. Each attack failed.

On October 17, Burgoyne surrendered to Gates, and 5,728 British soldiers lay down their arms—all of which were soon in the hands of the always arms-deficient rebels. British soldiers marched off into captivity while Burgoyne returned to London under parole. The colonists gained not only their first great victory of the war but also their first allies (5) among Britain's enemies. When France and other European countries saw that the American rebellion might very well be successful, they began sending support.

Back in London, Burgoyne defended his conduct and blamed his failure on the lack of support from Howe and St. Leger. The English were not happy with the defeat, prompting Parliament to make a motion "to condemn the state and condition of the army which surrendered at Saratoga." Even though removed from his military and government positions, Burgoyne continued to draw his general's pay.

In 1782 Burgoyne's political friends regained power and returned him to active duty as the commander of the British army in Ireland. A year later, after another change in political leadership, he returned to civilian life and left public service. In his final years he continued to write various literary and dramatic works. He died on June 4, 1792, and is buried in Westminster Abby.

Burgoyne was equally mediocre as a politician and as a soldier. Described as brilliant and brave or as vain and undependable, Burgoyne was a man whose character probably lay somewhere in between. His ranking in the top third of this list results not from his successes but for his loss at Saratoga. It was Burgoyne's surrender at Saratoga that turned the tide of the American Revolution in favor of the rebels.

34

LOYALISTS

1775–1783

Not all Americans favored taking up arms against Great Britain for the sake of independence. Only about a third of the population supported the Rebellion while another third preferred to be left alone, satisfied to live their lives under whatever government was in control. Still another third actively opposed the idea of an independent United States and remained loyal to King George III (20). These Loyalists had significant influence on the progress of the conflict and on the strategy of both sides.

Loyalists, also known as Tories, opposed the Revolution for many reasons. Some felt a loyalty to their king and believed Britain had legitimate reasons to rule and tax the colonies without representation. Others, such as the king's officers and other beneficiaries of the Crown, opposed the Revolution because it threatened their livelihood.

Yet others—men who considered themselves cultured because of education, wealth, or title—believed the Revolution had little chance of success, and they remained loyal to the Crown to secure their positions.

Loyalists tended to be older, wealthier, and better educated than those who favored independence. Yet support for the king came from all social-economic backgrounds. Recent emigrants, especially those from Scotland, tended to remain loyal to the Crown. Quakers claimed pacifism but withheld their crops and food supplies from the rebels so they could sell to the British, causing George Washington (1) to refer to Quaker areas of Pennsylvania and New Jersey as "the enemy's country."

Anglican Church leaders and their congregations also mostly sided with the king. Samuel Seabury, an Anglican clergyman from Westchester County, New York, explained, "If I must be enslaved let it be by a King at least, not by a parcel of upstart lawless Committeemen. If I must be devoured, let me be devoured by the jaws of a lion, and not gnawed to death by rats and vermin."

British sympathies were the strongest in New York, New Jersey, and Georgia generally and in the population centers like New York City and Savannah, specifically. Other concentrations were in Pennsylvania, North Carolina, and South Carolina. By the end of the war, New York City and Long Island had the largest concentration of Loyalists, many of whom were refugees from other regions. New England remained the "cradle of the Revolution" and had the fewest Loyalists within its borders. At no time, however, did those loyal to the king outnumber the rebel Americans in any of the thirteen states.

Treatment of the Loyalists varied. In some cases and areas, rebels harassed them and on occasion tarred and feathered them before the *Declaration of Independence* (14). After July 4, the Americans considered the Loyalists rather than themselves to be traitors. About 80,000 Loyalists left their homes and property and either returned to England or moved to Canada or other British possessions. Several hundred thousand others concentrated in areas in America under British control while still others—those who were not too vocal in their support of the king—remained in their homes.

Many Loyalists also stepped forward to defend their personal beliefs in support of the king and their own self-interests. About 50,000 enlisted in Loyalists' regiments during the conflict with about 10,000 in uniform at any one time. Loyalists also took the lead in organizing Native American (99) opposition to the rebels and in encouraging slaves to flee their masters and join the British in exchange for their freedom. All of this mixed together to foster intense hatred between Loyalists and the rebels, producing some of the bloodiest battles of the war when Loyalists units met the Continental Army (7) and rebel militias (53) on the battlefield.

While the Loyalists contributed to the British efforts, their very presence also hindered the movements of the Redcoats and often overextended their defenses. When British forces withdrew from Boston and the town's Loyalist civilians demanded to go with them, accommodations had to be made. Instead of immediately sailing to capture New York City in a timely fashion, General William Howe (15) had to first sail to Halifax, Nova Scotia, to insure the safety of the Loyalists there. Again, the Loyalists taxed the British in the winter of 1776 when Howe had to widely disperse his army in order to protect Loyalists communities in New Jersey at Trenton, Brunswick, Bordentown, and Princeton. This maneuver allowed Washington to execute successful winter attacks against Trenton (8) and Princeton that greatly raised the flagging morale of the Americans. When the war moved to the Southern states,

British and Loyalist units had to man garrisons at remote locations to protect those still loyal to the crown. As a result Americans were able to concentrate their forces against specific, and often numerically inferior, targets.

The British also had to deal with and make arrangements for slaves. When the British finally evacuated New York City in 1783, they took along 7,000 Loyalist civilians, who in turn evacuated their own slaves as well as those who had fled bondage from rebel owners. Several hundred other slaves were transported as freemen to live in London and about 4,000 were taken to Nova Scotia where they were given land. About a third of these former slaves eventually returned to Africa to settle in the British colony of Sierra Leone. Most, however, remained in bondage to be dispatched to sugar cane plantations in British Caribbean colonies.

The Americans confiscated land and other properties from Loyalists during and immediately after the Revolution. It was not uncommon for officers—especially those who had had little property before the war—to be rewarded for gallant service with an estate or plantation previously belonging to a family loyal to the king. Some Loyalists eventually secured compensation from the British. By 1790 that government had honored 4,118 claims by those who had lost property to the victorious Americans.

The majority of Loyalists remained in the United States after the war, and by the mid-1780s many more who had gone into exile returned. While not warmly welcomed, neither were they persecuted. No former Loyalists were tried for treason, and, in fact, many reentered mainstream America to regain their prewar status and success. The Anglican Church remained out of favor until it reorganized as the Protestant Episcopal Church. Pastor Seabury, who had called the rebels "rats and vermin" at the beginning of the war, became the church's first Episcopal Bishop in America.

Thus, the Loyalists both helped the British by providing man power and supplies and hindered them by overtaxing their resources to protect Loyalist settlements. The balance of their influence places them in the middle of this list.

35

DANIEL MORGAN

American General

1736–1802

Daniel Morgan, by employing brilliant battlefield tactics and emphasizing marksmanship, influenced nearly every battle of the American Revolution. Rough, uneducated, and defiant, Morgan earned a loyal following from his subordinates and established himself as one of the best field commanders of the conflict.

Born in 1736 in Hunterdon County, New Jersey, as the grandson of a Welsh immigrant and son of an ironworker, Morgan received little formal education. He left home at age seventeen after an argument with his father and moved to Virginia where he found work as a farm laborer. In 1755 he served as a civilian wagon teamster in the ill-fated British offensive against Fort Duquesne, Pennsylvania, during the French and Indian War. In the British withdrawal, Morgan distinguished himself by helping evacuate the wounded, and he also met a Virginia militiaman named George Washington (1).

The next year Morgan argued with a British officer who responded by striking the teamster with the flat of his sword. Morgan struck back with his fist, earning himself a beating with a horse whip. The incident left Morgan with a life-long hatred for British officers, but he continued to serve for much of the French and Indian War. In 1758 he suffered a musket-ball wound to the mouth that cost him all his teeth on one side.

After the war Morgan did well financially as a farmer near Winchester, Virginia. He was quick, however, to lay down the plow and pick up his musket to serve as a militia lieutenant in fighting Native Americans in Pontiac's War near Detroit in 1763–1764 and again in Lord Dunmore's War along the Virginia-Pennsylvania border in 1774.

Upon learning of the outbreak of the Revolution in Massachusetts, Morgan accepted a commission as a captain in the Virginia militia on June 22, 1775. He immediately enlisted ninety-six men and in only twenty-one days marched his company to join the Boston Siege (50). The following September he joined General Benedict Arnold's march toward Quebec in the Canada Invasion (84). Morgan and

his men fought well at Quebec and, when Arnold was wounded, the former teamster took command of the Americans. Forced to surrender, Morgan remained a prisoner of the British until his exchange in the fall of the following year.

On November 12, 1777, Morgan accepted a colonelcy in the Continental Army (7) in command of a Virginia regiment. He raised a unit of 500 sharpshooters armed with rifles rather than inaccurate smooth-bore muskets. During his recruitment Morgan printed broadsides of life-size figures of British officers—some reports say including King George III (20)—and accepted only those men who could hit the target at a hundred meters distance. Because Morgan well remembered being horse-whipped some two decades earlier, he frequently ordered his marksmen "to aim for the epaulets," adornments worn only by officers.

Morgan and his riflemen joined Washington in New Jersey where he covered the rear during the American withdrawal southward. In correspondence of the time, Washington called Morgan's organization "the Corps of Rangers," one of the first uses of the name Ranger in the American army.

Washington dispatched Morgan's Rangers to assist General Horatio Gates (31) the following September in blocking British General John Burgoyne's (33) advance down the Hudson River. Morgan and his men played an important role in the British defeat at the pivotal Battle of Saratoga (3), when Morgan's men turned back the British attack at Freeman's Farm on September 19. At a second battle on the same ground on October 7, one of Morgan's marksmen killed British General

Simon Fraser and many of his subordinate officers, forcing the remaining Redcoats to withdraw. After surrendering to Gates, Burgoyne remarked, "Morgan's men were the most famous Corps of the Continental Army. All of them crack shots."

Morgan spent the winter of 1777–1778 with Washington at Valley Forge (39) and then led the pursuit of the British after the Battle of Monmouth (59) in June 1778. In July 1779, Morgan submitted his resignation due to what he claimed were health reasons. More likely it was because of his displeasure for being passed over for a brigade command awarded Anthony Wayne (38). Congress directed Morgan to return to active duty in June 1780 to assist Gates, who was then fighting in the Southern theater. Without promise of a promotion to general, Morgan did not comply with the orders. Only when he learned of the American defeat at Camden, South Carolina (65), the following August did he set aside his grievances, don his uniform, and head south.

Congress rewarded Morgan with an appointment as a brigadier general in October. The next year Morgan led half the army in the South, now under the overall command of Nathanael Greene (4), in a fight-and-withdraw campaign that led to his classic victory over British Lieutenant Colonel Banastre Tarleton (44) at the pivotal Battle of Cowpens, South Carolina (18), on January 17, 1781. Both before and during the fight Morgan displayed his personal bravery by leading from the front and his abilities to motivate his soldiers.

On arrival at Cowpens, Morgan stated, "On this ground, I will defeat the British or lay down my bones." To his militiamen, many of whom were nearing the end of their enlistment, he announced, "Just hold up your head, boys, three fires [musket shots], and you are free, and then when you return to your homes, how the folks will bless you, and the girls will kiss you for your gallant conduct."

In February 1781, Morgan resigned from the army for what he again claimed were health reasons, but it was likely over his differences with Greene on how to conduct the remainder of the campaign. Morgan retired to an estate awarded to him by the State of Virginia that formerly belonged to a Loyalist (34) near Winchester. Over the years he added to his farm until it covered a quarter million acres. He briefly returned to uniform at the request of Washington to command militia troops against opponents of liquor taxes in the Whiskey Rebellion of 1794.

Morgan served as delegate to Congress from Virginia from 1797–1799 but declined to run for reelection due to his failing health—real this time. He died on July 6, 1802, and is buried in Winchester's Mount Hebron Cemetery.

The "Old Wagoner," as he was called, was far from fitting the stereotype of a gentleman who usually occupied the high officer ranks. Morgan earned his generalship and reputation by fighting hard, selecting and motivating his troops, and promoting the importance of good marksmanship. He was the kind of man one might want to join for a drink and an officer who one would definitely like by his side in combat. His direct participation at Saratoga and Cowpens provided the leadership in two of the Revolution's pivotal battles elevate him into the top half of this list.

36

KINGS MOUNTAIN,
SOUTH CAROLINA
October 7, 1780

The Battle of Kings Mountain, fought on the border of South and North Carolina, gained the Americans their first victory against the British offensive in the Southern states. In the fight between rebel militiamen and Loyalists (34), the Americans achieved one of their most overwhelming victories of the war. Kings Mountain, followed by the Battle of Cowpens (18) three months later, provided the turning point in the Revolution in the South and ensured the success of the American War for Independence.

After the occupation of Charleston (47) in May 1780 and the crushing defeat of the Americans at Camden (65) the following August, British General Charles Cornwallis (22) thought that he had neutralized Georgia and South Carolina, and he planned to push northward into North Carolina. The only remaining resistance of any consequence in South Carolina lay along its border with North Carolina in the far northwestern portion of the state. American militiamen, particularly those from the regions west of the Appalachian Mountains, were not fully committed to supporting the Revolution, but they were opposed to their fellow colonists who fought for the British. In what was more a Carolina Civil War than a revolt against England, the rebel Americans raided outposts manned by Loyalists.

Cornwallis marched into North Carolina on September 9, 1780, and established his forward base on September 26. To protect his flank, he dispatched an army of 1,100 well-trained Loyalists under the command of British Major Patrick Ferguson (94) on a screen to the west. Along the way Ferguson issued an announcement to the rebel militias, warning them not to resist or he would, "Lay waste to their country with fire and sword."

The order enraged the Carolinians. Those directly in Ferguson's path stood fast while militias from frontier settlements to the west picked up their muskets and headed eastward. These "Over Mountain Men" provided their own weapons and rations to swell the rebel ranks to about 900 men. In an unusual and nearly always disastrous organization, the rebels had no central command structure. Colonels John Sevier, Isaac Shelby, William Campbell, and other officers maintained separate commands that did not report to each other or to a senior headquarters. Despite this

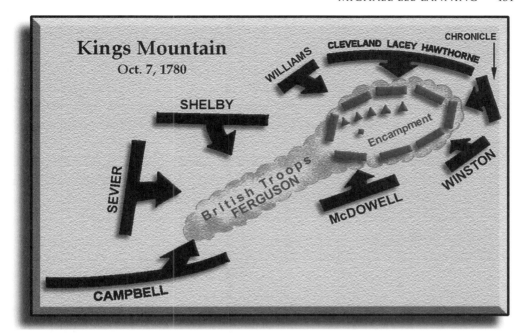

Kings Mountain
Oct. 7, 1780

CHRONICLE

CLEVELAND LACEY HAWTHORNE

WILLIAMS

SHELBY

SEVIER

British Troops
FERGUSON

Encampment

WINSTON

McDOWELL

CAMPBELL

command relationship, or lack thereof, the officers closely cooperated and agreed that their best course of action was to attack Ferguson and his Loyalists rather than wait.

On the morning of October 7, 1780, the rebels closed on Ferguson's encampment on Kings Mountain located about halfway between Charlotte and Spartanburg, South Carolina. Ferguson had selected excellent defensive positions for his 950 men on "boot heel"-shaped high ground, concentrating his troops on the boot's toe in the north and heel in the south.

By mutual agreement the independent rebel commanders each assumed responsibility for attacking a portion of the hilltop, and by noon the rebels had surrounded the Loyalists and moved into firing range. The rebels, most armed with rifles rather than muskets, made no effort to charge but instead from behind the protection of rocks and trees began pouring accurate fire into the enemy positions. Among the sharpshooters was John Crockett, father of the future famous frontiersman David.

William Campbell ordered his Virginians forward, instructing, "Shout like hell and fight like devils." Their resultant cries on Kings Mountain may very well be the precursor to the later famous Rebel Yell of the War between the States in the next century.

After several hours of sustaining causalities, Ferguson determined that his position was untenable and ordered a bayonet charge down the hill. The rebels, without bayonets themselves, simply fired a final volley and retreated. When the Loyalists stopped, the rebels resumed their accurate fire, driving the Redcoats back to their original positions. Subsequent bayonet charges produced the same results.

Ferguson rode throughout his defensives blowing a silver whistle to rally his troops. When he was killed by at least eight rifle balls, the Loyalists surrendered. Initially, the rebels, with memories of Waxhaw Creek (74) and other Loyalist massacres, gave no quarter. Only the firm leadership of the militia commanders prevented a bloody massacre of prisoners and wounded alike.

Few of the Loyalists escaped. On the battlefield lay 157 dead and 163 wounded. Prisoners totaled 686. The victors hanged nine of the captives either for treason in changing sides earlier in the conflict or for past crimes including arson and the murder of civilians. Rebels casualties numbered 28 killed and 62 wounded.

Just why Ferguson decided to make a stand rather than fight his way back to the main British army at Charlotte is unknown. Perhaps he thought Cornwallis would send reinforcements who never arrived or maybe the British major simply believed he could easily defeat the poorly organized rabble of rebels. Whatever his rationale, he paid for his mistakes with his life and gave the Americans their first victory against the British Southern offensive.

Henry Clinton (17), commander of British troops in the rebellious colonies, recognized the far-reaching influence of Kings Mountain. He later called it "the first link of a chain of evils that followed each other in regular succession until they at last ended in the total loss of America."

The Battle of Cowpens followed this "first link of a chain" three months later to provide the true turning point in the South and ultimately the Revolution. Kings Mountain, while certainly influential, was more a fight between neighbors than of Rebel against Redcoat. The American militiamen of the South did deliver their best performance of the war at Kings Mountain. Despite their lack of an overall commander, the individual rebel militia battalions and companies fought with a single purpose and bravery not exhibited on other battlefields where they had a central command structure and the support of the regular army. Kings Mountain helped rally the sagging morale in the Southern states and convinced many of the Over Mountain Men to continue to the fight for independence. Kings Mountain, indeed an important link in the chain to final victory, ranks only behind Cowpens and Guilford Court House (26) in influence on the war in the South.

37

GERMAN MERCENARIES (HESSIANS)

1775–1783

German mercenaries, better known as Hessians, served with their British employers in every major campaign of the Revolutionary War, earning a reputation as adequate fighters and willful plunderers. While these soldiers of fortune filled a need for man power for the British, their presence angered the Americans and helped unite the rebels.

European countries had traditionally employed mercenaries to fill the ranks of their armies to fight the mercenaries hired by their enemies. The mercenaries' only common language was that of combat. At the conclusion of the Seven Years' War in 1763, thousands of mercenaries and regular soldiers returned to their homes in search of new employment opportunities.

The sheer numbers of these former soldiers, especially in the nearly 300 different regions and principalities that composed the German states, led the princes who controlled these areas to realize they had a great income-producing commodity. By creating regiments of veterans and young men coming of age in the provinces, they could hire out these units at profitable rates. The export of these soldiers would not only provide a steady income but also reduce the number of subjects who faced unemployment.

At the outbreak of the hostilities in America, the British thought their army in North America could quickly quell the Rebellion. It was not until the shocking Battle of Bunker Hill (23) in June 1775 that they realized that they had to enlarge their army in the colonies if they were to prevail. This proved difficult because, at the time, the military service with its harsh treatment of soldiers was unpopular in Great Britain. As a result, King George III (20) had to look outside his home islands for additional warriors.

The English monarch initially contacted his old ally Russia for help, but Catherine the Great decided she did not need British gold in exchange for the use of her regiments and turned down the offer. King George then approached the German states and found several of them much more receptive, some needing the income to assist their subjects and others simply wanting to fund their own excesses. One prince had seventy-four children and desperately needed new sources of income to maintain his lifestyle.

Prince Frederick II of Hesse-Cassel negotiated with King George to provide more than 16,000 soldiers. Leaders of other German principalities—including Hesse-Hannau, Brunswick, Anspach-Beyreuth, Anhalt Zerbst, and Waldeck—committed an additional 14,000. Because Hesse-Cassel provided the bulk of the soldiers, their senior commanders led the mercenary army which became known to both the English and the Americans as Hessians.

On January 15, 1776, the representatives of King George and the German princes signed a lengthy contract agreeing to amounts, terms, and payment. Not everyone in England welcomed the news of the contracts. In a House of Commons debate, Governor Johnstone declared, "Shall we despise the history of all those nations from Carthage downwards who have lost their liberty by employing foreign troops and recur to those silly arguments which have always been used as the reason for the introducing them."

News of the agreement between the British and Germans met with outrage among the American rebels. Most believed their dispute with King George was an internal, "family" affair and resented the introduction of what they considered barbarous foreigners into the affray. When the United States issued its *Declaration of Independence* (14) on July 4, 1776, the document noted, "[King George] is at this time transporting large armies of foreign mercenaries to complete the works of death, desolation, and tyranny already begun with circumstances of cruelty and perfidy scarcely paralleled in the barbarous ages, and totally unworthy the head of a civilized nation."

Despite the hostility directed toward them by both the British and the Americans, the Hessians performed well in North America. They played an important role in both the New York and Philadelphia campaigns in 1776 and 1777. The Hessians were, however, also the victims of George Washington's (1) surprise attack against Trenton (8) and Princeton in late 1776 that regained momentum for the Rebellion. While the battles in New Jersey may have reenergized the Americans, they did not bring an end to the war. The Hessians continued to fight for five more years.

The German mercenaries generally acclimated to their situation. When they had difficulties getting replacements from their home provinces, they welcomed escaped African American slaves into their ranks, mostly as musicians and support personnel. The German mercenaries even remained in America for a year after the British surrender at Yorktown (2). King George still had money, and the German princes were more than willing to continue to be paid for their armies even if they were now serving a lost cause.

After the Americans and British signed the Treaty of Paris (69) in September 1783, the German regiments finally sailed home. However, only 17,000 of the 30,000 Hessians who served in America returned to their native provinces. Nearly 8,000 lay in graves in America—about 1,000 victims of battle wounds and the rest of illness and disease. The remaining 5,000 deserted their units either to join the quarter-million German immigrants already prospering as farmers and merchants in eastern Pennsylvania or to accept promises of free land offered to them by the Continental Congress (10).

In the more than 200 years after the American Revolution, debate continues over why the British—the world's most powerful country—could not quell a rebellion by the American colonists, and much of the argument rightly centers on the use of the German mercenaries. Hessian soldiers, fighting for their monarchs rather than themselves or their own national interests, were often reluctant soldiers at best. They symbolized the British difficulty of being unable or unwilling to sufficiently man their armed forces to fight their own battles.

The use of the mercenaries united the rebels—an effect recognized even by senior British officials. Lord Chatham, speaking to the British Parliament on November 20, 1777, declared, "If I were an American, as I am an Englishman, while a foreign troop was in my country, I would never lay down my arms; never, never, never."

Their very presence had a strong influence on both sides in the Revolutionary War. Ultimately the use of the German mercenaries proved that countries must fight their own wars. Because of their performance on the battlefield and impact as a unity force, the Hessian mercenaries earn a spot in the top half of this list.

38

ANTHONY WAYNE

American General

1745–1796

Anthony Wayne combined detailed tactical planning with bold execution to become one of the most effective and efficient American commanders in the Revolutionary War. His personal courage and aggressiveness earned him the title of "Mad Anthony," but he was not a reckless leader. His formalization of basic training for recruits and his repetitive drill and maneuver practices resulted in rebel units that performed well in most of the war's major battles and campaigns.

Born on January 1, 1745, in Chester County, Pennsylvania, Wayne was the son of a prosperous landowner and tanner. After only a few years of formal education, he joined a survey and land-speculation company in Nova Scotia. When this venture failed, Wayne returned to Pennsylvania and helped his father manage the family businesses. He served in the colonial assembly for two years beginning in 1774. At the outbreak of the Revolution in 1775, Wayne accepted a colonel's commission and assumed command of the 4th Pennsylvania Regiment. In March 1776, he accompanied the relief expedition to aid the Canada Invasion (84) and on June 8 led the American attack against the British at Three Rivers. During the American withdrawal southward, Wayne covered the rear as the Americans retreated back toward Fort Ticonderoga. Wayne assumed command of the defenses upon his arrival there.

In September 1777, Wayne, now a brigadier general in command of a division, joined George Washington (1) at the Battle of Brandywine Creek (72). Although forced back with the other rebel units by the British attack, Wayne's troops fought well. Wayne withdrew his 1,500 men to nearby Paoli where, on September 21, British troops, operating with knowledge from spies and deserters about Wayne's positions and numbers, made a night attack with bayonets, swords, and muskets turned as clubs. Caught by surprise and suffering 150 causalities, Wayne rallied his troops to save most of the command and all of its artillery.

Rumors spread across the colonies that the loss at Paoli had been the result of negligence on the part of the American commander. Wayne demanded and received a court-martial that fully acquitted him. The court announced in its findings that

Wayne "did every duty that could be expected from an active, brave, and vigilant officer, under the orders he then had."

In early October, Wayne commanded his division in a failed attack against Germantown (48) before joining Washington at Valley Forge (39) for winter camp. Wayne led an expedition the following February in search of food and recruits and proved that his logistical abilities matched his tactical skills. When the British occupiers of Philadelphia withdrew back toward New York in the summer of 1778, Wayne assisted General Charles Lee (79) in blocking their route. Although the British escaped during the following Battle of Monmouth (59), Washington commended Wayne "whose good conduct and bravery through the whole action deserves particular commendation."

A year later Wayne received permission to neutralize the most northern British fort on the Hudson River at Stony Point (88). The fort, standing on a 150-foot cliff surrounded on three sides by water and manned by 600 defenders with seven batteries of artillery, provided a formidable target. Adapting lessons learned at Paoli, Wayne drilled his soldiers in the tactics of night attack with bayonets while keeping their objective secret to prevent the British learning his plans from spies. The Americans reached the fort on July 16, 1779, undetected following a rapid march. After a fierce thirty-minute battle, in which Wayne received a head wound but remained in the fight, the Americans hauled down the British colors. Sixty-three Redcoats lay dead—the remainder of the garrison, prisoners. Wayne's casualties numbered fifteen dead and eighty wounded. In his report to Washington, Wayne stated, "The fort and garrison... are ours. Our officers and men behaved like men who are determined to be free."

The origin of the nickname "Mad Anthony" is undocumented. It could have been from his bold, aggressive actions or his quick temper. Some claim it was a phrase shouted by a drunken soldier to identify his unit and commander. The most likely source is probably the head wound he suffered at Stony Point that left him with occasional epileptic-like seizures. Whatever the source, the nickname entered history after the victory at Stony Point.

In 1780, Wayne assumed command of West Point (30) and increased its defenses to prevent British capture after the discovery of the treachery of Benedict Arnold (85). Wayne's leadership in January 1781 helped peacefully end a mutiny of soldiers protesting extended enlistments and poor food. He then organized a force of 800 men to march southward to assist Marquis de Lafayette (46) against Charles Cornwallis (22) in Virginia. After Cornwallis surrendered at Yorktown (2) in October, Wayne joined Nathanael Greene (4) to liberate South Carolina and Georgia from the last British strongholds and to pacify the hostile Creek and Cherokee Indians in the region.

Wayne left the army in November 1783 as a brevet major general to spend time on his Pennsylvania estate and on a rice plantation awarded him by the grateful state of Georgia. He later served in the Pennsylvania assembly and then in the House of Representatives as a Congressman from Georgia in 1790. On April 13, 1792, President George Washington recalled Wayne to active duty as a major general, making him the senior officer in the army. Over the next three years he recruited and trained a force that defeated the Indians in the Ohio River Valley and opened that territory for white settlement.

After his return to Pennsylvania, Wayne died—probably from complications of gout—on December 15, 1796, at Fort Presque Isle (now Erie). In 1809 his remains were disinterred and removed to St. David's Episcopal Church Cemetery in Randor, Pennsylvania. Legends claim that several of the old general's bones were lost along the road that is now covered by State Highway 322. Every January 1st, during the general's birthday, his ghost is said to wander the old pathway in search of his lost bones.

Legends aside, Wayne was one of the most competent commanders of the war on either side. Washington did not hesitate to place Wayne in the thick of the fighting or to dispatch him on the most difficult missions. Temperamental and bold enough to merit the title of "Mad Anthony," he was sufficiently modest to refer to "we" or "ours" rather than "I" or "my" in his dispatches. His techniques of standard training for recruits and his well-planned and well-executed tactics significantly influenced many battles and the outcome of the Revolution. Only the senior American commanders—Washington, Gates (31), Morgan (35), and Greene—outrank him.

39

VALLEY FORGE, PENNSYLVANIA

December 19, 1777–June 18, 1778

The American encampment at Valley Forge, Pennsylvania, during the winter of 1777–1778 became the symbol of the spirit of the Revolution and the resilient, brave men who gained independence for the United States. During those long months the army camped there they faced harsh weather, hunger, few supplies, disease, and a formidable nearby enemy. The rebels not only survived but also emerged from the camp for the summer campaign more organized, better trained, and highly motivated to continue the fight.

Throughout the war, neither the British nor the Americans conducted extended military operations during the winter months, preferring to wage their battles in advantageous weather. After the British offensive in Pennsylvania in late 1777, both sides went into winter encampments in mid-December. Following a final skirmish at White March, the British, who had the advantage, took up quarters in Philadelphia while George Washington (1) had to find a location in the rural countryside for his already suffering troops.

Washington selected a site 20 miles northwest of Philadelphia in an area named for a nearby iron forge. Even the march to Valley Forge was not easy. Washington wrote, "You might have tracked the army from White Marsh to Valley Forge by the blood of their feet."

Valley Forge had little to offer in the way of amenities, never mind luxuries. There was no village or even barns for protection from the weather. Neither was there a nearby source of food or supplies for the rebel army of 10,000. The Schuylkill River to the north and two nearby hills provided an easily defendable position while thick forests surrounding the valley provided building materials and fuel. However, many soldiers were already ill or so poorly clothed they could do little to assist in the construction of huts and cabins.

Supplies were slow to arrive or did not come at all. Vegetables were nonexistent and meat and bread in short supply. In the early weeks most of the nourishment for the soldiers came from "firecake," a tasteless mixture of flour and water cooked over open fires. Along with hunger, diseases such as pneumonia, dysentery, typhus, and typhoid further depleted the rebel ranks. In the early months at Valley Forge as many

as 40 percent of the soldiers were considered unfit for duty. Sickness and disease killed 2,000 during the long winter.

Upon his arrival at Valley Forge, Washington wrote, "Unless some great and capital change suddenly takes place… this army must inevitably… starve, dissolve, or disperse." The army had little, but it maintained its faith and confidence in Washington and the other Continental Army (7) leaders. While the soldiers chanted, "No pay, no clothes, no provisions, no rum," they did not mutiny and few deserted. Washington dispatched foraging parties to gather food and clothing. When his quartermaster general failed to procure sufficient provisions, Washington placed one of his most trusted officers in charge. Nathanael Greene (4) soon made significant progress in feeding and clothing the soldiers. He later wrote to Washington, "God grant we may never be brought to such wretched conditions again."

Washington meanwhile planned spring operations and recommended to the Continental Congress (10) improvements in the officer corps, cavalry, administrative support, and recruitment. He also placed Friedrich von Steuben (62) in charge of developing and initiating a training program when the Prussian arrived at the camp in February.

By spring ample supplies were reaching the camp and recruits reported to replace those soldiers lost during the long winter. On May 5, 1778, General Orders reached

Valley Forge announcing the alliance with France. Six months after the first hungry, tired, and nearly defeated Americans arrived at Valley Forge, they marched out of the encampment a fit and ready army prepared and motivated to continue the Revolution.

In the more than two centuries since the American army's winter there, Valley Forge has become an almost sacred site, symbolizing the struggle for independence. The army did indeed suffer and face great hardships, but much of the real story about Valley Forge has been glamorized over the decades. In reality, most of the suffering in the camp was a direct result of graft and corruption by American civilian contractors and suppliers and plain mismanagement by the army quartermaster system itself. Farmers near Valley Forge sold their meat and grain in Philadelphia to the British who paid with hard currency rather than to the rebels who gave promissory notes or nearly worthless paper money. As bad as the conditions were, the winter of 1777–1778 was actually milder than normal. Only a year later, the rebel army wintered in Morristown, New Jersey, in conditions that were much worse than Valley Forge.

Not all days at Valley Forge were marked by starvation or the ravages of disease. Wives, as well as other female camp followers, joined the soldiers there, and they all entertained themselves with sing-alongs, staged plays, and drink when spirits were available. There is even a record of the officers participating in games of cricket.

The Continental Army marched into Valley Forge nearly defeated, but with the leadership of Washington, Greene, von Steuben, and others, left in the spring prepared to continue the fight. They faced five more years of challenges and bloodshed, but the united, confident army that came out of Valley Forge had won an important victory—not one on a battlefield but one of will, the will to endure and win.

Valley Forge was a disaster that morphed into a rejuvenated army. While its "bloody footprints in the snow" became a powerful propaganda tool that won support for the Revolution, its vivid symbol remains more famous than influential and ranks only in the middle of this list.

40

BERNARDO DE GALVEZ

Spanish General

1746–1786

Bernardo de Galvez ranks as the most influential Spaniard in the American Revolution. Even before Spain entered the war, Galvez—as the governor of Louisiana—impeded British trade along the Mississippi River and Gulf Coast and assisted American agents in securing supplies for the Revolution. When Spain declared war against Great Britain in 1779, Galvez led military expeditions that eliminated British settlements on the Mississippi and captured British forts along the Gulf of Mexico. His successes secured 200 miles of the coast from New Orleans to Pensacola for the Spanish.

Born in the Malaga Province of Spain on July 23, 1746, into a family that had served the Spanish crown with distinction for generations, Bernardo de Galvez entered military service at age sixteen. He fought in the war against Portugal where he earned a lieutenant's commission. Before his seventeenth birthday, Galvez sailed to Mexico as a part of a military inspection tour. He stayed to campaign against Native Americans along the Rio Grande and Gila Rivers in what is today the southwestern United States. Wounded several times in battle, he became the commandant of the Northern Mexican province of Sonora in 1770. In 1772 Galvez returned to Spain and subsequently served in France and in the campaign against Algiers, where he was again seriously wounded. After a brief time as an instructor in the Spanish military academy, Galvez returned to North America on February 1, 1777, as the governor of Louisiana with the rank of colonel.

Galvez found Louisiana in turmoil. Originally settled and claimed by the French, the vast area had been ceded by France to Spain in 1763 to compensate for their loss of Florida to the English in the Seven Years' War. Although it did not possess a legal claim to Louisiana, Great Britain had established settlements north of New Orleans at Baton Rouge and Natchez. The British had also established forts to defend their territory in West Florida at Mobile and Pensacola.

As the governor of Louisiana, Galvez hindered British commerce between and among their Mississippi River settlements as he disrupted other commercial ventures—including slave trade—on the Gulf Coast. Galvez sympathized with the Americans in their quest for liberty but even more specifically sided with them because they opposed his British enemies. He openly received American agents and assisted with their import of arms and goods to support the Revolution. When Spain declared war against Great Britain on June 21, 1779, Galvez switched from his covert actions to overt operations against the English. An intercepted message from London to the British commander in Florida gave Galvez the advantage of knowing the strength and intentions of his opposition on the Gulf Coast.

Galvez, now a brigadier general, recruited locals and soldiers of fortune as well as free blacks and slaves to strengthen his militia. As he readied his army of 1,400, he secured herds of cattle from Spanish settlements in Texas to feed his troops. In the fall of 1779 he marched northward to neutralize the British garrison at Baton Rouge and then continued on to do the same at Natchez.

After briefly returning to New Orleans to acquire 600 more men for his army and several warships and transports for his navy, Galvez marched to Mobile to besiege the city, forcing its surrender on March 14, 1780. In the spring of 1781, Galvez, now in command of 7,000 troops, continued his offensive into Florida and lay siege to Pensacola, which fell on May 10, 1781. A year later, Galvez loaded his army aboard his transports and sailed around the Florida Keys to capture the British naval base at New Providence in the Bahamas on May 8, 1782. When the war finally ended in 1783, Galvez was preparing an attack on the last British stronghold in the Caribbean at Jamaica. He joined the representatives who negotiated the Treaty of Paris (69) and helped draft the final document that granted the Gulf Coast to Spain.

The American Continental Congress (10) cited Galvez for his contributions to the Revolution while Spain rewarded the general with the military and civil governorship of Cuba. In 1785, Galvez moved to Mexico City to become the viceroy of all of New Spain. During his reign he began construction of the Cathedral of Mexico, the largest church in the Western Hemisphere. He endeared himself to the local population, both Spanish and native, by contributing part of his own fortune to purchase food and other supplies when the country was struck by famine and disease. Galvez promoted education, leniency instead of the previously harsh punishment of criminals, and mapping of the Gulf Coast.

In the late fall of 1786, Galvez, forty years old, became ill and died on November 8 in Mexico City. Rumors spread that Galvez had been poisoned on orders from the Spanish court, which feared his popularity in Mexico might lead to a revolt for independence like that in the former English colonies. No evidence to support these stories has ever surfaced. Galvez is buried in a crypt in the wall of Mexico City's Church of San Fernando. Before his interment his heart was removed and placed in an urn to repose in the Cathedral of Mexico.

Galvez most definitely influenced the outcome of the Revolution. Although little known or remembered today in the United States—other than by a Texas city, island, and bay named Galveston in his honor by one of his mapping expeditions—Galvez is clearly the most influential Spanish contributor to the Revolution. His actions not only secured the Mississippi Valley and Gulf Coast for Spain but also diverted British soldiers and naval assets from the war against the rebels, taking pressure off the Continental Army (7) and navy. He easily ranks above soldiers of fortune such as the Marquis de Lafayette (46) from France and Friedrich von Steuben (62) from Prussia but below French army commander Jean Baptiste de Rochambeau (24) and François J.P. de Grasse (27) in overall influence on the outcome of the American Revolution.

41

NAVAL OPERATIONS

1775–1783

Naval operations played a secondary role in the American Revolutionary War despite the fact that the British had the reputation of being the most powerful navy in the world. Instead of taking advantage of this prowess, the British initially subjugated their naval power to needs of land commanders, handicapping their fleets into poorly coordinated and ineffective transportation and resupply vessels. The Americans, on the other hand, began the conflict with no naval assets and ended the war with only a few vessels. Not until the entry into the fighting by the French in 1778 and later by the Spanish and the Dutch did the battle at sea become significant and, therefore, influence the outcome of the Revolution.

Many British citizens thought their navy and its complement of sailors and marines should be able to smash the Rebellion given the condition of the poorly armed Americans who were mostly concentrated on the Atlantic coast and its estuaries. At the outbreak of the war, Britain had 131 warships of the line and 139 smaller battle and support vessels. The problem was that most of the vessels had been launched or refitted during the Seven Years' War more than a decade earlier. These ships were in a sad state of repair with poorly trained and ill-equipped crews. As a result, only 39 man-of-wars were available during the first year of the war for operations in North America.

The unfortunate conditions of the British navy were fortuitous in comparison to the status of the American "navy." Given that it had no ships of its own, the Continental Congress (10) took the expedient measure of granting Letters of Marque to privateers (61) authorizing privately owned ships to capture British merchants and sell them along with their cargos. In the summer of 1775, George Washington (1) organized a small fleet of six armed schooners and a brigantine to attack enemy supply ships and to protect his own cargo vessels during the Boston Siege (50).

"Washington's Navy" took 35 prizes before disbanding in 1777 while other privateers captured more than 600 British vessels, mostly merchants, during the conflict. Individual American ships occasionally raided beyond American shores, including a successful attack against Nassau in the Bahamas in March 1776 that captured much-needed gunpowder stores. Captain John Paul Jones (58) emerged as the country's

first naval hero with his defeat of the major British warships HMS *Drake* on April 24, 1778, and the HMS *Serapis* on September 23, 1779. Jones also led a successful raid on the English port of Whitehaven in 1778. None of these operations, however, proved to be any more than a nuisance to the British.

As the war progressed, the British repaired old vessels and launched new ones, expanding their fleet to a total of 468 ships of the line and smaller war and support vessels. With little or no opposition at sea, the British navy focused on supporting land operations in the war's early years, evacuating the army from Boston to Halifax in April 1776 and then returning it to New York for the successful invasion at Long Island the following June. A year later the navy again ferried the British army south for its invasion of Pennsylvania, which led to their occupation of Philadelphia.

Naval warfare in the Revolution moved from a secondary role to center stage only when France entered the war on the side of the Americans in 1778. In April, France dispatched a fleet of sixteen ships from Toulon to North America under the command of Charles d'Estaing (92). These ships, in ill repair and with poorly trained crews, took several months to cross the Atlantic. The French commander decided not to attack the British fleet in New York harbor and sailed on to support rebels' operations against Newport, Rhode Island (82). Threatened by an approaching British fleet and damaged by a storm, Admiral d'Estaing sailed away to Boston, leaving the American ground army with no naval support. This disastrous operation left many Americans strongly resenting d'Estaing and severely strained early Franco-American relations.

In November 1778, after waiting out the Caribbean hurricane season in Boston Harbor, d'Estaing sailed for the West Indies (45). The Americans' anger became even more acute at what they thought was abandonment by the French. Actually the move opened up a new front that forced the British to divert ships and troops to defend their possessions in the Caribbean.

The British challenges at sea expanded somewhat with the entry of Spain into the war in 1779. Spain, which had also let its navy deteriorate in peace time, could muster only fifty ships, and many of these were barely seaworthy. Other than to draw British vessels away from America to defend their home islands and the West Indies, which might have supported the rebellion, the Spanish navy did little to influence the war in the United States.

The entry of the Netherlands into the war in 1781 likewise required the British to spread their fleet to include defense of the North Sea tradeways, but the Dutch did not directly influence the land war in America either.

The French continued their direct support of the American land efforts in the midyears of the war, but their fleet failed to stop the British occupation of Savannah, Georgia (80), in October 1778 and again failed to recapture the port city a year later. In the spring of 1780, the French fleet was once again unsuccessful in supporting the defense of Charleston, South Carolina (47).

It was not until the war's final months that the French navy had a significant impact on the outcome of the Revolution. The American army, supported by French ground troops under the command of General Jean Baptiste de Rochambeau (24), surrounded the British army under General Charles Cornwallis (22) at Yorktown, Virginia (2). The French fleet, led by Admiral François J.P. de Grasse (27), joined them off the coast to block a British retreat or reinforcement by sea. When a British fleet tried to evacuate Cornwallis's army, the French met them at Chesapeake Capes (13) in September 1781. After a brief battle, the French turned the British away, forcing Cornwallis to surrender the following month.

The Revolutionary War gave birth to the U.S. Navy, officially established by the Continental Congress on October 19, 1775, and the U.S. Marine Corps, established on November 10. Despite the proud and effective service of these two organizations over the next two centuries, neither significantly contributed to the outcome of the Revolution. On the other hand, both the British and America's allies' navies played a more important role, but they, too, had only a minor influence on the land war.

Ultimately, it was the soldier with his musket and bayonet who was the dominant influence on America's gaining its independence.

If this ranking considered only the first half of the war, naval operations would rank near the end of this list. However, the events in the war's final years, particularly the influence of the French fleet on the final battle at Yorktown, elevate naval operations to a midlist ranking.

42

JOHN EAGER HOWARD

American Lieutenant Colonel

1752–1827

John Eager Howard fought in all the major battles of both the Northern and Southern theaters, earning accolades from his senior commanders as one of the most outstanding regimental commanders of the American Revolution. A master of infantry tactics and a man never hesitant to order the use of the bayonet, he garnered praised for his calm and bravery under fire.

Born into a wealthy planter family in Baltimore County, Maryland, on June 4, 1752, Howard pursued a college education before volunteering for military service at the outbreak of the Revolution. Commissioned a captain in the Maryland militia, he saw his first sustained combat at White Plains, New York (77), in October 1776. Promoted to major, he fought at Germantown, Pennsylvania (48), a year later and then participated in the battle of Monmouth, New Jersey (59), as a lieutenant colonel in the summer of 1778.

Howard joined General Horatio Gates (31) to lead the 2nd Maryland Regiment at the disastrous Battle of Camden, South Carolina (65), in August 1780. He then remained in the Southern theater when Nathanael Greene (4) replaced Gates and became one of the new commander's favorite subordinates. Dispatched by Greene to join Daniel Morgan (35) at Cowpens, South Carolina (18), Howard commanded "the third line" of Continental Army (7) defenders who broke the British advance with a bayonet charge on January 17, 1781. In his post-battle report, Morgan wrote that Howard's attack "was done with such address that the enemy fled with the utmost precipitation….We pushed our advantage so effectually, that they never had an opportunity of rallying." The Continental Congress (10) agreed with Morgan and rewarded Howard a silver medal.

The young lieutenant colonel next led his Maryland regiment in the battles that neutralized British efforts to control the interior of South Carolina, including Hobkirk's Hill on April 25, 1781; Ninety-Six (91) in May and June 1781; and Eutaw Springs (63) on September 8, 1781. At the latter battle Howard was wounded severely enough to take him out of action permanently. He returned to Maryland where, although he never completely recovered from his wounds, he continued his public service. In 1788 he served as a delegate to the Continental Congress and then as governor of his state until 1791. For the next four years he sat as a state senator before election to the U.S. Congress in 1796. He then became a U.S. Senator until 1803. In 1795 he turned down an invitation by President George Washington (1) to become his secretary of war, but three years later accepted promotion to brigadier general in the expanding U.S. Army. In 1814 he formed a volunteer corps of veterans to defend Baltimore when he learned the British had taken Washington, DC, in the War of 1812.

Howard ran as the vice presidential nominee with presidential candidate Rufus King of the Federalist Party in 1816. When he lost that election, he resumed his business interest in Baltimore where he owned much of the land that the growing city eventually occupied. Howard died on October 12, 1827, at his home and is buried in Baltimore's Saint Paul's Church cemetery.

Little known or remembered outside his home state—except for mention in their official song, "Maryland, My Maryland"—Howard displayed extraordinary talents during the war that contributed directly to its outcome. Henry "Light Horse Harry" Lee, commander of cavalry in many of the battles in the Southern theater, observed Howard in the midst of much of the conflict. Lee later wrote, "This officer was one of five lieutenant colonels on whom Greene rested throughout the hazardous operations to which he was necessarily exposed by his grand determination to recover the South, or die in the attempt. We have seen him at the Battle of Cowpens seize the critical moment and turn the fortune of the day; alike conspicuous though not alike successful at Guilford and the Eutaws; and at all times, and all occasions, eminently useful. He was justly ranked among the chosen sons of the South."

Lee continued by describing Howard's bravery and temperament, stating, "Trained to infantry service, he was invariably employed in that line, and was always to be found where the battle raged, pressing into close action to wrestle with fixed bayonet. Placid in temper and reserved in deportment, he never lessened his martial fame by arrogance or ostentation, nor clouded it with garrulity or self-conceit."

General Greene joined Lee in praise of the Maryland regimental commander in a letter he composed to a friend that he had Howard hand-deliver. Greene wrote, "This will be handed to you by Colonel Howard, as good an officer as the world affords.

My own obligations to him are great—the public's still more so. He deserves a statue of gold no less than the Roman or Grecian heroes."

As one of the most remarkable regimental commanders of the Revolution, Howard earns a place on this list for his own actions and attributes. Although he rarely led more than 300 infantrymen at any one time, Howard was the kind of commander whom the rebel enlisted men respected and followed without question. His ranking is elevated to the top half of this list as a representative of those hundreds of other majors and lieutenant colonels who, as midlevel leaders, executed the plans of their generals to secure the independence of the United States.

43

LEXINGTON AND CONCORD, MASSACHUSETTS

April 19, 1775

Differences between American colonists and the British government became acute during the decade following the French and Indian War. The British demanded that the colonists pay for that conflict and taxed all aspects of their commerce accordingly. The Americans demanded more latitude for profit-making, and by the early 1770s many supported separation from the crown. They stockpiled arms and supplies in the event of war. On April 19, 1775, a detachment of British soldiers marched from Boston to seize a reported colonial arms supply near the village of Lexington. The local militia responded, and shots were fired. The fight continued to Concord and then followed the British retreat route back to Boston. The American Revolution had begun.

By the mid-eighteenth century, Great Britain looked to its American colonies as a source of raw materials and of revenues through duties and taxes. Discontented emigrants from the Old World had established the North American colonies, bringing with them their rebellious, independent spirit that soon rankled at British rule and regulations. Harsh taxes and trade restrictions imposed by the British on the colonists to pay for the French and Indian War further fanned the growing flames of rebellion. When in 1765 the British imposed the Stamp Act (19) on the colonists, taxing all colonists regardless of their location or station, they inadvertently unified the Americans in a common cause.

Opponents to the Stamp Act formed secret societies or adapted previously organized social and political clubs to oppose the tax. One of the larger organizations, the Sons of Liberty, took direct action by attacking stamp agents and destroying their stamps and records. When the British finally repealed the Stamp Act in 1766, the Sons of Liberty did not disband but rather continued to meet to oppose British control. By 1772, they had evolved into the Committees of Correspondence that initiated communications among like-minded groups in each of the thirteen colonies. In 1774, the committees convened the First Continental Congress (10).

While they were supposedly organized specifically for political purposes only, the colonists began to horde arms and ammunition in the event of future military operations. On September 1, 1774, British troops, on the orders of General Thomas

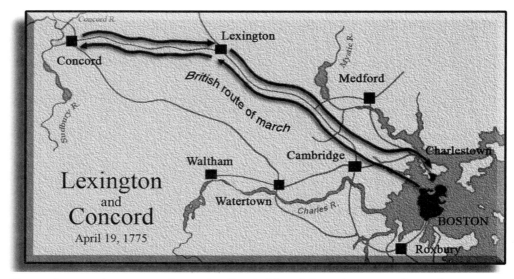

Lexington and Concord
April 19, 1775

Gage, destroyed an arms depot in Cambridge, Massachusetts, where they met no resistance.

Despite the setback, the colonists continued to stockpile military supplies as more and more Americans favored independence from Great Britain. On April 18, 1775, General Gage, having learned of a new cache of arms and munitions, issued the following order in Boston to the 10th Regiment of Foot: "Having received intelligence that a quantity of ammunition, provisions, artillery, tents, and small arms have been collected at Concord, for the avowed purpose of raising and supporting a Rebellion against His Majesty, you will march with the Corps of Grenadiers and Light Infantry put under your command, with the utmost expedition and secrecy to Concord, where you will seize and destroy…all military stores whatever."

Rebel agents in Boston learned of the order, and William Dawes and Paul Revere (98) rode toward Concord warning the villagers en route that "the British are coming." By the time the column of 700 British soldiers reached Lexington, 16 miles from Boston, early on the morning of April 19, militiaman Captain John Parker had 70 "Minutemen" assembled on the town's common.

British Major John Pitcairn rode forward on his horse and demanded, "Disperse, ye rebels, disperse!"

Both sides stood their ground. According to some reports, Parker—rather than reply to Pitcairn—ordered his soldiers, "Stand your ground, men. Don't fire unless fired upon; but if they mean to have a war, let it begin here!"

Finally, the Americans, keenly aware they were vastly outnumbered, started to walk away, but they did not lay down their muskets. Suddenly, a single shot rang out, and then several, followed by a general volley from the British infantry. Who fired first remains undetermined, and it actually may have been an accidental discharge. Whatever the origin of the shot, a brief firefight followed, leaving eight Americans dead, including Parker, and ten wounded militiamen. The British suffered a single man wounded in this first battle of the American Revolution.

The confident British continued their march to Concord, where they were only partially successful in destroying the rebel stores and provisions before Minutemen from surrounding villages converged on the area. As many as 4,000 rebels soon outnumbered the British. After a brief skirmish at Concord's North Bridge that killed 14 Redcoats, the British hastily retreated back to Boston.

Unhampered by any rules of warfare and angered by their losses at Lexington and Concord, the Americans sniped at the retreating British from behind fences, trees, and buildings. By the time the British reached their garrison in Boston, they had suffered 73 killed, 174 wounded, and another 26 missing. American casualties totaled 49 dead, 41 wounded, and 5 missing.

The battles at Lexington and Concord were not decisive. They were, however, "the shots heard around the world," the opening armed engagements of the American Revolution. The brief fights proved to the rebel colonists that, despite their small numbers and lack of regular military training, they could stand against the British regulars.

Lexington and Concord would rank even higher on this list but for the simple fact that if the Revolution had not begun there, it would have occurred elsewhere. The Americans were ready for independence and prepared to fight for it. Many battles lay ahead, including the Boston Siege (50) and the pivotal engagement at Saratoga (3) before the final victory at Yorktown (2), but the United States of today can trace its origins those first shots fired at Lexington Green and Concord's North Bridge on April 19, 1775.

44

BANASTRE TARLETON

British Lieutenant Colonel

1754–1833

The youthful Banastre Tarleton established himself as the finest British cavalry leader of the Revolutionary War while earning the reputation as a ruthless and cold-hearted soldier. Both respected and resented by his fellow Redcoats, Tarleton became the British officer hated most by the Americans. Although he remains controversial on both sides of the Atlantic, Tarleton serves as an example of the junior officers of the British army who made a difference in many battles and campaigns.

Banastre Tarleton was born on August 21, 1754, to an upper-middle-class family in Liverpool; his father earned his living as a merchant, ship owner, and slave trader. Tarleton graduated from Oxford University and, instead of studying law as his father wanted, chose to purchase a commission in the cavalry and entered the army on April 20, 1775. Upon completion of his training, Tarleton volunteered for duty in North America and arrived in time to participate in the Charleston Expedition of June 1776.

Later that summer he sailed north with General Henry Clinton (17) and joined the 16th Light Dragoons. Tarleton accompanied the patrol that captured Charles Lee (79) in New Jersey on December 13, 1776. Over the next three years, Tarleton performed well enough to advance in rank to lieutenant colonel as he established himself as a superior leader of cavalry.

Tarleton's first remarkable performance came on July 2, 1779, when he led 360 horsemen northeast from White Plains, New York, in a raid against a rebel camp at Pound Ridge. He made the 64-mile round-trip in twenty-three hours, gaining sufficient surprise to successfully scatter the Americans, seize their weapons and supplies, and capture their regimental flag.

Not until Tarleton joined the Southern campaign under Charles Cornwallis (22) in 1780 would the young cavalryman become a hero to the British public and a villain to the American rebels. In command of the British Legion composed of American Loyalists (34), Tarleton joined the second expedition against Charleston (47) where his cavalry screens helped seal off the port city and force its surrender. In

the aftermath of the siege, Tarleton pursued and caught retreating rebel units near the border between North and South Carolina. In the ensuing battle at Waxhaw Creek (74) on May 29, Tarleton's horsemen broke the rebel defensive line and killed both the wounded and the prisoners. Before the British officers regained control of their men, about 100 rebels—many unarmed and unresisting—died by saber, bayonet, and musket. Tarleton returned to Charleston with three rebel battle flags and the spite of the Americans who called him "the Butcher" and "Bloody Ban." After Waxhaw Creek, soldiers of both sides referred to the execution of wounded and prisoners as "Tarleton's Quarter."

After the overwhelming British victory at the Battle of Camden (65) on August 16, 1780, Tarleton once again successfully pursued the retreating Americans and garnered more accusations of indiscriminate killing of those seeking to surrender. Over the next months, Tarleton unsuccessfully fought the rebel partisans Francis Marion (60) and Thomas Sumter (83) before rejoining Cornwallis in his offensive into North Carolina. With orders to protect the British western flank, Tarleton engaged a rebel force at Cowpens (18) on January 17, 1781. The Americans, commanded by Daniel Morgan (35), totally defeated the British. Only Tarleton and a few subordinates escaped.

Back within British lines, Tarleton faced criticism and animosity from his fellow, elder officers who resented the young man's fame and doubted that he had the experience and maturity to lead large commands. Fortunately for Tarleton, Cornwallis did not share the doubts of these officers, and only two weeks later the cavalry lieutenant colonel was again leading horsemen against the rebels. After several minor battles, Tarleton led his men in repeated cavalry attacks and proved his personal bravery at Guilford Court House, North Carolina (26), on March 15, 1781. In an early assault, Tarleton lost two fingers to either a saber or musket ball. Despite the injury, Tarleton stayed in the saddle only to be wounded again.

Over the next months Tarleton led cavalry raids against the American rear and screened the flanks of Cornwallis's advance into Virginia. When the Americans and French surrounded them at Yorktown (2) in October, Tarleton commanded the garrison on the north side of the York River at Gloucester before the surrender. Taken prisoner, Tarleton received treatment different from the other captured officers. As gentlemen, the Americans invited the defeated British officers to dine with them after their surrender. Tarleton was the only one of his rank who did not receive an invitation. The Americans took no legal action against him for any perceived war crimes, but neither did they forgive him.

Paroled in early 1782, Tarleton returned home and remained in the army while also holding a seat in Parliament. Over the years he advanced in rank to full general but never again played a significant role in combat. In Parliament he was best known for his opposition to the Abolitionists and his support for the slave trade, a profession in which his brothers in Liverpool still participated.

The short, red-headed Tarleton stood for several portraits after his return to England, the best-known depicting him in full uniform with his four captured rebel battle flags at his feet. Just how he managed to get these prized bits of cloth home is a mystery. Maybe he hid them among his personal possessions when captured, or perhaps he had already sent them back to England before the war ended.

By the time of his death on January 23, 1833, Tarleton's deeds in the Revolutionary War had been mostly forgotten in Britain, but he remained a villain to the now independent Americans. Tarleton had no children, but his possessions, including the flags, remained in his family over the passing decades. On November 11, 2005, Sotheby's of New York announced that they had been commissioned by British Captain (Retired) Christopher Tarleton Fagen, the great-great-great-great nephew of Banastre Tarleton, to auction the four captured battle flags. Sotheby's held the sale on United States Flag Day, June 15, 2006. Pre-auction estimates put the flags at a value of $4 to $10 million. When the gavel fell, the high bid, by "an undisclosed bidder," had reached $17.3 million. Sotheby's later revealed that the flags would stay in the United States where the young Banastre Tarleton had taken them in battle more than 225 years earlier.

Despite the bitter feelings toward Tarleton, he more than earned the title of the best British cavalry officer of the war. His youthful enthusiasm and lack of experience in conventional warfare employed by the British on the Continent allowed Tarleton to readily adapt innovative tactics and execute excellent horse-mounted operations. He understood how to fight partisans, aware that ruthlessness was often required to defeat the rebels.

45

WEST INDIES

1775–1783

The role of the island colonies of the West Indies receives little mention in the histories of the American Revolution, but that oversight does not diminish how they directly and indirectly influenced the outcome of the war. None of the islands joined the rebellion; however, their rich resources tantalized the interest and military might of Great Britain and other European countries that eventually joined the war. Britain, France, Spain, and Holland all fought in the West Indies, not only to maintain their current possessions but also to establish claims on additional territories for leverage in postwar peace negotiations. For the Americans, the West Indies played an influential role because they diverted both British land and naval power away from the battlegrounds of the United States.

European countries had established colonies throughout the Caribbean during the two centuries preceding the American War for Independence. Employing slaves imported from the African continent, a relatively few number of English, Spanish, French, and Dutch colonists carved out huge plantations on several islands and exported great wealth back to their home countries. The thirteen American colonies maintained trade with the West Indies, particularly those islands that were in the hands of the British.

West Indian islands existed in a state of nearly constant turmoil during the decades prior to the Revolutionary War. Their garrisons of meager military forces left them vulnerable to naval attack by other countries as well as by privateers and pirates. Still, the riches were so abundant as to be sufficient for all, so the West Indies settled into a generally accepted and recognized colonization. Britain claimed the Bahamas, Jamaica, and Grenada; the Spanish flag flew over Cuba, Santo Domingo, and Puerto Rico; the French possessed Haiti, St. Lucia, Martinique, and Guadeloupe; the Dutch staked out St. Eustatius, and the Danes St. Croix.

When the Americans declared their independence in 1776, they hoped the British colonies in the West Indies would join the fight against the Crown and possibly become part of the union of states. The English colonists in the Caribbean, however, had no desire to participate in the Rebellion for several reasons. First, they feared a rebellion among their own large number of slaves but, more importantly, as island residents, knew they would be nearly powerless to resist the omnipresence of the British naval power. So vulnerable were they to sea invasion that even the fledging American navy later invaded the Bahamas—even if it was more of a raid for gunpowder and supplies than the establishment of a lasting occupation.

The West Indies languished outside the major combat ongoing in the United States and its nearby waters until France allied with the United States in May 1778 and Spain joined the war against the British the following year. The French dispatched a fleet into the Caribbean to protect their possessions and to forcefully take those claimed by Great Britain. British Secretary of State George Germain (9) initially thought he could defend his West Indian possession with small army detachments, but his naval advisors insisted that only a naval flotilla could match up against the French fleet. As a result, ships previously supporting British operations along the Atlantic Coast of the rebellious colonies were diverted to the Caribbean.

Offensive operations by Spanish general Bernardo de Galvez (40) along the Gulf Coast in 1779–1780 pushed the British out of Louisiana, Alabama, Mississippi, and Western Florida. Galvez's threat against East Florida and the West Indies forced even more British warships to the Caribbean and away from supporting battles with the Americans.

The tropical islands of the West Indies were far from paradise for either residents or naval invaders. Disease, including malaria and yellow fever, thinned the ranks of defender and attacker alike. The east-to-west trade winds that dominated the region for most of the year were factors for the navies that depended strictly on sail power. Furthermore, the hurricane season from July through November threatened fleets regardless of their flag, a fact that encouraged most navies to evacuate the area during that period.

For the entirety of the war, naval commanders in the Caribbean were reluctant to risk their vessels and men for a cause they little understood or where risks outweighed possible gain. As a result, navies of both sides shied away from battle, and no large scale sea engagement occurred during the conflict. Most of the operations by all sides resembled more of a chess match than a military operation as each country tried to establish claims for the future negotiation of treaties and agreements.

Ultimately, most of the Caribbean islands remained in the hands of their original possessors. Some occupied islands were exchanged in postwar treaties for other islands or for fishing rights in far-away seas or other remunerations. Britain, France, Spain, and the Netherlands maintained possessions in the region for more than a hundred years, and their flags continue to fly over several of the isles today.

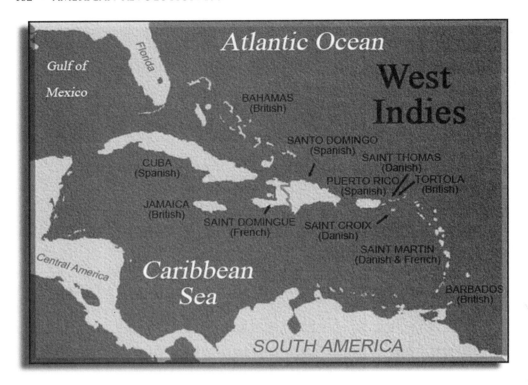

The Americans did not gain possessions in the Caribbean with the Treaty of Paris (69) that ended the war. It would take more than another century and the Spanish American War of 1898 for the United States to lay claims to islands of the West Indies. While the Americans did not benefit by occupying Caribbean territory at the end of the Revolution, the conflict over the area greatly influenced the actual conduct of the war. Every British ship, sailor, and soldier diverted to the West Indies meant one less vessel and man the Americans had to fight on the battlefields of their home states. Arms and supplies sent to the Caribbean likewise were not available for use against the rebels.

The influence of the West Indies is so intertwined with the influence of the American allies (5), the two are almost inseparable and indistinguishable. While the West Indies do not rate as high a ranking on this list as the American allies themselves, they were remarkable as a theater that drew away British assets at no cost and little effort on the part of the American patriots.

46

MARQUIS DE LAFAYETTE

American General

1757–1834

Marquis de Lafayette arrived in America as a teenage junior officer to receive a commission as a major general in the Continental Army (7). Initially accepted for his possible influence in securing aid from France for the Rebellion, Lafayette quickly earned the respect of the rebels for his battlefield leadership and for his personal friendship with George Washington (1). By the end of the Revolution, both the United States and France considered him a hero, and he remains one of the best-known figures of the Revolutionary War.

Marie Joseph Paul Yves Roche Gilbert du Motier, Marquis de Lafayette, was born on September 6, 1757, at Chavaniac into a wealthy, aristocratic French family. When he turned two, his father died in a battle against the English, and in 1770 he inherited the family fortune upon the death of his mother and grandfather. Lafayette entered the Royal Army in 1771 and advanced in rank to captain as he gained experience but saw no combat in infantry and dragoon units. Disenchanted with the French royal court system, he became interested in the upheaval against British authority in the American colonies.

In July 1777, Lafayette arrived in Philadelphia via South Carolina, presenting himself before the Continental Congress (10) and offering to serve in the Continental Army without pay or promise of specific command. Even though Lafayette was only nineteen, spoke few words of English, and lacked combat experience, Congress saw the advantages of including a French aristocrat as a friend of the Revolution and granted him a commission as a major general.

Lafayette met with Washington in August and the two began an immediate and warm friendship. The young Frenchman served on Washington's personal staff and on September 11, 1777, showed his bravery and leadership at the Battle of Bandywine Creek (72) where he was wounded.

On November 1, Washington wrote to the Continental Congress requesting permission to place the young Frenchman in a field leadership position. He began by lauding Lafayette's support for the Revolution and concluded, "…he is sensible, discreet in his manners, had made great proficiency in our language, and from the dispositions he discovered in the battle of Brandywine possesses a large share of bravery and military ardor."

In December, with Congress's permission, Washington placed Lafayette, whose English was becoming proficient, in command of a division of Virginians. Lafayette spent the winter with Washington at Valley Forge (39) and in the spring made plans for an invasion of Canada to secure support of the French settlers there. When the expedition was cancelled due to a lack of supplies, Lafayette rejoined Washington to lead a division at the Battle of Monmouth (59) on June 28, 1778.

For the remainder of the year Lafayette served as a field commander while also encouraging an American-French alliance. When France joined the Americans in their war against Britain, Lafayette became a liaison to the French fleet led by Charles d'Estaing (92), who arrived off Rhode Island in July 1778. The following January, Lafayette returned to France to encourage the commitment of additional troops and supplies to the Americans. France received him as a hero and honored him with parades and the promotion to colonel in the French army. Lafayette returned to the United States in April 1780 with the news that France was dispatching an army under Jean Baptiste de Rochambeau (24) to America.

Late in the year, Lafayette rejoined the army in the field in an unsuccessful attempt to capture traitor Benedict Arnold (85). He then resumed command of a division and participated in the final battles that led to the encirclement and surrender of General Charles Cornwallis (22) at Yorktown (2) in October 1781. During this period the Frenchman enhanced his reputation for battlefield leadership and earned accolades for his tactical abilities.

Near the end of the war Lafayette wrote, "Humanity has won its battle. Liberty now has a home." He then sailed for France in December 1781 where he was promoted to major general and again hailed as a hero. Back home, Lafayette continued to support American causes, remaining friends with American ambassadors Benjamin Franklin (25) and Thomas Jefferson (87). Lafayette also became a strong proponent of a National Assembly and the establishment of a constitutional monarchy during the years preceding the French Revolution. This, of course, lost him favor with the

French court. He fell further in popularity with the people when he led a French National Guard unit that used force to end a street riot.

In 1784, Lafayette returned to America for a brief visit with his old friend Washington. Back in Paris he became a member of the Assembly of Notables in 1787 and two years later assumed command of the National Guard. In 1792 he became the leader of French forces in the war against Austria but was forced to give up this position when France's own revolution took control of the government. Lafayette attempted to flee Europe for America but was captured by the Austrians, who held him a prisoner. Napoleon Bonaparte finally freed him five years later and forgave him for his support of the royalty.

Lafayette returned to France in March 1800 to find his fortune had been confiscated by the rebels. For the next decade and a half he lived the quiet life of a farmer before returning to Paris to play a role in the abdication of Napoleon in 1815. Lafayette then spent the rest of his life in political and military positions. He again visited the United States in 1824 where he was greeted as a hero. Lafayette died in Paris on May 20, 1834.

Lafayette remains today a hero of the American Revolution with his name prominently included in accounts of the period. Some historians claim that the Frenchman came to America out of frustration with his own country's military and political problems, but others speculate that he fought the English to avenge his father's death. He may have been driven by a youthful sense of adventure. His supporters note that he served without pay and, in fact, loaned $200,000 (more than $4.5 million in today's dollars) of his own money to support the American Revolution, while his detractors point out that Lafayette was later reimbursed for his loans and received full back pay for his time in uniform as well as a large land grant.

Whatever his motivations, Lafayette contributed to the success of the Revolution. As a valued friend of Washington, an apt battlefield division commander, and an unofficial ambassador to and from France, he significantly influenced the outcome of the Revolution. He is well-deserving of his honored place in American history and his placement in the upper half of these rankings.

47

CHARLESTON, SOUTH CAROLINA

February 11–May 12, 1780

The siege and battle of Charleston, South Carolina, in the winter and spring of 1780 ended with the largest surrender of American forces in the entirety of the Revolutionary War. Its aftermath left all of South Carolina in the hands of the Redcoats and cleared the way for the British to neutralize the support for the Rebellion in the Southern states. The Battle of Charleston also left General Charles Cornwallis (22), who would ultimately lose the region as well as the war to the Americans in the battle of Yorktown (2) less than eighteen months later, in command of the British Army in the South.

At the outbreak of the Revolution, British commanders planned to occupy Southern ports and pacify that area of the colonies before concentrating their efforts in the North. Their first effort in June 1776 focused on Charleston, where they met not passive resistance but an army that turned back their force at Fort Sullivan and battered their fleet on the shoreline. Deciding that the South might not be as easy to pacify as first believed, the British turned northward to fight the Rebellion and George Washington (1).

The British initially found success in the North and soon occupied both New York City and Philadelphia. However, after their disastrous defeat at Saratoga (3) in October 1777, the British once again decided to shift their efforts to the South, where they believed they would find support from the large number of Loyalists (34) residing there. They also thought that neutralizing the South would cut off a primary source of man power and supplies for the Rebel army in the North.

To accomplish this goal, the British relied on their superior sea power to both transport and resupply their army in the South and thus concentrated their initial efforts on capturing the major seaports in Georgia and South Carolina. In late 1778 the British accomplished their first objective by taking Savannah (80) and then moved into and occupied the Georgia interior.

The British turned back an American-French effort to retake Savannah the next year, but in the plodding way that typified Redcoat operations, it was not until early 1780 that they decided to expand their holdings into South Carolina. Leaving Savannah's defenders in place, General Henry Clinton (17) sailed south from New

York with 8,500 soldiers and 5,000 sailors aboard ninety troop transports and fourteen man-of-wars. With his fleet blockading the harbor, Clinton landed his infantry about 30 miles south of Charleston at Saint John's Island on February 11, 1780. Over the next six weeks, the British pushed the rebel defenders back toward the city.

By March 29 the American army of 5,500, about half regulars and half militiamen, occupied only a three-mile defensive line around Charleston's land approaches. General Benjamin Lincoln (76), American commander of the Charleston defenses, had established a strongpoint of 500 men led by General Isaac Huger at the crossroad at Monck's Corner to maintain an outlet for communications and possible escape from the city.

During the early morning hours of April 14, a British cavalry and infantry force led by Lieutenant Colonel Banastre Tarleton (44) made a night attack that surprised and quickly overran Monck's Corner. Lincoln and his Charleston defenders were now besieged and cut off from escape. Clinton tightened his lines and moved against the city while also bombarding it with field and seaborne artillery. By May 8 the British had advanced their lines to the very edge of the city. As part of their preparations for a final assault, the British peppered the city with heated artillery shells known as "hot shots" that started multiple fires. On May 11, Charleston's officials asked Lincoln to approach Clinton for terms of surrender.

At 11:00 a.m. the next morning, the Americans surrendered, their colors cased in covers prepared to be turned over to the victors. Under their surrender terms, their band could play neither American nor British music, so the beaten army marched to a Turkish tune to relinquish all weapons, ammunition, powder, and other military supplies to their captors. Most of Charleston was saved from the torch, but the city and its residents would remain under British control for the remainder of the war.

During the siege and battle for Charleston, 89 Americans were killed. The 189 wounded in the campaign joined the nearly 5,500 prisoners. Material losses included—by British count—5,316 muskets; 15 regimental colors; more than 33,000 rounds of small arms ammunition; at least 40 cannons; 8,000 artillery balls; and 376 barrels of gunpowder. The irony was that most of the materiel was destroyed in an explosion caused by British negligence a few hours after the American surrender. The loss of the supplies and men, however, were much more critical to the Americans than to the British.

With his mission accomplished, Clinton sailed back to the comforts of New York, leaving Charles Cornwallis in charge. His orders were for Cornwallis to maintain control of Charleston, neutralize all of South Carolina, and then march toward North

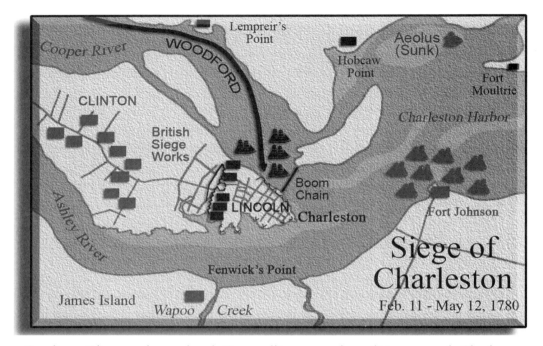

Siege of Charleston
Feb. 11 - May 12, 1780

Carolina. Clinton also ordered Cornwallis to parole militiamen and Charleston civilian leaders. Cornwallis did so but added the condition that the parolees swear an oath to the Crown and be prepared to join the British forces if necessary. This requirement furthered resistance and encouraged many of the militiamen to return later to the American lines and rejoin the rebel army.

Lincoln and most of his officers were soon exchanged for British prisoners of equal rank. Few of the regular enlisted soldiers were so fortunate. While militiamen were paroled, the Continental Army (7) troops were interned on prison ships in Charleston Harbor where sickness and disease decimated their ranks until the end of the war finally brought freedom for the few survivors.

While the later Battle of Camden (65) provided the British a more decisive battle-field victory, Charleston produced the most American prisoners and captured stores of the war. Had this tremendous loss in manpower and materials happened to the Americans earlier in the conflict, it might have ended the Rebellion. However, by 1780 the French had allied with the Americans, and the lost weapons and munitions were eventually replaced by France and its allies.

The influence of the Battle of Charleston on the American Revolution is one of the most difficult of all to assess. The aftermath of the battle left Cornwallis in command, and many of his subsequent errors led to Britain's defeat and America's independence. Charleston also caused Washington to send General Horatio Gates (31) with an American army to meet Cornwallis. After Gates failed at Camden, the very apt General Nathanael Greene (4) took command of the rebels in the South and led them to the final victory at Yorktown. For these reasons, Charleston ranks in the middle rather than at the top or bottom of this list.

GERMANTOWN, PENNSYLVANIA

October 4, 1777

After a succession of losses in New York and Pennsylvania that led to the British occupation of the American capital at Philadelphia, George Washington (1) was determined to take the offensive and destroy, or at least weaken, the Redcoat army. On October 4, 1777, he launched a four-column night assault against British forces at the village of Germantown, Pennsylvania. The complexity of the plan, poor timing, and bad luck caused the attack to fail, but it proved to the Americans that they could take the war to the British, increasing their morale and confidence. Furthermore, the boldness of the Americans impressed the French and encouraged their recognition of the new republic.

Following their defeat on Long Island (32) and the loss of New York, the Continental Army (7) withdrew into New Jersey. When British General William Howe (15) moved against Philadelphia in the fall of 1777, Washington tried to block his advance at Brandywine Creek (72) but failed, allowing the British to occupy the city. Washington suffered more casualties than Howe at Brandywine Creek, but he could gather replacements from neighboring states much more rapidly than additional British soldiers could be transported from England. With this in mind, Washington planned a surprise attack to destroy Howe's weakened army and bring a successful conclusion to the Revolution, a bold offensive that would also encourage his troops, for whom defensive-only operations were routine.

After his victory at Brandywine Creek, General Howe occupied Philadelphia on September 26 and then dispatched 9,000 of his troops north of the city. Howe's army camped in and around Germantown, a small village that ran narrowly along Skippack Road from Mount Airy in the north to the intersection of School Lane in the south.

Washington, aware that the British did not expect an attack and had not prepared more than basic defensive positions, planned on a four-pronged night assault with his 8,000 regulars and 3,000 militiamen. General Nathanael Greene (4) would lead the center and main attack against the crossroads of Skippack Road and School Lane. General John Sullivan's (71) column would attack from the north around Mount Airy and Generals William Smallwood and John Armstrong would envelop Howe's flank to the southeast. All four columns were to be in position no later than 5:00 a.m. for a coordinated cannon and musket attack followed by a bayonet assault that would sweep across the British camp, killing or capturing the entire army.

Howe felt secure in his Germantown camp, not believing the Americans were strong enough to mount an attack. When informed by Loyalist (34) spies of Washington's concentration of troops and movement, Howe responded by only posting sentries a few hundred yards beyond the village and warning them to be especially vigilant.

Washington advanced at sundown on October 3, but all four columns moved slower than planned. It was not until dawn the next morning that Sullivan's column struck British pickets at Mount Airy and drove them south down Skippack Road. The British soldiers, however, retreated only as far as an abandoned stone mansion, known as Chew House, where they barricaded the doors and windows. American musket and cannon fire failed to neutralize the 120 Redcoats in their stronghold, stopping Sullivan's advance. The rebels lost at least 70 men killed or wounded.

By the time Greene's column neared Germantown from the northeast, the morning fog and smoke from the fight around Chew House caused some of his men to exchange fire with those of Sullivan's command. In the confusion both columns withdrew. Meanwhile Howe deployed his main force along School Lane to face the advancing Americans. Few of these British soldiers ever had to fire a shot. The rebels' northern and center columns were stopped and even firing on each other; a British counterattack was pouring musket fire into Greene's flank; and the two southern columns had yet to reach the battlefield. At this point, Washington called off the attack and retreated toward what would be his winter headquarters at Valley Forge (39). A British column followed, but in his usual reluctance to fight, Howe turned them back to Germantown after a pursuit of only 5 miles.

The Americans left behind 152 dead and 400 prisoners. Another 521 suffered wounds in the fight. British casualties totaled 520 killed, wounded, and captured.

Some of the immediate blame for the American loss was placed on Adam Stephen, a division commander in Sullivan's column who had gone off course and fired into Greene's troops. On November 20, Washington approved the recommendations of a court-martial that convicted Stephen and dismissed him from service for "unofficer-like behavior" and for being drunk during the attack. This setback proved fortuitous when Washington replaced Stephen with a young Frenchman, Marquis de Lafayette (46), who performed heroically during the remainder of the war.

While some analysts blamed Stephen for the defeat at Germantown, others recognized major inherent problems. First, there was the fog and then the valiant stand by

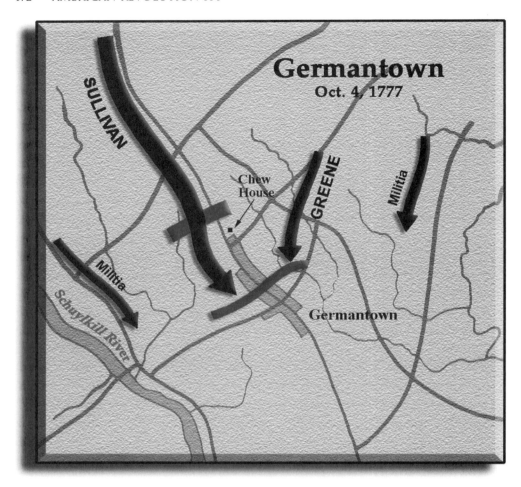

Germantown

Oct. 4, 1777

the British at Chew House that stopped Sullivan's column. Both of these incidents were influential, but Greene's late arrival also played a key role. Most importantly, however, the ultimate reason for failure lay in Washington's plan itself. A coordinated night attack by four columns separated by as much as 7 miles was not realistic for the most highly trained army, not to mention relatively inexperienced Continentals and militiamen. In itself the plan was brilliant on paper but nearly impossible to execute. Even the fog that some blamed for the failure likely assisted the rebels. If it had not covered the rebel advance, British pickets would have spotted them earlier, allowing Howe more time to prepare his defenses.

Even though the Americans were again sent into retreat, most of the troops and their commanders felt that victory had almost been theirs. Except for the dark of the night, the fog, the British stand at Chew House, and just plain bad luck, most believed they would have swept the field and then marched on to Philadelphia. While this is highly unlikely, the American troops felt good about themselves for taking the offensive.

Washington's initiative at Germantown, combined with Horatio Gates's (31) victory over John Burgoyne (33) at Saratoga (3), gained the attention of the French. Now convinced that the American rebellion had a chance of success against their longtime English enemies, the French planned for a treaty of alliance with the United States.

Germantown, a complete battlefield defeat, ultimately led to success for Washington. His army came away confident and this offensive helped to gain the assistance of France. While not nearly as important as Saratoga during the same month or Yorktown (2) that ended the war, Germantown was more influential than the Brandywine Creek skirmish that preceded it and of about the same influence as the battles in the Southern theater that led to the final victory.

49

GUY CARLETON

British General and Governor of Canada

1724–1808

Guy Carleton was the individual directly responsible for Canada's remaining loyal to the Crown rather than joining the Revolutionary War. As the governor of Canada and the Province of Quebec during the first three years of the American Revolution, he exerted his leadership skills to set that country on the course he thought best. His battlefield command as a major general turned back the Americans in their Canada Invasion (84) in late 1776. After the British surrender at Yorktown (2) five years later, Carleton became the commander in chief of British forces in North America and successfully evacuated the remaining British army, refugees, and Loyalists (34) from New York.

Born in Strabane, County Tyrone, into a prominent Irish family, Carleton entered the army as an ensign on May 21, 1742. He steadily advanced up the ranks to colonel and served with General James Wolfe in the capture of Quebec in September 1759 during the French and Indian War. For the next two years, he distinguished himself on far-flung battlefields from Belle Isle off the French coast to Havana, Cuba. In September 1766 he returned to Quebec as the province's lieutenant governor. Although he had no experience as a civil administrator and limited knowledge of Quebec, he had friends in Parliament and the court. King George III (20) backed Carleton for the position, declaring the soldier "a gallant and sensible man."

A year after his return to North America, Carleton became governor of the Province of Quebec and governor general of Canada. Three years later Carleton sailed home to return to active military service as a major general. In June 1774, he argued before the House of Commons in favor of the Quebec Act (19)—legislation that he had helped draft—that would extend Canadian boundaries south to the Ohio River and grant French Canadians freedom to continue to practice their Catholic religion.

The Quebec Act greatly enhanced Carleton's popularity in Canada where he was welcomed back as governor in January 1775. When General Thomas Gage relinquished command of his forces in the rebel colonies to General William Howe (15),

Carleton also assumed the duties of the independent commander of British troops in Canada.

Carleton believed that the French Canadians, subservient to the Crown since their defeat in 1763, would readily fight against the rebels, while the Americans thought they would join the pursuit of liberty as their fourteenth state. Neither Carleton nor the Americans were correct in their assessments.

Because he was so certain his Canadian militia would rise to defend their territory against the Revolutionaries, Carleton dispatched most of his British regulars to join the fight in New England. Meanwhile the Americans had invited Canadians to send delegates to the Continental Congress (10). Both were disappointed. Carleton later wrote to British Secretary of State George Germain (9) about his Canadian subjects, explaining, "I think there is nothing to fear from them, while we are in a state of prosperity, and nothing to hope for when in distress; I speak of the people at large; there are among them who are guided by sentiments of honor, but the multitude is influenced only by hopes of gain, or fear of punishment."

In early 1776, with reluctant Canadian militiamen, some Native American (99) allies, and a few British regulars, Carleton managed to stop the American invasion at Quebec. He then pursued the rebels back into New York before being turned back to Canada after the Battle of Valcour Island (28) in October. Carleton's political opponents in London accused him of being too cautious in pursuing the rebels and insisted he should have advanced all the way to New York City. His more influential friends commended Carleton for saving Canada, promoted him to lieutenant general, and nominated him for knighthood.

Carleton requested additional British regulars for another offensive into New York. He wanted to control the Hudson River Valley and separate the former Northern and Southern colonies. When the British leadership selected Carleton's second in command, John Burgoyne (33), to lead the offensive, the angry and disgruntled governor tendered his resignation and demanded to be recalled to England on June 27, 1777. Over the next year, while awaiting the arrival of his replacement, Carleton loyally supported Burgoyne even after his defeat at Saratoga (3) in October. Carleton continued his civil duties until he finally sailed for England in July 1778.

Back home Carleton served as commissioner of public accounts until the General Charles Cornwallis (22) surrendered at Yorktown in October 1781. The loss of their former American colonies caused a change in government in England, and one of the new administration's first acts was to return Carleton to America. With the support of King George III, who called Carleton "the best officer" in the army, the former governor of Canada returned as the commander-in-chief of British forces in North America on May 5, 1782.

Carleton's instructions were to attempt "to reconcile and reunite" the colonies with Great Britain, but the war for American independence had already been won by the rebels. All that was left for him to do was to evacuate the remaining British soldiers and their supporters safely from New York City. Ordering his subordinates to remain on duty until every man, woman, and child who wanted to leave the United States had moved to British soil, Carleton evacuated 30,000 soldiers and 27,000 refugees, including Loyalists and several thousand escaped slaves. Carlton departed New York on November 25, 1783.

Three years later Carleton returned to Canada to once again become the governor of Quebec, where he remained popular and respected. In 1796, Carleton left his post and sailed for England and retirement. He died at Stubbings in Berkshire on November 10, 1808.

Carleton may well have been Britain's most able general, and the Revolution might have ended differently had he been in overall command at an earlier date. While Carleton himself admitted that the Canadians had little interest beyond their own welfare, his influence was critical in keeping them from joining the Americans or beginning their own rebellion. His actions before the war, during its early years, and throughout its last months clearly earn him a place in the middle of these rankings.

50

BOSTON SIEGE

April 19, 1775–March 17, 1776

In the opening phase of the Revolutionary War, the Boston Siege by the Americans prevented the British army from moving among the New England colonies and eventually forced their evacuation from the city. The long siege failed to achieve complete victory because the British maintained naval superiority and kept their sea avenues open. More significant, the siege provided the opportunity for both the Americans and the British to establish their attitudes and objectives for the following conflict.

Upon the conclusion of the Rebellion's opening battles at Lexington and Concord (43) on April 19, 1775, the colonial militias pursued the retreating British toward Boston. When the British soldiers reentered the city, the militiamen took up positions across the narrow piece of land known as Boston Neck, blocking the major route of entry into or egress from Boston. General Thomas Gage, the commander of the 2,000 British forces in the city called for reinforcements from Canada and Great Britain by way of the open waterway. By the end of May, his numbers had risen to 6,500.

Meanwhile, the Massachusetts Provincial Congress called for the enlistment of 30,000 men, 13,600 from the colony and the others from Connecticut, Rhode Island, and New Hampshire. They were to replace the veteran militiamen who were nearing the end of their enlistments. Only about half of the requested numbers were actually recruited, but by June there were more than 15,000 militiamen occupying positions around Boston under the command of General Artemas Ward.

This "Army of Observation," as they called themselves because they were not yet willing to openly admit they were in rebellion against King George III (20), occupied three specific areas. A third of the militiamen camped on the right wing around Roxbury in the south to guard Boston Neck. A center sector manned the village of Cambridge to the west, and the left wing prepared defenses along Charleston Neck in the north.

The British faced several quandaries. Although they had open access to the sea, they suffered a shortage of food and supplies that required rationing to feed and maintain the 6,500 soldiers and 17,000 civilian residents of Boston. At the same time, many British officials still hoped for a peaceful resolution to the uprising. On June 12, General Gage issued a proclamation offering a pardon to the rebels with the exception of a few key leaders. When he received no response, Gage decided to take action. He ordered the occupation of the unoccupied Dorchester Heights southeast of the city. Before his army could comply, the Americans, acting on information from spies within the city, moved across Charleston Neck to the north and occupied Bunker and Breed's Hills outside Charlestown.

On June 17, the British crossed the narrow waterway between Boston and Charleston and attacked the Americans at what became known as the Battle of Bunker Hill (23). The British finally prevailed by pushing back the Americans, but the rebels reformed to secure Charleston Neck and maintained the siege, which now became stalemated.

Back in Philadelphia, the Continental Congress (10) was meeting to decide the future of the American colonies. Understanding that the colonial militias (53)—which had varied enlistment periods and lacked overall leadership—could not maintain the fight, the Congress appointed George Washington (1) as commander of the newly designated Continental Army (7) and dispatched him to Boston to take charge. Washington arrived outside Boston on July 3 and immediately strengthened positions and reorganized and trained his army. He found his men generally well-fed but many with inferior arms and short of ammunition and powder. Other than reoccupying Bunker and Breed's hills, with no opposition from the British, the lines remained stalemated on into the fall and winter.

Washington's major challenge was to recruit new soldiers. To Joseph Reed, Washington's former military secretary and presently a member of the Continental Congress, the general wrote, "Search the vast volumes of history through, and I much question whether a case similar to ours is to be found; to wit, to maintain a post against the flower of the British troops for six months together, without powder, and then to have one army disbanded and another to be raised within the same distance of a reinforced enemy."

On February 16, Washington proposed a surprise attack against the British defenses across the ice-covered Back Bay. His subordinates disagreed, believing that the British were more numerous than Washington's estimate and that the Continental Army's shortage of artillery would doom any attack. Washington listened to his officers and cancelled his plans, but he continued to look for ways to take the fight to the British. The answer to his quest was already arriving via a sled train of captured cannons led by Henry Knox (12) from recently captured Ticonderoga (52).

Despite the intentions of the British to occupy Dorchester Heights early in the siege, the high ground overlooking the harbor remained held by neither side. On March 2, Washington launched a series of diversionary attacks around Back Bay while he positioned men and artillery on Dorchester Heights. Aware that digging defenses on the Heights would be difficult, if not impossible, because of the frozen ground, Washington prepared heavy timber frames that could be filled with bales of hay and barrels containing sand to provide instant fortifications.

During the night of March 4–5, the Americans executed their plan with few obstacles other than the physical difficulty of wrestling their cannons up the slopes. The next morning the British awoke to find rebel artillery poised above their ships

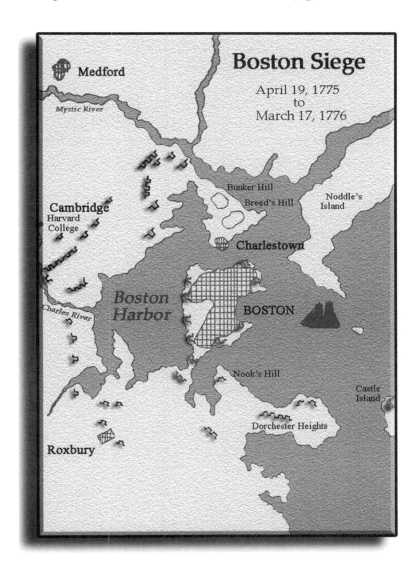

in the harbor and overlooking the city itself. British General William Howe (15) remarked to a subordinate, "The rebels have done more in one night than my whole army could do in months."

The British options were now few. They could attempt a direct attack against Dorchester Heights into the rebel strength, but that would surely fail. They could remain in Boston, but the artillery locations on the Heights could shell their vessels in the harbor while the British ships could not elevate their guns sufficiently to return fire. Their only viable option was to use their navy to evacuate the army by sea.

Although no formal agreement was made, the Americans allowed the British to evacuate Boston unmolested as long as they did not burn or otherwise destroy the city. From March 7 until March 27, about 11,000 British soldiers and sailors departed Boston for Halifax, Canada. More than a thousand Boston Loyalists (34) joined them. Washington entered Boston on March 20 to find sixty-nine much-needed cannons as well as stores of medical supplies and blankets left behind. The eight-month siege of the port city, including the Battle of Bunker Hill, had cost the Continental Army fewer than 250 dead. Boston, as well as Massachusetts, remained free of British troops for the remainder of the Rebellion.

Washington did not linger in Boston to enjoy his victory. He correctly assumed that the British would soon move against New York, and so he maneuvered his army overland to counter the threat.

Before the Boston Siege, neither the colonists nor the British were sure if the Rebellion would continue or possibly be settled by negotiations. Afterward, both sides knew the war would be long, bloody, and settled only by victory or defeat. Lexington and Concord provided the first shots, but Boston offered the first extended campaign that unified the Continental Army and established Washington as its leader. The siege was the first great step on the road to Yorktown (2) and independence, an event well worthy of its ranking in the middle of this list.

51

JOHN ADAMS

American Statesman

1735–1826

The writings and speeches of John Adams encouraged the Rebellion and defined the liberties on which the new nation was founded. As a leader in the Continental Congress (10), he helped produce the *Declaration of Independence* (14) and select George Washington (1) as the commander of the Continental Army (7). Near the end of the war Adams served as ambassador to France, and his negotiating skills in reaching the Treaty of Paris (69) helped add territories and rights for the Americans.

Upon his birth on October 19, 1735, at Braintree, just south of Boston, Adams began a privileged life in a family that had been in America since 1640. Adams graduated from Harvard University in 1751 and briefly taught school in Worcester where he found his students to be "little runtlings" with scant knowledge or interest in learning. He studied law and by 1758 was back in Braintree with his own office. His practice often took him to Boston, where he became acquainted with many of the city's and colony's leaders, including his distant cousin Samuel Adams.

Adams's discussions with his cousin and Boston leaders about the Stamp Act of 1765 (19) furthered his already growing concerns about British rule. He wrote anonymous articles published in local newspapers about the origins of freedom, saying that the rights of Englishmen, whether in England or in the colonies, were derived from God and not from the king or from Parliament. Back in Braintree, Adams prepared the formal protest for the village against the Stamp Act, writing that the tax was an unconstitutional levy and "no free man can be separated from his property but by his own act or fault." Other towns throughout New England adopted Adams's Braintree protest in various forms.

In 1768 Adams moved permanently to Boston where he continued his law practice while also attending meetings and discussions with those who opposed various aspects of British rule. Adams believed that everyone, regardless of crime or cause, deserved legal representation. He defended John Hancock against a charge of smuggling and defended the British soldiers accused of the Boston Massacre (93). Adams put honesty and the law—he claimed to have the only compete printed set of British statutes in the colonies—above all else.

Despite his belief in liberty, Adams had doubts about mob violence and concerns about a direct break from Great Britain. These thoughts, along with an unknown illness, caused him leave Boston in the spring of 1771 to return to Braintree. After a little more than a year of recovery, Adams returned to Boston with a renewed zeal for liberty. He approved of the Boston Tea Party in December 1773 and began to believe that independence might be both possible and necessary.

Massachusetts selected Adams, now thirty-eight, as a representative to the Continental Congress on June 14, 1774. In his early months in Congress he helped draft letters of protest to England and a declaration of rights of colonists. By 1775 Adams had come to the conclusion that the British would not grant further rights or ease taxation, causing him to join those who favored independence. Aware that Massachusetts and New England alone could not stand against the British, Adams led the way for the appointment of George Washington to command the Continental Army, in part because he was from Virginia and brought support from the South.

When Richard Henry Lee moved that Congress declare independence from Great Britain on June 7, 1776, Adams was the first to rise to second the motion. The next day he joined Thomas Jefferson (87) and three others in drafting the *Declaration of Independence*. Adams deferred most of the writing to Jefferson, but he was instrumental in getting the Congress to approve the final document.

Adams then joined the newly formed Board of War where he labored to equip the army in the field and to conduct early, unsuccessful peace conferences with the British. On October 26, 1777, Adams left Congress to become the commissioner to France with the task of negotiating a commercial and military alliance. By the time he arrived in Europe, the previous delegates had already secured an agreement, so he sailed back to the United States. Arriving back in Braintree in August 1779, he attended the Massachusetts Constitutional Convention where he prepared much of the state's future constitution.

In February 1780, Adams returned to France to prepare for the peace treaty negotiations that would end the war. Adams, in his usual straight-laced manner, clashed with the French and angered fellow American Benjamin Franklin (25) by commenting on his personal behavior. When the talks with the British stalled, Adams traveled to the Netherlands on December 29, 1780, as the U.S. minister. There Adams secured Dutch recognition of the United States and negotiated a loan as well as commerce treaties.

On October 26, Adams went back to France to play a key role in producing the Treaty of Paris document that formally ended the war. During the negotiations Adams insisted on and secured for the U.S. fishing rights off the Canadian coast and the westward extension of the old colonial borders.

After the ratification of the treaty, Adams toured Great Britain and then stayed as the U.S. minister to that country. He did little to improve American-British relations given his personality and the English bitterness over losing the colonies. During this time Adams wrote the three-volume *Defense of the Constitution of the United States,* which, while unpublished, was often cited in the U.S. Constitutional Convention of 1787.

Adams returned to Braintree in 1788 to become a gentleman farmer and continue his writing. In 1789 his fellow Americans elected him the first vice president of the United States, a position he declared in a letter to his wife to be "the most insignificant office that ever the invention of man contrived or his imagination conceived." In 1796 Adams defeated his old friend Thomas Jefferson to become the second president of the United States. Jefferson, in turn, defeated him in the election of 1800, creating difficulties between the two that interrupted their friendship. They reconciled a dozen years later to renew a correspondence that now provides rich insights into their personalities and the times.

After leaving office Adams retired to Quincy, Massachusetts. He lived long enough to see his son John Quincy Adams become the sixth president of the United States in 1825. Adams died in Quincy on July 4, 1826—the fiftith anniversary of the *Declaration of Independence.* Unaware that his old friend had died a few hours earlier, Adams's last words were "Thomas Jefferson." Adams is buried in Quincy's United First Parish Church.

Described as honest and direct by his friends and as vain and irritable by his detractors, Adams was a complex man whose firm beliefs in liberty and his country stood above all his other characteristics. He joins Jefferson and Franklin among the few on this list who influenced the Rebellion as civilian politicians and diplomats rather than as soldiers and sailors. Adams's quill pen and ink well greatly influenced the start of the revolt and the treaty that ended it. However, the war was won by muskets and blood, not pen and ink, causing his ranking to be in the second rather than the first half of this list.

52

TICONDEROGA, NEW YORK

May 10, 1775

Ticonderoga was not a battle or even a skirmish. In fact, it was little more than an armed robbery where only one shot was fired and only one casualty suffered a minor bayonet wound. Despite this lack of combat, the American capture of Ticonderoga provided the primary source of heavy artillery, shot, and gunpowder for the Continental Army (7), a feat that led to their later successful Boston Siege (50).

The French had established the first military fortification on the western shore of Lake Champlain in October 1755 named Fort Carillon. During the French and Indian War, the British unsuccessfully attacked the fort on July 8, 1758, withdrawing after suffering nearly 2,000 casualties. When the British returned the next year, it became evident that they would prevail, so the French destroyed much of the fort and withdrew to Canada on July 26, 1759.

Renaming the site Fort Ticonderoga, the British fortified the installation, as it became known as the "gateway to the continent" and the "Gibraltar of America" for its importance of guarding the most direct route from Quebec to New York. By the outbreak of the Revolutionary War, however, the fort was in disrepair and its British garrison numbered only two officers and forty-eight men commanded by Captain William Delaplace. Half of the command was recently arrived reinforcements from Canada led by Lieutenant Jocelyn Feltham.

As the news spread among the American colonies about the battles of Lexington and Concord (43) on April 19, 1775, the colonists who supported the Revolution realized that their militias were extremely short of gunpowder and completely without heavy artillery. Leaders in Connecticut and Massachusetts began separate and uncoordinated efforts to organize units to seize the British garrison and armory at Ticonderoga.

In Hartford, Samuel H. Parsons and Silas Deane organized a company of about fifty local volunteers and then contacted Ethan Allen in Bennington, Vermont, to request that he and his Green Mountain Boys join the expedition. On May 7 the Hartford company linked up with about a hundred of Allen's men at Castleton, 15 miles east of current Whitehall, New York. Another fifty men led by John Brown and James Easton arrived from Massachusetts. The next day the combined force elected

Allen as their commander and planned their attack. The main body was to move to Hand's Cove, near what is now Orwell, on the eastern side of Lake Champlain, about 2 miles from Fort Ticonderoga, while the two other detachments were to gather boats to cross the lake.

Meanwhile Benedict Arnold (85) had presented a similar plan to the Massachusetts Committee of Safety and received a colonel's commission and permission to recruit 400 men. Before Arnold began his enlistments, he learned of the Connecticut force and quickly journeyed to join them. When he arrived at Castleton on May 9, he was accompanied only by a single manservant, but he nevertheless presented his commission papers and claimed command of the entire force. Most of the soldiers objected, the Green Mountain Boys threatening to return home if Arnold assumed command. Allen and Arnold met, and, while the exact details of their arrangement are not known, they did agree to proceed together. Arnold marched with Allen at the head of the column; whether he shared command or just accompanied him is not known.

When the expedition reached Hand's Cove, the officers discovered that only enough boats for about a third of the force had been found. Allen feared the British would learn of their presence and he would lose the element of surprise. He ordered eighty-three men into the boats and set off across the lake at 2:00 a.m. on May 10. Wind and rain slowed the flotilla but provided concealment of the men and noise.

A sentry challenged Allen and his small force when they landed. He attempted to shoot his musket, but it misfired in the damp. Another sentry fired a single shot that hit no one while a third sentry spilled the only blood of the "battle" when he slightly wounded James Easton with his bayonet. Allen next encountered Lieutenant Feltham from whom he demanded a surrender. About this time Captain Delaplace appeared and agreed to give up. Although Allen did not mention it until 1779, he then claimed he demanded the surrender "in the name of Great Jehovah and the Continental Congress."

Included in the store of captured weapons and equipment were eighty-one cannons, six mortars, thousands of cannon balls, and tons of gunpowder. In the fall, with the Revolution rapidly escalating, Henry Knox (12) and a detachment of rebels hauled the artillery pieces down Lake George and then overland to join in the Boston Siege. More than fifty of the captured cannons made their way on what Knox called the "Noble Train of Artillery." Their placement of the heavy guns on Dorchester Heights overlooking Boston directly influenced the eventual British evacuation of the city.

In addition to the arms and equipment, the rebels also captured several lake ships anchored near the fort that later contributed to the rebel victory at Valcour Island (28) in October 1776. Subsequent raids against small British garrisons, including

Crown Point and St. Johns, added even more arms, powder, and supplies to the bounty seized at Ticonderoga. The Americans rebuilt and reinforced Ticonderoga but were unable to hold the fort against a British offensive, led by John Burgoyne (33), launched from Canada in July 1777. Ticonderoga stayed in British hands the rest of the war, having little further influence. Its much-needed heavy guns had been removed to Boston for future use by the Continental Army. With the British defeat at Saratoga (3) the following October and the shift of the war's focus to the South, Ticonderoga was no longer important to the Revolution.

Neither Allen nor Arnold greatly benefited from their roles at Ticonderoga. The Green Mountain Boys soon voted Allen out of command, and he played no further role in the war. When Allen departed Ticonderoga, Arnold declared himself the

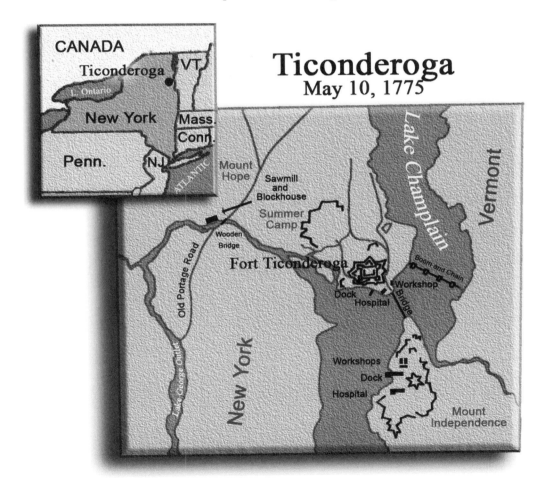

commander of the fort. Several weeks later, reinforcements arrived with notice from the Massachusetts authority that Colonel Benjamin Hinman would take over the fort's leadership. Arnold resigned his Massachusetts command in what became the first of several incidents he perceived as the slights that eventually led to his turning traitor against the Revolution.

Ticonderoga directly influenced the American success at Boston and, thus, the remainder of the Revolution. Its cannons and gunpowder were desperately needed. While not ranking with Saratoga or major battles in the South, Ticonderoga opened the way for the success of the Revolution and merits placement in the middle of this list.

53

AMERICAN MILITIAS

1775–1783

Massachusetts militiamen fired the first shots of the American Revolution and then besieged the British garrison at Boston (50). They and their fellow militiamen from other states fought well at Bunker Hill (23), Bennington, Saratoga (3), and Kings Mountain (36), but overall their performance was much less than stellar. Inadequately trained, undisciplined, and poorly led, the militias proved unreliable throughout most of the war, causing regular Continental Army (7) commanders to neither respect nor trust these part-time soldiers.

When the English settlers first arrived in North America, they sought safety in numbers and banded together in villages. As the Native Americans (99) became more hostile, the colonists built small forts and formed militias. Each colony had its own rules about military service, but generally each required every able-bodied man from age seventeen to sixty to assemble on a regular basis to train to defend their village. Militiamen usually provided their own weapons and selected their leaders by popular vote. Discipline was lax, and the frequency of drills and training depended on real or perceived threats of attack.

These militias proved successful in the limited operations against the crudely armed and loosely organized Native Americans. It was not until they fought against conventional forces in the French and Indian War of 1754–1763 that their lack of will and discipline became apparent. When the militia units joined the British regulars against the French and Native Americans, they performed poorly in battle and deserted more often than they fought. British General James Wolfe wrote of the American militiamen, "They are the dirtiest most contemptible cowardly dogs that you could conceive. There is no depending on them in action. They fall down dead in their dirt [excrement] and desert by battalions, officers and all."

In the decade leading up to the American Revolution, militias improved somewhat—the most progress being made by those in villages outside Boston. As the colonists' anger grew against Great Britain and talk of independence increased, militia units intensified their training and stockpiled arms and ammunition. Some units took oaths promising to assemble in "a minute's notice" in the event of need. These

"Minutemen" were the soldiers who gathered at Lexington and Concord (43) to fight the first battles of the war.

Minutemen and other militiamen from New England then staged the Boston Siege. It was militia units that stood against charge after charge of the British at Bunker Hill before finally being forced from their defenses. With the arrival of spring, many of the militiamen who were farmers left the ranks to return home to plant their crops. The Continental Congress (10) realized that the diminishing ranks and the lack of a central control could only be resolved with a united armed force. In June, George Washington (1) rode to Boston as the commander of the newly authorized Continental Army. Washington was not happy with what he found. On August 20, 1775, he wrote his cousin Lund Washington about the militias, "In short, they are by no means such troops, in any respect, as you are led to believe of them from the accounts which are published, but I need not make myself enemies among them by this declaration, although it is consistent with the truth…they are exceedingly dirty and nasty people."

Despite his feelings, Washington integrated many of the militiamen into the regular army, believing that with experience and proper training they could and would make acceptable full-time soldiers. Militia units that remained under the control of their state officials usually joined the regular army only for operations in their local areas. While the Continental Army conducted the major operations, fought the influential battles, and suffered the bulk of the casualties, the militias provided marginal reinforcement. On occasion the militia units were activated for periods of one to six months and became subordinate to regular army commanders. Even then they often failed to show up for duty, causing regular officers to say, "It was easier to raise the dead than a militia company."

There were exceptions. Militias commanded by John Stark (68) performed well at Bennington—even though they were operating against the orders of regular General Horatio Gates (31) to delay their attack. Militias also joined Gates at Saratoga and fought successfully.

Washington's favorite subordinate and future commander of the Southern theater, General Nathanael Greene (4), explained the differences between part-time soldiers and regulars. He wrote, "The militia were not sufficiently fortified with natural courage to stand the shocking scenes of war, to march over dead men, to hear without concern the groans of the wounded, I say few men can stand such scenes unless steeled by habit and fortified by military pride."

In a letter to Congress on September 24, 1776, Washington exclaimed, "To place any dependence upon the militia is assuredly resting upon a broken staff."

He later expanded his thoughts on the part-time soliders, writing, "No militia will ever acquire the habits necessary to resist a regular force. The firmness requisite for the real business of fighting is only to be attained by a constant course of discipline and service. I have never yet been a witness to a single instance that can justify a different opinion, and it is most earnestly to be wished that the liberties of America may no longer be trusted, in any material degree, to so precarious a dependence."

In the Southern theater the militias performed better when participating as guerrillas. At Kings Mountain, South Carolina, in August 1780, militia units surrounded and defeated a British and Loyalist (34) force, but even after such successes, militiamen still tended to desert the lines after the first shots were fired. Continental Army commanders at Cowpens (18), Guilford Court House (26), and Eutaw Springs (63) learned to position their militia units where their avenues for running away were limited by waterways or other terrain features. Daniel Morgan (35) used the tactic of placing his militia on the first line of defense and telling them they could retreat after firing three volleys.

During the war, a total of 145,000 citizen soldiers served in their state militias. Despite their overall poor performance, the militia concept remained in place after the war ended and Congress disbanded the Continental Army, evolving into today's National Guard.

The militias did favorably contribute to the independence of the United States. Farmers and villagers picking up arms and resisting the British at Lexington and Concord began the war, and these citizen soldiers occasionally provided substantive support to the regulars. As for the militiamen themselves, their inadequacies and failures were the result of poor organization, training, and leadership rather than any particular fault of their own. They, however, by no means had nearly as much influence on the outcome of the Revolution as did the Continental or British armies (11), or even the Hessians (37) or Loyalists (34).

54

POPULATION AND RESOURCES

1775–1783

If one looks at statistics alone, the British should have subdued the American Revolution handily in 1776. They certainly had the man power and resources to do so. Britain had a population more than three times that of the United States, and the empire possessed far greater wealth and vastly superior military forces. The British, however, faced long supply lines and communications difficulties in fighting a trans-Atlantic war. They also had enemies throughout Europe who supported any opposition to the British Crown. The American colonies, on the other hand, appeared statistically to have all the disadvantages. Nearly a third of their own population remained loyal to the king (34), they had no monetary system, and they had no national army or navy. However, the Americans did possess the advantages of fighting for a cause, superior commanders, and the home territory. These factors held great sway over the conflict as it evolved.

In 1775 the British Isles boasted a population of about 7,500,000 of which 2,300,000 were of the age, gender, and health to serve in the armed forces. The American colonists numbered only 2,350,000 and fully half a million were black slaves. Native Americans, generally considered hostile rather than friendly, were not included in the total. Of the total white population, only 600,000 men were eligible to bear arms. Most sources note that about a third of this population of potential soldiers remained loyal to Great Britain while another third remained neutral, leaving about 200,000 men for the American military.

In 1774 the British had a standing army of 17,500 soldiers and a navy of 100 ships manned by 16,000 sailors. At the outbreak of the Revolution, the British Parliament authorized an increase in the army to 55,000 soldiers and the navy to 270 ships manned by 28,000 sailors. Furthermore they approved funding to hire an additional 30,000 Hessian mercenaries (37).

On the other side of the Atlantic, the Americans had no regular army and could only field state militias with varying levels of training and discipline. They had a single warship with a minimal crew. Their resources to arm and equip an army and navy were nonexistent. For every dollar the United States either possessed or could collect, the British had a thousand.

These seemingly overwhelming population and resource advantages were balanced by several other factors. While the British had an abundance of senior officers who were veterans of the French and Indian War and Seven Years' War, that conflict had ended a dozen years before. By the time the shooting started again, many of the best officers had left the service and few of the enlisted men in the ranks, who would experience the brunt of the fighting, had ever heard a shot fired in anger. Furthermore, the royal and Parliamentary leadership of the past decades had passed to much less qualified leaders, including King George III (20). On the American side stood leaders like George Washington (1) and Nathanael Greene (4) who understood the simple strategy that all they had to do was remain in the field in order for the United States to continue to exist. The British had to achieve complete victory; the Americans only had to survive. In this, the American field commanders had the support of able diplomats like John Adams (51) and Benjamin Franklin (25).

Great Britain faced the difficulty that their empire was not fully committed to a war to crush the Rebellion. Many British citizens had no desire to see their "American cousins" killed or wounded. Some thought that the revolt could be resolved diplomatically; others lobbied that the money for war expenses could better be spent at home.

The British had to face former enemies who sought opportunities to gain revenge. Long-oppressed Ireland was a tinderbox ready to explode, requiring the British to maintain garrisons throughout the Green Isle. European countries—especially France, Spain, and the Netherlands—were strengthening their own military forces. Under the theory of "the enemy of my enemy is my friend," France secretly provided the Americans arms and supplies before officially allying with them in May 1778.

Compounding all these problems for the British was the time factor—the time required to deliver troops and supplies to North America, to receive news from the war front, and to get new orders back across the Atlantic. A ship sailing from London took two full months to cross the Atlantic. The return trip, with the prevailing westerly winds, reduced the crossing to one month. A message from England to North America might very well require four months for a response because once a message reached land it still might take weeks to reach a commander in the field. The fastest land transit for a message was via mounted messenger who could cover at best 50–60 miles per day—and that required frequent changes of horses. British supply and communications ships were also plagued by both weather and American privateers (61) early in the Rebellion and French warships in its later years. Some messages were delayed; others never delivered.

Americans had their own challenges. It took the Continental Army (7) several years to evolve into a decent force in the midst of ongoing operations and fighting.

They had the advantages of experience and motivation. Many of the Americans were veterans of skirmishes against the Native Americans, but, more importantly, they knew that if the Rebellion failed, they would be treated as traitors. That is not to say that the Americans were united and focused. Officers maneuvered for rank and fame, and petty differences often distracted them from the mission of the war. On several occasions the enlisted men threatened mutiny if they were not properly fed and paid. In every crisis, Washington's personal leadership took the forefront in maintaining a degree of stability.

Washington and the Continental Congress (10) also faced the problems of thirteen states that were far from being in agreement. Regional differences reigned. New Englanders and Southerners did not like or trust each other. Many manufacturers and suppliers saw the Continental Army as a source of income rather than the protector of their liberties. Inferior products at inflated prices often left the American soldier hungry and in rags.

Despite all the odds, the Americans believed they were fighting for a noble cause. The numbers who stepped forward to secure the liberty and independence of others were fairly small, and they paid dearly. About 25,000 Americans died in battle or from disease during the Revolution—about 1 percent of the total population of

the newly declared nation. Today, the United States as the single world superpower continues to rely on a few to protect the masses. If 1 percent of today's American population died in battle, it would total more than 3,000,000 dead.

Had the British put down the Rebellion, their success would be credited to their advantages in population and resources. Had the Americans failed in their bid for freedom, their disadvantages in population and resources would have been blamed. However, the will of the Americans turned their few positives in leadership and home field into victory. The population and resources very much influenced how the war was fought. The final American victory negated the British advantages, placing population and resources in the middle rather than near the top of these rankings.

55

GEORGE ROGERS CLARK

American General

1752–1818

George Rogers Clark, with fewer than 200 soldiers, subdued the Indians in the Illinois Territory and defeated the British in the area. Clark's victories in Illinois gave the Americans claim to the Northwest Territory at the end of the Revolutionary War, earning the newly independent United States the vast region that eventually became all or parts of five states. Never defeated in battle, Clark secured the distinction of the most influential leader on the frontier during the Revolution and the lasting title of "Father of the Northwest."

Born on November 19, 1752, on his family's modest farm near Charlottesville, Virginia, Clark had little formal education as a boy. He did have access to books and was well read. His later journals reflect a writing ability above average for the times. As a teenager Clark learned surveying from his grandfather and at age twenty journeyed west into unclaimed territory that was to become Kentucky. Over the next four years, Clark surveyed and claimed land for himself as well as friends and neighbors back in Virginia. He then returned home and guided his fellow Virginians into Kentucky.

In 1774 Clark joined the military in battles against the Native Americans in western Pennsylvania and eastern Ohio during Lord Dunmore's War. The end of the conflict established a temporary peace in the area, but the most important aspect of the conflict was that it provided combat experience for Clark and many of the participants in the pending Revolution.

Indian resistance to the white settlers in Kentucky resumed two years later at the outbreak of the Revolutionary War. Clark approached Patrick Henry, governor of Virginia, requesting that Kentucky be recognized and protected as a separate Virginian county. Otherwise, Clark said he would seek status for Kentucky as a state. After some debate, the Virginia Assembly welcomed Kentucky as its most western county, appointed Clark a major to command the militia, and authorized 500 pounds of gunpowder to defend the territory.

Back in Kentucky, Clark found his settlements under severe pressure from the Indians who were now supported and supplied by their British allies headquartered in Detroit and commanded by Governor Henry Hamilton. Over the next months, Clark recruited militiamen, but he could only muster 150 soldiers because Kentucky was sparsely populated and not all of the settlers supported the Revolution. Despite his small force, Clark gathered his company at Fort Pitt, Pennsylvania, and on June 26, 1778, headed westward by boat on the Ohio River.

On July 4, Clark's small force surprised the British and Indian occupants of a fort and major supply point at Kaskaskia in western Illinois and forced them to surrender without anyone firing a shot. Clark promised the many French residents of the area privileges of "American citizenship" for their support. Faced with the American militiamen's muskets and the news that France was now an ally of the Revolution, the Frenchmen readily joined Clark and brought with them the support of other nearby French communities, including Vincennes in western Indiana. Clark also negotiated a peace treaty with surrounding Indian tribes and secured their neutrality in his subsequent fights with the British. He then personally took charge of the defense of Kaskaskia while leaving a subordinate in command of Vincennes.

When Governor Hamilton in his Detroit headquarters learned of Clark's capture of Kaskaskia and Vincennes, he assembled an army of about 500 British soldiers and Indians and set off south down the Maumee and Wabash Rivers. On December 17, Hamilton easily recaptured Vincennes but decided to send his Indian allies home and postpone an attack against Kaskaskia until spring.

Aware that he could not defend Kaskaskia against a reinforced Hamilton in the spring, Clark decided on an immediate attack despite the harsh winter conditions. To Governor Patrick Henry he wrote that if he failed "this country and also Kentucky is lost."

On February 6, 1779, Clark departed Kaskaskia at the head of 172 men, about half Frenchmen who had joined his militiamen. Despite freezing cold and a countryside so flooded that his drummer boy often floated atop his drum, Clark pushed on for seventeen days—two weeks longer than the journey would have taken under normal conditions. When the Americans neared Vincennes on February 23, Clark ordered his company flag bearers to march back and forth behind a small hill to make the British think his force was far larger. He then ordered his best riflemen to open fire at the British cannon gun ports in the defensive walls.

The gunfire inflicted few casualties, but Hamilton's mixed force of regulars, French conscripts, and Indian allies were reluctant to stand and fight. On February 24, Hamilton surrendered to Clark, who then dispatched his captives under heavy guard to Virginia. Clark immediately planned for a spring offensive of his own to capture Detroit, but the campaign never took place because of a lack of supplies and reinforcement from Virginia.

Clark was rewarded with promotion to brigadier general, but the eastern section of the country had little interest in the Western Theater. For the remainder of the Revolution, Clark and his militiamen conducted limited campaigns from their headquarters at Fort Nelson, near present Louisville, Kentucky, to neutralize Indian uprisings.

Although Clark had occupied only a small part of the Trans-Allegheny region that reached north from the Ohio River to Canada and from Pennsylvania to the Mississippi River, his claim was sufficient to force the British to cede the entire area to the United States in the Treaty of Paris (69) that finally ended the war in 1783. Clark,

with fewer than 200 men and at almost no cost to the Continental Congress (10), had increased the United States land mass by more than a quarter.

After the war Clark received a grant of 8,049 acres in southern Indiana and served on a board to survey and allot land to other veterans. Clark, however, was never again financially solvent. He had borrowed funds to fit and supply his army during the war that he was not able to pay back. Much of his land was sold to reimburse his debtors and eventually he was left with only a small gristmill on a few acres near Clarksville, Indiana. He never married. William, his younger brother by eighteen years, became the famed co-leader of the Lewis and Clark Expedition early in the nineteenth century.

In 1809, Clark suffered a stroke and, no longer able to work, moved in with the household of his brother-in-law William Croghan at Locust Grove near Louisville. Clark died there of another stroke on February 13, 1818, and was buried in a family plot. His remains were moved to Louisville's Cave Hill Cemetery in 1869.

During and immediately after the Revolutionary War, Clark received little recognition. The Western Theater was just too far from the Atlantic Coast, and those in the East did not yet realize the future importance of the Northwest Territory. Critics, including James Wilkinson (100), attacked Clark for his actions against several out-posts along the Mississippi during his campaigns held by fellow belligerent Spain.

Subsequent decades and centuries have been much kinder to Clark, now considered the "Father of the Northwest." With limited assets, he stabilized the western frontier and secured a vast region for the United States. If this list ranked the influence on the future of the United States rather than just on the Revolutionary War, Clark would merit a spot near the top. Since it does not, Clark ranks in the middle.

56

AFRICAN AMERICANS

1775–1783

From the shots that felled Crispus Attucks at the Boston Massacre (93) in 1770 to the formal end of the war in 1783, black Americans played a significant role in the fight for the independence of the United States—both on land and at sea, for the Americans and for the Crown. African Americans served with the Revolutionaries and with countries allied with the rebels as well as in the ranks and in support of the British. War-time service did advance the status of African Americans in the United States somewhat, but their contributions did not end slavery, leaving most blacks still in bondage and unable to enjoy the rights of "life, liberty, and the pursuit of happiness" as promised in the *Declaration of Independence* (14).

Black Africans have played important roles in the Western Hemisphere since the first visits by Europeans. At least one man of African heritage sailed with Christopher Columbus on his 1492 voyage. Another accompanied Columbus on his last voyage in 1502. Blacks also joined the military expeditions during the early sixteenth century when Vasco de Balboa crossed Central America to the Pacific Ocean, served with Hernando Cortes when he conquered the Aztecs in Mexico, and assisted Francisco Pizarro in his conquest of the Incas in Peru.

The first blacks in North America arrived as slaves of the Spanish who attempted to establish a colony on the coast of today's South Carolina in 1526. After only a few months, the effort failed, and the survivors returned to the Caribbean. Two years later a black slave accompanied Cabeza de Vaca's exploration into the American Southwest.

English colonists did not bring slaves when they initially established colonies during the early seventeenth century in Massachusetts and Virginia. The first black slaves joined the Virginia colony on August 20, 1619, when a Dutch ship anchored off Jamestown and sold the colonists twenty men and women recently captured in Africa.

Over the next decades the demand for slaves in America increased with the need to clear land and to farm tobacco and other crops. Faced with the threat of attacks from Native American tribes, the colonial governments initially provided military training for slaves and included them in their militias. As the number of blacks reached critical mass, however, the white colonists ended this practice for fear of slave rebellions. In 1639 the General Assembly of Virginia established militia laws that stated, "All persons except Negroes to be provided with arms and ammunition or be fined at the pleasure of the Governor and Council." By the end of the century, all the colonies had excluded blacks from serving in the military.

These laws were frequently set aside in times of major Indian problems when blacks were allowed to serve, mostly as laborers and support personnel but occasionally as infantrymen. In the French and Indian War, the British and their American colonists actively recruited blacks to fill the ranks. Their wages went to their owners and, while a few were freed for their service, most returned to bondage after the war.

By 1775 the population of the English colonies in America totaled about 2,500,000—500,000 of whom were Africans or of African decent. A few freemen of color lived in the North, but in the Southern colonies, where field crops benefited the most from indentured labor, slaves constituted almost 40 percent of the population. White Americans paid little attention to the issue of slavery other than its favorable impact on the economic development of the colonies. Not until they themselves felt oppressed by increased British control and taxation did some Americans question their own position as oppressors and the morality of owning fellow human beings. Crispus Attucks sacrificed his life standing up against the British in Boston and earned some recognition for blacks. The initial drafts of the *Declaration of Independence* in 1775 contained language damning slavery and extending liberty to all. Objections from Southern delegates, however, forced the deletion of the paragraphs.

Although they faced exclusion from the objectives of the Revolution, blacks participated in the war from its very beginnings. Several black militiamen were in the ranks at Lexington and Concord (43) in April 1775 and one of the first Americans to die was Prince Esterbrook, a black soldier. A month later Massachusetts officials determined that freemen could continue to serve but slaves would be excluded because their service "would be inconsistent with the principles that are to be supported, and reflect dishonor on this colony." Despite the edict, at least two black soldiers fought at the Battle of Bunker Hill (23) the following June with one, Salem Poor, being officially commended for his brave performance.

Shortly after George Washington (1)—a Southerner and slave owner—assumed command of the Continental Army (7), he issued an order on July 9, 1775, instructing his recruiters not to enlist "any stroller, Negro, or vagabond." Washington again published orders the following November specifically excluding slaves from his army, but he allowed those already in uniform to remain. Washington's officers supported the decision, as did slave owners who did not want to risk valuable property in combat.

Unlike the Americans, the British welcomed blacks into their ranks. They were happy to recruit African Americans to augment their personnel shortages created by worldwide commitments and by the long supply lines that hindered the timely arrival of replacements. The British also sensed how divisive slavery was among white Americans and wished to exploit the situation.

On November 7, John Murray, the Earl of Dunmore and the royal governor of Virginia, issued a proclamation, "I do hereby…declare all indentured servants, Negroes, or others free, that are able and willing to bear arms, they joining His Majesty's troops, as soon as may be, for the more speedily reducing the Colony to proper dignity." Within a month, 300 escaped slaves joined Lord Dunmore's Ethiopian Regiment, donning uniforms inscribed with the slogan "Liberty to Slaves." Over the next few months, more than 30,000 slaves crossed the lines to serve with Dunmore or in other British and Hessian (37) units.

Pressured by the loss of slaves to Dunmore and the increasing shortage of available white recruits, Washington issued orders in December 1775, and again in February 1776, allowing free blacks to enlist, but he still barred slaves from the army. Some commanders paid little attention to the status of blacks and enlisted them or just ignored the order altogether, so desperate were they to fill their ranks.

In September 1776 the Continental Congress (10) issued instructions for the states to provide an additional eighty-seven battalions. Congress understood the difficulties the states would have in filling these quotas, and when they asked for an additional sixteen battalions three months later, their request stated that requirements could be filled "by drafts, from their militias, or in any other way."

The states, except those in the Deep South, took this as permission to recruit slaves—with added guarantees to owners that they would be compensated for all blacks freed or killed. By mid-1776, African Americans served in nearly every battalion in the Continental Army as either infantrymen in regiments recruited in the North or as servants and support personnel in the Southern regiments. Reports by British officers noted that most of the units they faced had several black faces in their ranks.

Washington, now more concerned with the possibility of losing the war than with his objections to slaves, also accepted their service, usually with a promise of postwar freedom. According to some reports, at least one black soldier accompanied

him in his personal boat when he crossed the Delaware River to attack Trenton (8) in December 1776. Blacks continued to serve in the Continental Army, integrated in white regiments, throughout the remaining battles in the North and the campaigns in the South. In 1779, Washington agreed to a request from Rhode Island to form two all-black infantry battalions. The resolution approving the battalions by the Rhode Island Assembly stated, "History affords us frequent precedents of the wisest, freest, and bravest nations having liberated their slaves and enlisting them as soldiers in defense of their country."

Allies of the United States also employed black soldiers. More than 600 black freemen and slaves recruited in the West Indies accompanied the French army that helped the Americans in their attempt to recapture occupied Savannah, Georgia (80), in 1779. Black soldiers made up at least 10 percent of the Spanish army led by Bernardo de Galvez (40) out of Louisiana to push the British from the Gulf Coast.

Along with their fellow soldiers who served on land, many African slaves and free-men also fought at sea as members of the navy or as privateers (61). Black sailors saw action in every major naval battle of the Revolutionary War, including on the crew of John Paul Jones (58) aboard the *Bonhomme Richard* that defeated the British *Serapis* in 1779. At least thirteen African Americans served as Continental or state marines.

Records of the American Revolutionary War do not provide exact information on the number of its black participants. Enlistment records, when kept, did not necessarily note the race of a soldier or sailor. However, estimates consistently place the number of black military veterans at about 5,000 of the total of 300,000 Americans who served in the conflict.

Another 1,000 served in Lord Dunmore's Ethiopian Regiment and in other British units. At least two-thirds of the 30,000 escaped slaves who joined the British contributed in various support roles. Despite American protests, the British evacuated the blacks who had supported them at the end of the war. Some 3,000 were resettled as freemen in Nova Scotia, and 1,200 sailed back to Africa to establish the free British colony of Sierra Leone. The majority, however, were returned to slavery and shipped to the West Indies. Generally, black slaves who fought on the American side in the war did receive their freedom as the states had promised. Many blacks even shared in the land grants made available to veterans. Through birth and the arrival of additional slaves from Africa, however, there were actually more slaves in the United States after the war than before.

African Americans proved their willingness and ability to fight throughout the Revolutionary War. While most white Americans quickly forgot the contribution of the blacks, some puzzled over a country based on freedoms that would continue to practice slavery. It would be an issue that would continue to divide America until finally settled with the Civil War nearly a century later.

Their contributions alone merit the inclusion of African Americans on this list. If the war had resulted in their freedom, they would rank near the top. Unfortunately, it did not, dropping African American to the middle of these rankings.

57

MOORES CREEK BRIDGE, NORTH CAROLINA

February 27, 1776

The Battle of Moores Creek Bridge pitted North Carolina colonists against each other. There the rebels fought the Scottish Loyalists (34) until most of the Loyalists were dead or captured. North Carolina would never again be ruled by the British. The battle rallied support for the Revolution throughout the Carolinas, increased enlistments in the militias, and motivated North Carolina to be the first of the thirteen colonies to instruct its delegates to the Continental Congress (10) to cast their votes for independence.

When news of Lexington and Concord (43), the Boston Siege (50), and the Canada Invasion (84) reached them, North Carolinians knew the Revolution would soon affect their territory. Like residents of the other twelve colonies, North Carolinians were fragmented about the Rebellion. About a third favored breaking from Great Britain while an equal number, mostly Scottish immigrants and wealthy Tidewater landowners, stood with the crown. Still another third, generally Quakers and German immigrants, simply wanted to be left alone.

In early 1776, the British decided to go on the offensive by taking the war into the Southern colonies. General William Howe (15) ordered General Henry Clinton (17) to sail south to meet at Cape Fear with reinforcements arriving from England. He was then to march inland to link up with Loyalists led by General Donald McDonald. The plan was to first pacify North Carolina and then turn south to capture the important port of Charleston, South Carolina.

McDonald assembled a force of 1,800 Loyalists in the Cross Creek area of central North Carolina and marched eastward on February 20, 1776. Most of the Loyalists carried muskets and bayonets, but a hundred or so relied on their lethal broadswords as their primary weapon. Both the Loyalists and the rebels dispatched messages to each other encouraging the other side to join its cause. Neither the rebels nor the Loyalists were swayed. When the Loyalists neared Moores Creek Bridge, about 10 miles north of Wilmington, they found the route blocked by 1,100 rebels under the official command of Colonel James Moore.

Because Moore was away from the bridge coordinating other militia movements, Colonel John Alexander Lillington took charge of the blocking force. Lillington initially prepared defenses on the far side of the bridge but then withdrew his troops to near-side positions with his two cannons aimed directly against the crossing. He also had the cross-planks of the bridge removed and applied grease to the remaining stringers.

Loyalist General McDonald fell ill during the march, so by the time his army reached Moores Creek, Lieutenant Colonel Donald McLeod had assumed command. McLeod, who did not anticipate much resistance, saw the abandoned defenses on his side of the creek and assumed the rebels had withdrawn. Exhausted from the long march, McLeod camped for the night to rest his men.

At dawn on February 27, with bagpipes wailing, the Loyalists advanced on the bridge with the leading company armed only with swords known as claymores. When they neared the partially destroyed bridge, they charged forward, shouting, "King George and broadswords!" Several slipped from the greased support beams into the creek to drown in the cold water, but the majority of their casualties resulted from the rebel cannon and musket fire at a range of only 30 yards. In a devastating matter of minutes, the rebels killed McLeod, several of his officers, and thirty of the Scots.

Lillington then ordered his engineers to replace the removed bridge planks and counterattacked across the creek. At the same time a rebel detachment forded the creek to flank the Loyalists and cut off their avenue of retreat. Over the next two days, the rebels rounded up more than 850 prisoners, including General McDonald, and confiscated weapons, wagons, and British sterling. Total rebel casualties amounted to one wounded and one dead.

Captured Loyalist officers were initially held in Halifax, North Carolina, before being transferred to confinement in Philadelphia. The North Carolinians were remarkably lenient with the captured Scots. Their Provincial Congress resolving that they were to be considered "erring brothers" rather than enemies, the North Carolinians took measures to care for their families and to protect their property. In contrast, the British General Howe declared North Carolina "in a state of rebellion" and ordered the disbandment of all forms of the colonial government. To entice the rebels back into the fold, he offered pardons to the rebel leaders, but at the same time he initiated actions to loot and burn rebel-owned properties.

Before the Battle of Moores Creek Bridge, many in North Carolina were unsure where they stood in regard to the Rebellion. After the rout some remained neutral but the majority cast their lot with the rebels. There was no doubt that North Carolina had joined the Rebellion. The rebel success in the battle not only brought the colony into the fight, but also it insured that it would no longer be ruled by the

British. When its delegates reached the 1776 meeting of the Continental Congress, they were the first of those from the thirteen colonies instructed to vote in favor of independence. Even though a few more fights would take place in the Tar Heel State, it remained mostly in the control of the rebels for the remainder of the war.

Moores Creek Bridge was important because it forced the British to abandon their plans to occupy North Carolina. They instead focused on an offensive against Charleston, South Carolina. In June the British and their Loyalist allies would be defeated at Charleston, returning the major battles of the war to the Northern theater for the next four years.

The battle of Moores Creek Bridge further united the Northern and Southern colonies against British rule. Although the Americans had not yet declared their

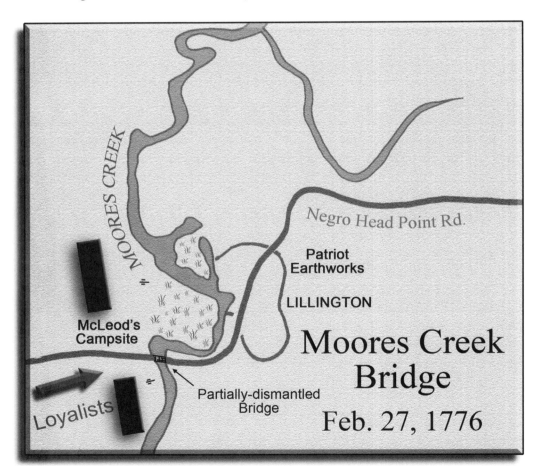

independence, the battle "burned the bridges" between the Mother Land and the colonies. Any hope for appeasement and reunification were fleeting and the declaration of July 4, 1776 (14), was nearing. For its role in this unification and advancement toward declaration of independence, Moores Creek Bridge gains a position in the middle of these rankings.

58

JOHN PAUL JONES

American Naval Captain

1747–1792

As the most successful American naval commander in the Revolutionary War, John Paul Jones displayed his seamanship and bravery in battles on the high seas as well as during raids on British land bases. While many questioned his character, Jones emerged from the war as America's most famous naval officer and its most influential, for he established the duties and traditions of future U.S. Navy officers.

Born on July 6, 1747, in Kirkcudbright, Scotland, to a gardener named John Paul, the boy who would become an American naval hero was his father's namesake. The young John Paul received little formal education before shipping out aboard a merchant vessel as an apprentice at age thirteen. For several years he participated in voyages between England, the West Indies, and the American colonies where his brother was a tailor. After two years and with the completion of his apprenticeship, John Paul briefly joined his brother in Virginia. He then sailed aboard a slave ship that operated between the African coast and Jamaica.

By 1769, John Paul had gained the captaincy of the merchant ship *John,* where he flogged a crewmember who later died from the ordeal. After being arrested for murder back in Scotland, John Paul was exonerated, and he returned to sea only to again face charges for killing an alleged mutineer in 1773 on the Caribbean island of Tobago. This time, instead of facing the charges, John Paul fled to Virginia where he changed his name to John Paul Jones to avoid further legal troubles.

At the outbreak of the Revolution, Jones offered his services to the Continental Congress (10). His friendship with several Virginia delegates resulted in his commission as a lieutenant in the newly formed U.S. Navy. On December 3, 1775, Jones, the man Thomas Jefferson (87) would later describe as "the principal hope of America's future efforts on the ocean," joined the crew of the thirty-gun *Alfred.* The following February, Jones used his knowledge of the Bahamas to assist in the capture of a large quantity of war materials in a beach raid at Nassau. On May 10, Jones assumed command of the twelve-gun sloop *Providence,* and the Continental Congress rewarded him with a promotion to captain on August 8, 1776. Sailing from

Delaware Capes on August 21, Jones and the *Providence* captured eight vessels and destroyed eight more during the next six weeks. In addition to cutting off British supplies meant for their army in North America, Jones and his crew profited by selling the prizes and their cargos.

In November, Jones returned to the *Alfred* and conducted successful operations off Nova Scotia. During this cruise Jones captured a British supply ship bringing winter clothing to the Redcoats in North America. Back in Boston, Jones found that, despite his success, there were those in Congress who thought his heritage and character too questionable to warrant further promotion.

Jones languished in Boston without a command until November 1777 when he took the helm of the *Ranger* to sail to France with news of the American victory at Saratoga (3). When Jones sailed into Quiberon Bay on February 14, 1778, flying the Stars and Stripes of the independent United States, the local French commander fired a cannon salute, the first rendered by a foreign power to the American colors.

From the end of February through May, Jones sailed the *Ranger* around the British Isles. His two raids against shore villages brought the American Revolution directly to the British homeland and created much controversy on why the vaunted British navy could not protect its own shores. On April 24, Jones attacked the HMS *Drake,* forcing the first surrender of an enemy warship to a U.S. Navy captain.

Jones returned to France where he spent a year awaiting for another command. Finally in August 1779 the King of France loaned him a former merchant vessel refitted with forty-two guns that Jones renamed the *Bonhomme Richard* in honor of Benjamin Franklin's (25) *Poor Richard's Almanac.* For a month Jones, accompanied by several French vessels, attacked British merchant warships off the English coast.

On September 23, 1779, the *Bonhomme Richard* encountered the HMS *Serapis* and other British vessels escorting merchant vessels off Flamborough Head, Yorkshire. Although outgunned by the faster, more maneuverable enemy ships, Jones ordered an attack against the *Serapis.* After several broadside shots, Jones maneuvered to grappling hook-range and tied the two ships together as both continued pointblank cannon fire.

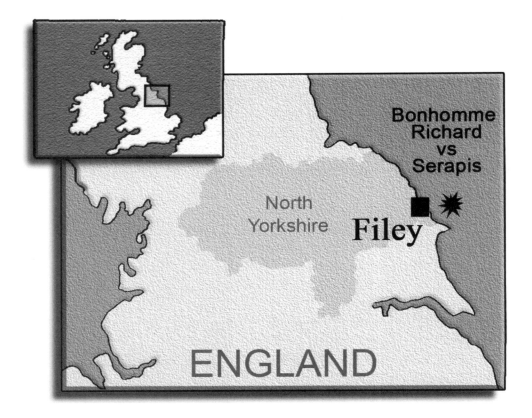

Over the next three and a half hours the two ships fought the most furious and bloody naval engagement of the war. Early in the fight with the *Bonhomme Richard* already in danger of sinking, the British captain asked the Americans if they had struck their colors in surrender. Jones replied with what became some of the war's and the navy's most famous words when he responded, "I have not yet begun to fight."

Jones then did indeed continue to fight and finally forced the surrender of the *Serapis*. With his own ship sinking, he transferred his colors and crew to the British vessel and sailed away.

In December, Jones took command of the *Alliance* and continued operations against the British. Upon his return to France in April 1780, the French honored him with a ceremonial sword and other accolades. A year later Jones returned to the United States where Congress voted him a thanks and the promise of the command of the seventy-four-gun *America* under construction in Portsmouth, New Hampshire. Delays in construction, however, prevented its launch before the war ended.

In the process of commanding ships and men, Jones established protocols that would become standard naval procedures after the war. In later years he elaborated on the procedures and responsibilities of a naval officer.

In 1783 Jones sailed back to France to act as a negotiator for prizes captured and held in French ports before sailing to Denmark in 1788 for additional prize negotiating. Between these assignments, Jones returned to the United States in 1787 where Congress presented him a gold medal—the only such honor to a naval officer for service in the Revolutionary War. In late 1788 Jones accepted a commission as an admiral in the Russian navy and fought well in their war against Turkey. Back in Paris, he died on July 18, 1792, and was buried in an unmarked grave. More than a century later, the U.S. Ambassador to France recovered remains he claimed were Jones's and had them escorted by a flotilla of U.S. Navy ships to North America. The remains were temporarily placed in the U.S. Naval Academy's Bancroft Hall in Annapolis, Maryland. His casket was finally placed in an honored crypt in the Academy's Chapel on January 26, 1913.

No one can question Jones's performance at sea or his personal bravery. However, his early actions that led to the deaths of two crew members and his name change when he settled in Virginia cast aspersions on his character. His reputation further suffered from his coarseness and propensity to encourage the attention of women admirers. Still, Jones easily ranks as the most influential American naval commander of the Revolutionary War. His defiant response, "I have not yet begun to fight," has become one of America's most famous quotations, and his writing on the responsibilities of naval officers remains today a part of the curriculum for American naval cadets. Jones's accomplishments were heroic but not overly significant to the outcome of the war because the navy was so small and ineffectual. His fame alone merits his inclusion on the list. His actual influence puts him into the middle third of these rankings.

59

MONMOUTH, NEW JERSEY

June 28, 1778

The day-long fight on June 28, 1778, at Monmouth, New Jersey, earned the distinction of being the longest battle of the Revolutionary War and the final major engagement in the Northern theater. Although it ended in a draw, the Americans under General George Washington (1) proved they could hold their own against the British in open battle. The fight also brought an end to the military career of American General Charles Lee (79) and popularized the legend of a female camp follower called Molly Pitcher.

With the defeat of the British at Saratoga (3) in October 1777 and the French recognition of the United States the following February, the British Commander General Henry Clinton (17) elected to evacuate Philadelphia and return to New York City to protect that important port. Washington, who had failed in his defense of the American capital of Philadelphia the previous fall, had been forced into winter quarters at Valley Forge (39). Despite the harsh weather, Washington used the time to train and prepare for further operations. When word reached him that Clinton was marching toward New York, Washington ordered his army to take the offensive.

The British and American armies each fielded about 13,000 men, but neither was able to concentrate its entire force. The British were spread over miles along their line of march while the Americans were strung over their own extended lines of pursuit. Initial efforts by the rebels concentrated on small units getting ahead of the British and destroying bridges and felling trees across roadways to delay the Redcoats. These tactics, combined with the unusually hot weather that had temperatures in the high 90s, successfully slowed the British column to less than 10 miles a day.

Meanwhile, Washington prepared to attack the British rear. Many of his subordinates, including his most experienced officer, Charles Lee, argued against the plan, citing the Continental Army's (7) vulnerability if they lost a major engagement. Washington, however, stood fast and ordered an assault with about half his army. Though initially opposed, Lee asked to command the main assault force when he learned its size. Despite Lee's ambition, he did not prepare for the attack, making no attempt to gather information on the British units, no effort to reconnoiter the surrounding terrain, and no study of available maps.

Advancing blindly, Lee caught up with the British rear early on the morning of June 28 near Monmouth Court House. Lee deployed his men with little knowledge about what they were facing. Although he quickly formulated a plan on the battlefield to envelope the British, he was unable to inform his subordinates of his thoughts. Clinton, fearing for his supply train, turned his army around and showered the Americans with artillery. Lee made little effort to resist, ordering a general withdrawal that quickly turned into an unorganized retreat.

Washington, hearing the artillery, rode forward and confronted Lee. After an angry exchange—including reports of profuse profanity by the usually mild-speaking Washington—the American commander sent Lee to the rear. Washington quickly reformed the retreating army into defensive positions and repeatedly beat back British assaults. At several points during the British attacks, the American lines wavered and nearly broke, but Washington, often exposing himself to the British guns, came forward to rally and reform the rebel defenses.

Over the long day, heatstroke downed about as many soldiers on each side as did ball and bullet. The British, as the active attackers, suffered even more than the rebels did from the heat, and by late afternoon Clinton called off the assaults. Washington

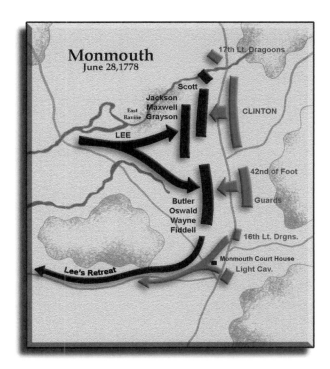

wanted to mount a pursuit of the British but found his soldiers too exhausted to continue the fight.

Clinton departed the battlefield for New York, satisfied that he had preserved most of his supply train and saved the bulk of his army. Although the day had begun poorly for the Americans, Washington had shown that his army could stand against the best of the British regiments. American casualties numbered about 460, but the British had suffered more than twice that number as well as losing part of their supply train.

Besides the direct influence of the battle, Monmouth provided one of the most enduring legends of the Revolutionary War. Throughout the conflict, various female camp followers contributed to the cause by bringing buckets or pitchers of water to the men on the frontlines. In the heat of the Monmouth battlefield, such water would have been most welcome. According to legend, the wife of John Hayes (or Hays) not only delivered pitchers of water but also took her husband's place as a cannon crewmember when he was wounded. In the battle's aftermath Mary (or Margaret) Hayes evolved into Molly Pitcher, the name that is an icon for all the brave women who supported their men and the Revolution.

Small skirmishes continued in Pennsylvania and New York while General Lee stood court-martial for his incompetence. A year later General Anthony Wayne (38) made a successful raid on the British fort at Stony Point (88) on the Hudson River, but for all practical purposes, the war in the North ended at Monmouth. Clinton concentrated his army in New York City while Washington took up positions nearby at White Plains. By July 20, both were in the same positions they had occupied two years earlier. The war was far from over, but now it moved to the South, where more battles over the next three years led to Yorktown (2) and independence.

Monmouth is actually more famous—as the war's longest continuous fight and as the last one in the North—than it was influential. While the battle did display the fighting abilities of the Continental Army and the leadership of Washington, most of Clinton's force succeeded in reaching New York. Even if Washington had not attacked, the British were already headed for New York City to defend against a possible offensive by the French fleet. The British leadership had already determined that the future of the conflict lay in the South where they expected more support from Loyalists (34). For these reasons the Battle of Monmouth ranks in the middle of this list rather than near the top with the more influential battles like Saratoga and future battles that led to Yorktown and final victory.

60

FRANCIS MARION

American General

1732–1795

Francis Marion was America's most famous partisan leader. For a period of months in 1780, he led the only rebel resistance to the British in South Carolina. *The Swamp Fox,* as Marion became known, subsequently fought as a militia leader with the Continental Army (7), displaying the same superior military skills that made him a successful guerilla leader. Poems, books, television shows, and movies have catapulted the Swamp Fox to a level of fame among the Revolutionary heroes exceeded only by that of George Washington (1).

Born in "midwinter" of 1732 on his family's farm in Berkley County, South Carolina, Marion was a small, sickly child. After a basic education, he went to sea at age fifteen—only to become shipwrecked. Surviving six days without food or water, and losing two of his shipmates before he could reach shore, Marion decided the life of a sailor was not for him. He returned to his family plantation near Georgetown, South Carolina, and settled into the life of a farmer. In early 1757, Marion joined the local militia as a private and participated in two campaigns against the Cherokees in the French and Indian War. During the campaigns against the Native Americans, Marion advanced in rank to lieutenant.

Back home after the war, Marion agreed with those who advocated more rights from Great Britain. In 1773 he purchased his own plantation on the Santee River 4 miles south of Eutaw Springs. In 1775 he served in the South Carolina Provisional Legislature and at the outbreak of the Revolution accepted a captain's commission in the militia on June 17. His unit assisted in the ouster of the royal governor and his Loyalist (34) supporters before joining the forces fortifying the harbor at Charleston.

Over the next three years, Marion advanced in rank to lieutenant colonel while participating in the battles at Fort Sullivan on Charleston Harbor in June 1776 and then in the attack against Savannah, Georgia, in the late 1779. In early 1780, Marion, now a regimental commander, returned to Charleston (47) to assist in the defense of the city against the latest British offensive. He narrowly escaped capture when the city fell the following May.

During command of his militia regiment, Marion earned the reputation as a strict disciplinarian who enforced high standards. With the rebel army's surrender at Charleston, Marion recognized that he could no longer engage the British with regular tactics and quickly adapted unconventional warfare activities. With a small group that varied from twenty to a hundred men, Marion harassed British lines of communications and supply. His men, all volunteers, served without pay and supplied their own horses and arms. They secured food and other supplies from local farmers and captured ammunitions and other necessities from the British and Loyalists.

When General Horatio Gates (31) arrived from the North on orders from the Continental Congress (10) to recapture Charleston, Marion offered his services. Gates, who had little use for partisan units, dispatched Marion on a scouting mission all but unrelated to his actual battle plans. As a result, Marion and his guerrillas were not present at the disastrous Battle of Camden (65) on August 16, 1780. While Gates did not have confidence in the partisan leader, the governor of South Carolina recognized Marion's performance and promoted him to brigadier general in the state militia.

With Gates and what remained of his army in full retreat into North Carolina, Marion and his small band, along with a similar unit led by Thomas Sumter (83), became the only rebel military presence in South Carolina. Over the next few months no British courier, supply train, or small garrison was safe from Marion's raiders. Striking quickly, usually under the cover of darkness, the partisans attacked and then melted back into their swamp strongholds and hidden camps.

British commander Charles Cornwallis (22) became so concerned with the partisan activities that he dispatched his ablest cavalry commander, Lieutenant Colonel Banastre Tarleton (44), to hunt down the guerrilla leader. Not only did Tarleton fail in his assigned task but also further alienated civilian South Carolinians by confiscating their crops and animals to keep them out of the partisans' hands. Marion also took supplies from the locals but always paid with vouchers that were honored after the war concluded.

Tarleton became so frustrated with his inability to capture Marion that he inadvertently provided the name that would make the partisan leader famous. After an unsuccessful pursuit for seven hours through 26 miles of swamp, Tarleton remarked, "As for this damned old fox, the devil himself could not catch him." From that time on Marion became "the Swamp Fox" about whom legend often exceeded fact.

When Nathanael Greene (4) arrived in South Carolina on orders from George Washington to resume conventional operations against the British, Marion rejoined the Continental Army in command of militia. He again served with distinction at the battles for Georgetown and Eutaw Springs (63).

At the end of the war, Marion resumed his position in the South Carolina State Senate. In 1784 his state honored him with the command of Fort Johnson on Charleston Harbor. Marion died at his Berkley County plantation on February 27, 1795, and is buried there.

Known as ruthless, moody, introverted, and only barely literate to his detracters and gentle, kind, and humane to his supporters, Marion actually possessed and dem-onstrated all those characteristics. Most importantly he was a capable field commander of both militia and partisan units. For a period of several months after the surrender of Charleston and the Battle of Camden, he was the most influential American military leader in South Carolina.

Marion's time as a partisan offered a morale boost to his fellow rebel South Carolinians. The "Marion Legend" began shortly after the war with the publica-tion of small books and a poem based on his escapades. As the years passed, Marion continued to capture the public's interest—much more so than Gates, Greene, or other accomplished military leaders. In the mid-1950s, a Walt Disney television series, *The Swamp Fox*, immor-talized Marion to a whole new generation. The 2000 movie *The Patriot*, based loosely on the partisan leader and starring Mel Gibson, added to the legend.

Overall, Marion's superior and laudable service as a militia commander and parti-san leader earn him a ranking slightly above his fellow guerrilla commander Sumter. His lasting fame elevated him to the middle of these rankings.

61

PRIVATEERS

1775–1783

The American colonies rebelled against the strongest sea force in the world, and they did so without a navy of their own. The Continental Congress (10) and some states authorized the commissioning of various sizes of warships, but by the time the United States officially declared its independence in 1776, the Americans had been able to muster a fleet of only 30 vessels. To enhance this "navy," the United States turned to a tradition more than five centuries old by issuing Letters of Marque to privately owned vessels, authorizing them to prey on British ships. Over the next six years, these "privateers" captured needed supplies for the Continental Army (7) and made prisoners of British replacements on their way to North America. By war's end American privateers had either sunk or captured more than 600 British vessels.

The history of privateering began in the thirteenth century when English King Henry III gave his approval for private vessels to attack French merchant ships on the condition the crown received half of the proceeds. These authorizations, begun in 1295, not only approved privateers but also detailed their responsibilities to the king. Over the following centuries other countries also issued these letters to private captains. Government officials saw the practice as an easy way to increase the size of their navies at no cost to themselves, while ships' captains appreciated the opportunity to secure legal wealth in a manner opponents to the practice considered to be piracy.

By the time the British became engaged in combat with France in 1756 in the Seven Years' War, privateering was an important part of their naval activities. During the conflict, British privateers captured more than a thousand vessels and brought French wartime commerce to a virtual standstill. Not all of the captured vessels, known as prizes, were taken by ships operating from British ports. The American colonists, especially those from the seafaring coast of New England, readily joined the privateer fleet and accounted for nearly a third of the French losses.

When the rebel colonies took up arms against Great Britain in 1775, funds for building naval vessels were sparse, and volunteers willing to fight against the powerful British armada were few. Members of the Continental Congress and state governments, remembering the success of privateers in the French and Indian War, issued Letters of Marque of their own. To insure against possible claims from neutral merchants or other innocent noncombatants who were not subject to the Letter of Marques, U.S. officials required that owners of privateers post bonds of $5,000 to $10,000. They also required that before any cargo or ship could be sold as prizes, the privateer had to present them before an Admiralty Court to prove the captured goods met the requirements outlined in his Letter.

Captains who owned their own ships quickly applied for Letters. Wealthy merchants and others provided funds to buy or build boats and hire crews in speculation of large returns. Experienced sailors and landlubbers alike, either anxious for profits or merely avoiding service in the Continental infantry, rushed to ports to crew privateers. Captains enticed volunteers with newspaper advertisements and broadsides.

An ad for the privateer *Deane* issued, "An invitation to all brave seamen and marines who have an inclination to serve their country and make their fortunes."

Once at sea privateers avoided British man-of-wars and focused on lightly armed merchant vessels. In an early success, the privateer *Lee*, commissioned by a personal letter from George Washington (1), captured the British merchant *Nancy* on November 25, 1775. Aboard the vessel were 2,000 muskets; 2,000 bayonets; 3,000 rounds of shot for 12-inch cannons; and hundreds of pounds of gunpowder. This latter commodity was in extremely short supply in the colonies, and the bayonets filled a void in the rebel armories.

Arms were not the privateers' only booty. In early 1776, American privateers captured several British transports ferrying more than 200 replacement soldiers from England to the rebellious colonies. By the end of the Revolution, the privateers, along with the U.S. Navy, took 16,000 British prisoners—one thousand more than those captured on land by the Continental Army.

Records are far from complete on the number of Letters of Marque issued by the Continental and state governments. Estimates rage from as low as 1,150 to as high as 2,500. Accurate counts are all but impossible because at any one time only about a third of this number were at sea. Some ships carried Letters from more than one source. From 1775 to 1783, American privateers captured or sank at least 600 British vessels, accounting for estimated prize money of $18 million—more than $300 million in today's dollars.

The American privateers' disruption to British shipping required armed escort vessels to accompany merchantmen in the war's latter years, but the Americans never remotely challenged the British rule on the seas. Not until France allied with the Americans and dispatched their fleet to North America did a balance of naval power shift. It is noteworthy that, despite promises of an added government bounty, privateers neutralized only sixteen British warships during the entire war. Also, once crewmen received their pay for a prize, they often were reluctant to return to sea—at least until they had spent all their money.

Critics of the American privateers claim that they were little more than authorized pirates who siphoned off able seamen from the Continental Navy and that much of their prize money went to individual investors rather than to the Continental treasury. It is true some cargos were sold in Europe and a few were purchased back by their original British owners.

Despite these critiques, privateers did contribute captured war materials as well as prisoners to the Revolution. They represented the United States along the Atlantic Coast and all the way to the Baltic Sea in search of their prizes. The privateers were one example of how rebel leaders, well aware that they faced the hangman if they failed, took desperate measures in desperate times. The U.S. Constitution of 1789, in Article I, Section VII, paragraph 11, permits Congress to issue "Letters of Marque," a note of approval and appreciation adopted by these victorious rebels.

The American Revolution was won on land, not at sea, but privateers did contribute to the ultimate victory. Their performance and contributions merit a ranking in the middle of this list.

62

FRIEDRICH WILHELM VON STEUBEN

American General

1730–1794

Friedrich Wilhelm von Steuben joined the Continental Army (7) at Valley Forge, Pennsylvania (39), in late 1777 and spent the winter training the soldiers in basic drill while he reorganized the layout and sanitation of the entire camp. He so impressed George Washington (1) that the general appointed von Steuben the inspector general of the army. His ability to organize and train the undisciplined soldiers earned him the title of "the first teacher of the American army" and his military capabilities as a division commander later helped him to contribute to the final successful campaigns of the Revolution.

The future American general began his life and service as the son of a junior officer in the Prussian army. Born on September 17, 1730, at Magdeburg, Prussia, he accompanied his father on a tour in Russia before returning to Germany for his schooling. At age seventeen he joined the army and served in the Seven Years' War as an infantry commander and staff officer. Near the end of the conflict, he advanced to the rank of captain and joined the General Staff of Frederick the Great before leaving the army in 1763.

For the next decade he served as an official in the royal court of Hohenzollern-Hechingen. Sometime during this period he gained the title of "baron," but there is no record if this was officially proclaimed or merely assumed by von Steuben. When the court he served dissolved from lack of funds, von Steuben journeyed to France in search of new employment. He found no success in resuming his military career although he offered his services to several European countries.

In the summer of 1777 in Paris, von Steuben befriended the French minister of war who introduced the Prussian to the American commissioner Benjamin Franklin (25). When the minister recommended von Steuben to Franklin, he thought a mere captain might not be acceptable to the American so he inflated his rank to "former lieutenant general in the King of Prussia's army." Von Steuben did not correct the claim, and Franklin, impressed with the officer and aware of Washington's shortage of qualified leaders, dispatched him to America.

Von Steuben landed at Portsmouth, New Hampshire, on December 1, 1777, accompanied by a secretary and an aide. The citizens of Boston lavishly entertained "the general" for several weeks before the Continental Congress (10), temporarily meeting at York, Pennsylvania, received him with honors and accepted his offer to volunteer for the American army. On February 23, von Steuben reported to Washington at his winter headquarters at Valley Forge. Washington recognized von Steuben's experience in training and organizational skills learned in the Prussian army. Even though the Prussian spoke only German and some French, Washington placed him in charge of drilling new and veteran militiamen.

Von Steuben formed a "model company" of one hundred men. Previously each man acted and reacted more as an individual than as a team member. Von Steuben repeatedly drilled them in marching, firing, and reloading until they acted in unison. When they failed to react appropriately, he shouted commands and profanities in German or French and had a junior officer, fluent in the languages, interpret his orders and threats. Once the model company met his standards, he dispatched its members to other units as cadre to teach their newly learned skills.

The Prussian then initiated a system similar to today's basic training for newly arriving soldiers that provided them instruction before they reported to their regiments. He also reorganized the heretofore haphazard arrangement of tents and other shelters into the neat rows of company and battalion streets that still typify U.S. military camps today. Von Steuben demanded kitchens be built on the opposite side of the camp from the latrines, greatly enhancing the camp's sanitation level and reducing sickness and disease. He later initiated a system of supply accountability, and while there is no official record, he likely advised Washington on how to fight the German Hessian (37) regiments hired by the British.

Washington was so awed by the Prussian's contributions that he secured a commission of major general for von Steuben from the Continental Congress and appointed him the army's inspector general. Von Steuben remained with Washington's staff during the Monmouth, New Jersey (59), campaign in the summer of 1778 and on through the following summer. During the winter von Steuben prepared and published the *Regulations for the Order and Discipline of the Troops of the United States*. These military regulations, better know as "the Blue Book," remained in use for the remainder of the war and beyond until finally being replaced in 1812.

Throughout his tenure on Washington's staff, von Steuben lobbied for a field command. Washington finally acquiesced and dispatched him to the Southern theater in 1780 to serve with Nathanael Greene (4) in the Carolina Campaign. At Yorktown (2) von Steuben commanded one of the three American divisions and remained in that

position for the duration of the war. After the Revolution came to an end, von Steuben returned to serve Washington as a military advisor before finally accepting his discharge on March 24, 1784.

The Pennsylvania legislature had declared von Steuben an American citizen in March 1783. He established residence in New York City and undertook an active social life as well as assuming leadership roles in church and veteran organizations. His business ventures were mostly unsuccessful and most of his finances came from loans against future compensation from the government for his wartime service. Finally in 1790, Congress granted him a lifetime annual pension of $2,800 (nearly $90,000 in today's money) and the state of New York gave him a large estate near Remsen. For the remainder of his life, von Steuben divided his time between his farm and New York City. A lifelong bachelor, he left his property to his two former military aides when he died on November 28, 1784. He is buried at Remsen.

Von Steuben came to America in search of a job rather than a cause, but it is not accurate to label him a mercenary because he served with no pay during the conflict. His later compensations were in no way extravagant. Despite many accounts of the war that refer to the Revolutionary army he trained as "rabble," von Steuben produced a skilled, organized force. While he was a great self-promoter and many later writers exaggerated his service, von Steuben did serve well and bravely. His influence, however, did not begin to match that of the senior commanders or of significant battles and events. While von Steuben is one of the best-known officers of the Revolution, he is more famous than influential. Still, his role as teacher and trainer earned him a place in the middle of this list.

63

EUTAW SPRINGS,
SOUTH CAROLINA

September 8, 1781

At Eutaw Springs, South Carolina, on September 8, 1781, the American commander General Nathanael Greene (4) lost the battle and won the war. The fight there further weakened a faltering British army in the South and forced it to retreat into Charleston. The battle was the last significant action before the victory at Yorktown (2) six weeks later that put the Americans in control of most of the United States and assured their independence.

In a series of battles in the first half of 1781, General Greene had not been able to defeat the British, but he had crippled their offensive operations. The Redcoats' efforts to neutralize the Southern states had failed. British General Charles Cornwallis (22) had retreated to the Northeast in hopes of either reinforcements or evacuation. The majority of the British forces who had stayed behind in the South concentrated their defenses in Charleston and Savannah. Scattered Redcoat units outside these two cities had assembled at Orangeburg, South Carolina, after the narrow British victory over Greene at Ninety-Six (91) that concluded in June 1781.

Greene had retreated from the Santee River where he rested his army, recruited replacements, and prepared to resume his offensive. Aware that George Washington (1) and his French allies were moving against Cornwallis in Virginia, Greene planned to prevent British troops still in South Carolina from reinforcing Cornwallis. He also hoped to end all enemy occupation of the interior of the Southern states.

When Greene moved toward Orangeburg, Lieutenant Colonel Alexander Stewart, who had replaced Lieutenant Colonel Francis Rawdon (73) as commander of the British field troops, fell back eastward so as not to be cut off from Charleston. His route paralleled the Santee River to a natural spring that flowed down a narrow creek a half mile to the main waterway. Stewart established his camp of 2,000 soldiers at this water source known as Eutaw Springs. Other than a single strong brick house with a high-walled garden, the site offered little in the way of defensive protection.

On the hot, clear morning of September 8, 1781, Greene advanced from the west with his militia on line to his front. The British, eating their breakfast, quickly formed their lines. After heavy musket fire by both sides, the American militia line faltered. The British immediately responded with a bayonet charge. The militia retreated as

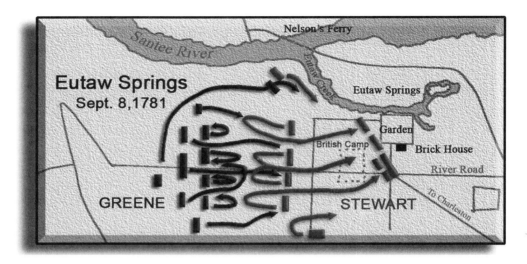

Greene ordered his second line—this one composed of Continental Army (7) infantry regulars and his cavalry—forward. They stopped the Redcoat advance and forced them into their own withdrawal. The Americans pursued only to be stopped by the British stronghold centered in and around the brick house and walled garden at the northeast of their camp.

Some of the Americans fired on the brick house but most stopped to loot the British supply trains and to eat the Redcoats' breakfasts still simmering in kettles on open fires. While the rebels enjoyed the food and spirits they found in the British wagons, Stewart rallied his troops for another counterattack. They charged out of the brick house and, with bayonets and musket fire, forced the rebels to retreat. In the woods to the west, Greene regained control and reformed his lines to stop the British advance.

Stewart broke contact and resumed his retreat toward Charleston. Although he could claim victory because he had forced the Americans from the field, Stewart left behind most of his 85 dead and many of his 351 wounded. American casualties totaled even more—139 killed and 375 wounded. Of the rebel casualties 17 officers had been killed and another 43 were wounded, including four of the six regimental commanders.

From all accounts both sides fought with discipline and bravery. Several stories reported that blood ran ankle-deep in places. The fact that the Americans paused to loot the British trains and eat their breakfast was not an indication of poor discipline; these troops thought that the battle had already been won. Also they had been on short or no rations for days and were nearing starvation.

Despite his defeat, Greene had accomplished his goal of forcing the British out of the interior of South Carolina. For five years the Redcoats had fought to control the Southern states and to prevent their resupplying the rebels in the North. Eutaw Springs marked their final failure to do so. When Stewart reached Charleston, the only British holdings in the South consisted of that city and Savannah, both surrounded by the rebels. With their land routes to the north blocked by Greene and the sea lanes now controlled by the French, there was no way for the British to resume their offensive or to attempt to reinforce Cornwallis in his final battle at Yorktown.

Eutaw Springs completed Greene's long, difficult mission to pacify the South. Although defeated in nearly every battle, he emerged victorious in the end, having earned the distinction of hero of the Revolution.

Eutaw Springs, one of the bloodiest battles of the Revolution, outranks the battle of Ninety-Six but falls below Cowpens (18) and Guilford Court House (26) that led to this final engagement.

64

BARRY ST. LEGER

British Colonel

1737–1789

Barry St. Leger earned the command of one of John Burgoyne's (33) invasion columns from Canada in the summer of 1777 only to be stopped and then turned back at the siege of Fort Stanwix and the Battle of Oriskany near Lake Ontario. His failure to continue his march southward contributed to Burgoyne's defeat at Saratoga (3) that served as a turning point in the war.

The records of St. Leger's life outside his time in uniform are sparse. Born sometime in the spring of 1737 into a Huguenot family in Ireland, St. Leger attended both Eaton and Cambridge. On April 27, 1756, he joined the 28th Foot as an ensign. A little more than a year later, he saw his first combat in the siege of the French fortress of Louisburg on Cape Breton Island. He then sailed to North America where he participated in the capture of Quebec in 1759 and the following year acted as a staff officer in the successful Montreal campaign. On August 16, 1762, St. Leger advanced in rank to major in the 95th Foot.

In the early months of the Revolutionary War, St. Leger served in various capacities in Canada. His distinguished service in the French and Indian War as well as in late frontier operations against the Native Americans led Burgoyne to recommend that George III (20) name now Lieutenant Colonel St. Leger to lead one of the invasion columns into New York.

Burgoyne's plan called for his main column to move south down the Hudson River while St. Leger's marched east to neutralize the rebels in the Mohawk Valley. Meanwhile, General William Howe (15) would lead a column north from New York City to gain support from Loyalists (34) in the region and to link up with Burgoyne at Albany. When the three columns came together, they would control the Hudson River Valley from New York to Canada, separating the New England states from the man power and supply resources of the other states. The generals believed that this operation could end the Rebellion.

St. Leger departed Montreal with a force of 1,000 Indians and 800 Loyalist militiamen and regulars on June 23, 1777. Within a month he had his army assembled at Oswego on the southeastern shore of Lake Ontario. He then marched southeast toward Fort Stanwix near the present town of Rome, New York, at an efficient rate of 10 miles per day, reaching there on August 2.

The British anticipated little or no resistance from the rebels, but they quickly discovered their intelligence about the Americans' resolve had been incorrect. Instead of a fort manned only by a few dozen rebels, St. Leger discovered that 550 Americans had been at work for weeks rebuilding the fort's defenses. An additional 250 rebel militiamen had arrived to reinforce the fort only hours before the British.

St. Leger, who had only four light artillery pieces and four small mortars, knew these weapons were too few and too impotent to breach the fort's walls. Instead of firing, he paraded his army before the fort in a show of strength. The revolutionaries were not impressed. Furthermore, seeing the Indians in St. Leger's ranks rekindled past animosities toward the Native Americans. The fort's defenders, commanded by Colonel Peter Gansevoort, prepared for a siege.

Throughout August 4 and 5, actions around the fort were limited to occasional sniper fire by each side. St. Leger improved and tightened his encirclement of Fort Stanwix but stopped when word reached him that a relief column of New York militiamen, led by General Nicholas Herkimer, was only 10 miles away. St. Leger quickly organized an ambush at Oriskany 6 miles southeast of the fort.

The British surprised the American column with withering musket fire at mid-morning on August 6. In a bloody battle that lasted over six hours, with several intervals of pouring rain, casualties were heavy on both sides. Although the battle ended in a stalemate, St. Leger claimed victory because he had turned back the rebel reinforcement column. When he returned to his camps around Fort Stanwix, he discovered his victory had come at a great cost. During his absence, rebel raiders from the fort had destroyed most of the British camps and supplies. Also, St. Leger's Native Americans, who had lost nearly a hundred warriors at Oriskany, were no longer interested in the fight.

St. Leger continued his siege. On August 23 word reached the British that another American relief column was on its way, forcing St. Leger to gather his force and retreat back toward Canada. The defenders of Fort Stanwix then joined the relief force and marched toward Saratoga, where they assisted General Horatio Gates (31) in defeating the column led by Burgoyne.

For the remainder of the war, St. Leger operated out of Montreal with small groups of raiders. Despite his loss at Fort Stanwix, the British promoted him to colonel in 1780. St. Leger then failed in an attempt to kidnap New York General Philip Schuyler in the summer of 1781. He was preparing to meet with Vermont officials at Ticonderoga a few months later in hopes of securing that region peacefully back under British control when he learned of Charles Cornwallis's (22) surrender at Yorktown (2). St. Leger abandoned his mission and returned to Montreal. He commanded British forces in Canada until 1784 when he sailed for England, where he left the army a year later and died in 1789.

From all accounts, St. Leger was an adequate soldier and even a proficient battlefield commander—at least in the French and Indian War. His performance in the American Revolution, however, was marked only by failures. When he turned back his column at Fort Stanwix he took away with him men who could have otherwise supported Burgoyne, and he left the rebel ranks intact to fight at Saratoga.

In reality, St. Leger did not have the man power or sufficient information about his enemy to accomplish the mission assigned to his second column. He performed as well as he could under the circumstances, but his defeat did contribute to the ultimate rebel victory at Saratoga. The extent of the influence of his failures is impossible to quantify, but the likelihood that he directly impacted the British defeat at Saratoga elevates him to the middle third of this list.

65

CAMDEN, SOUTH CAROLINA

August 16, 1780

The Americans lost a crucial battle at Camden, South Carolina, on August 16, 1780. In the aftermath of the fight, the British increased their hold on South Carolina and opened the way for their invasion and occupation of North Carolina. The battle also saw the end of the military career of American General Horatio Gates (31) and the rise of General Nathanael Greene (4) as commander in the Southern states.

Following American successes in the Northern theater—at Trenton (8) and Saratoga (3)—and France's entry into the war, the British turned their efforts to the Southern states in an attempt to quell the Rebellion. In the spring of 1780, the British dispatched a force commanded by General Henry Clinton (17) to South Carolina. With his ships blockading the harbor, Clinton put his land forces ashore near Charleston (47) and began an offensive against the port city. On May 12, Clinton accepted its surrender. Three weeks later he returned to New York, leaving General Charles Cornwallis (22) in command with orders to subjugate the remainder of South Carolina.

Rebel resistance against the British in the state was now reduced to partisan activities by small forces led primarily by Francis Marion (60) and Thomas Sumter (83). On July 25 the Continental Congress (10) ordered General Horatio Gates, the hero of Saratoga, to organize an army in the North around 1,100 veteran Continental Army (7) soldiers and march southward. Along the way 2,000 militiamen from Virginia and North Carolina joined the rebel column.

Gates never paused long enough to organize, train, or supply his army. By the time he reached South Carolina, his troops were a mass of hungry and disgruntled men ready to desert. Despite the problems, Gates continued the march toward Charleston, believing the element of surprise was on his side and fearing that the British would have time to reinforce their army if he delayed.

On the other side, Cornwallis had only two-thirds of the troops that Gates commanded but decided to take the offensive. Acting on intelligence about Gates's route of march, he moved the bulk of his army of 800 regulars and 1200 Loyalists (34) northwest of Charleston about 110 miles to the British base at Camden. After resting briefly and learning that the Americans were close, he marched northward despite the approach of darkness. Gates, aware the British were on the move, ordered his tired troops to continue their march. In the late evening of August 15, the two armies clashed about 7 miles north of Camden.

The lead elements of the two armies skirmished intermittently until dawn. At daybreak Americans and British faced each other along a line on low, sandy hills with thinly spaced pine trees, cleared farm fields, and small swamps between two small creeks. Gates had his Continental regulars from Delaware and Maryland, commanded by General Johann DeKalb, on the right flank; he had assigned the Virginia militia under General Edward Stevens to the left wing; and he had placed the North Carolina militia, led by General Richard Caswell, in the center.

Cornwallis attacked. His left flank struck DeKalb, but the regulars held their line against the Redcoats. In the center, however, the North Carolina militiamen fired only a volley or two before withdrawing. The rebels from Virginia on the left flank saw the center fall back, and they joined the retreat without firing a shot. Colonel James Webster, the commander of the British right wing, followed the retreating militiamen and then swung to his left into the flank of DeKalb. The regulars, now fighting on their front and side, were soon overwhelmed. Of the 900 regulars, an estimated 650 were killed or captured. Among the dead was DeKalb, who died from eleven gunshot and bayonet wounds.

Gates and his headquarters, located to the rear of the American line, joined the rapidly retreating militiamen. The best evidence has him not slowing down until he was 70 miles from the battlefield. He did not successfully reorganize what remained of his army until they reached Hillsboro, North Carolina—200 miles from the Camden battlefield.

Cornwallis ordered his cavalry commander Lieutenant Colonel Banastre Tarleton (44) to pursue the rebels now fleeing in full panic. Along the way he killed at least 150 and captured twice that number. The annihilation of Gates's army was so complete that his exact casualties are unknown. Best estimates show that about 1,000 Americans were killed, wounded, or missing with another 1,000 taken prisoner. The British victors suffered only 68 dead, 245 wounded, and about 60 missing.

The battle at Camden was the most costly defeat in relative man power for either side during the entire war. On a comparative basis of numbers committed against casualties sustained, it is the bloodiest battle in American military history. The American defeat was complete. Gates, although eventually cleared of any misconduct by Congress and allowed to rejoin the army, never again commanded combat troops. His stellar reputation, so deservedly won at Saratoga, now lay in shambles marked with incompetence.

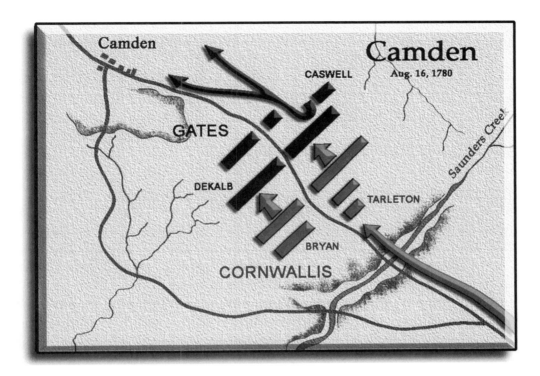

Cornwallis's victory at Camden confirmed for him and the British that the success in defeating the Rebellion was indeed in the South. George Washington (1) understood the significance of the defeat and the panicked aftermath. He ordered his trusted subordinate Nathanael Greene to assume command of what was left of the rebel army in the South. It would be Greene who recruited replacements and led the American army in a series of battles that resulted in the final victory at Yorktown (2).

As a battle, Camden was important only for the short-term damage sustained by the Continental Army. Its real influence was the demise of Gates and the rise of Greene who would have the command ability to reorganize, recruit, and revitalize the army in the South into a force that would ultimately defeat the British.

66

JOHN TRUMBULL

American Colonel and Painter

1756–1843

John Trumbull served as an aide to several of the senior American commanders early in the Revolution, but his real influence on the war and its aftermath came from his paintings of people and events of the conflict. His art contains the likenesses of many of the Rebellion's participants not recorded elsewhere. Trumbull's renditions of influential events are the lasting and, in many cases, the only images of the war, earning Trumbull the title of "Painter of the Revolution."

Born on June 6, 1756, in Lebanon, Connecticut, into the family of the colony's royal governor, Trumbull graduated from Harvard University in 1773 as the youngest member of his class. Despite a childhood accident that cost him an eye and his father's desire for him to become a minister or attorney, Trumbull wanted to draw and paint. After briefly teaching school in his hometown, he studied art under John Singleton Copley, the leading portrait painter in the colonies at the time.

At the outbreak of the Revolution, Trumbull joined a Connecticut militia unit and marched to join the Boston Siege (50). The son of the only royal colonial governor to side with the rebels, Trumbull witnessed the Battle of Bunker Hill (23) from nearby Roxbury, but he did not participate in the actual fight. Later he met George Washington (1) who thought the young artist's drawing skills might prove useful in sketching enemy positions. The general made him a junior aide-de-camp on July 27, 1775.

Trumbull joined the staff of Horatio Gates (31) in a similar capacity a year later. After brief service in upstate New York, he received a colonel's commission in the regular Continental Army (7). Angered that Gates dated the commission three months after his appointment to that rank, Trumbull resigned his commission on April 19, 1777, and moved back to Boston where he continued his study of art. Trumbull briefly returned to the army as an aide to John Sullivan (71) in the Newport, Rhode Island (82), campaign of August 1778.

Back in Boston, Trumbull resumed his painting once more and in 1779 decided to study under Benjamin West, one of Europe's most distinguished artists. Carrying a letter of introduction from Benjamin Franklin (25), Trumbull sailed first to France and then to London, where West had his gallery. Initially the English paid little attention to a rebel veteran in their mist, allowing Trumbull to go about his studies. However, when the Americans arrested John Andre as a spy on October 2, 1780, British officials retaliated and arrested Trumbull on November 8, threatening to hang him for espionage. West and other artists interceded to gain Trumbull's release, but he had to leave the country, which he did the following June.

Trumbull remained on the Continent until the end of the war and then returned to London in 1784 to resume his studies under West. Over the next two years he focused his brush on depicting major events of the Revolution and completed *The Battle of Bunker Hill* and *The Death of Montgomery at Quebec*. He also began painting *Declaration of Independence* in which he captured the faces in portrait of thirty-six of the fifty-six signers over the next eight years. While working in West's studio, he also completed *Surrender of Lord Cornwallis at Yorktown, Death of General Mercer at the Battle of Trenton*, and the *Capture of the Hessians at Trenton*.

In Paris, Trumbull reproduced many of his painting as engravings but found little market for the copies. He stayed with Thomas Jefferson (87), who was in Paris to negotiate treaties, but declined an offer to become the future president's private secretary. Trumbull returned to America in 1789 and began painting portraits in New York, starting with Washington. Over the next five years, Trumbull established himself as the best artist of his time, receiving great praise for his subtle glazes and fluid brush strokes.

Trumbull applied for government grants and backing to continue his series of Revolutionary War paintings, but he met with no success. Disappointed, he sailed to London in 1794 as the secretary to John Jay in treaty negotiations. For the next ten years he did little to practice or to hone his skills as an artist.

Back in New York in 1794, Trumbull tried to revive his art career, but much of his talent had atrophied during his decade of inactivity. Few of his works during this period match his earlier pieces. He returned to Europe in 1809 and did not return to the United States until 1815.

In his absence the British had burned much of Washington, DC, including the Capitol, during the War of 1812. Trumbull again lobbied for a commission to decorate the repaired Rotunda with enlargements of his original paintings. In

March 1817, Congress commissioned Trumbull to execute four paintings to be "Commemorative of the most important events of the American Revolution." The choice and the size of the paintings were left to President James Madison (78) who requested *The Surrender of John Burgoyne*, *The Surrender of Lord Cornwallis*, *The Declaration of Independence*, and *The Resignation of Washington*. Madison also asked for the paintings to be 12-feet-by-18-feet in size with life-size figures.

Over the next seven years, Trumbull produced the paintings and delivered them to Washington at a cost of $8,000 (about a quarter of a million dollars in today's money) each. Trumbull did not replicate his original paintings, brushed on canvases only about 20-inches-by-30-inches, to the new, huge format with the same quality as the earlier works. Not accustomed to painting in such a large format and already far past his prime as an artist, Trumbull produced images that appeared flat.

Trumbull, disappointed with the criticism of his Capitol paintings, became even more cantankerous. From 1817 to 1835 he served as the president of the American Academy of Fine Arts in New York City. In 1831, Trumbull signed an agreement with Yale University to turn over his paintings for a permanent exhibit in a building named the Trumbull Gallery in exchange for an annuity of $1,000 (about $32,000 in today's dollars). Trumbull died in New York City on November 10, 1843. His remains are buried beneath his Yale University Art Gallery in a tomb with the inscription, "To his country he gave his sword and pencil."

In an age before photography, John Trumbull produced detailed, extremely accurate paintings that remain today the very images of the Revolutionary War. His twelve paintings of the conflict, along with the hundreds of portraits of its participants, are the most important sources of visual information on the Revolution. His influence extends even to United States currency today. An engraving of his portrait of Alexander Hamilton graces the $10 bill and his *Declaration of Independence* is on the back of the $2 currency.

If this were a list of people influencing the recorded history of the war, Trumbull would rank near the top. However, this list consists of characters and events that directly influenced the Revolution. Trumbull's military service was largely insignificant, and it was not until after the war that his paintings came to national and international renown. Still, from schoolbooks to the Capitol, Trumbull's vision of the American Revolution is shared by all today, earning him a place in the latter half of this list.

67

PAY, RATIONS, UNIFORMS, AND MEDICINE
1775–1783

Monetary reward, food, clothing, and medical care have been inducements for military service since the beginnings of armed forces. These compensations lured both rebel and Redcoat alike to don the uniform of their countries, but most soon discovered that not all promises were delivered and that the dangers of being a soldier vastly outweighed the benefits.

The Americans established their own monetary system even before they declared their independence. On June 22, 1775, the Continental Congress (10) resolved to finance the war with paper currency backed by the "Spanish milled dollar." Congress initially authorized the printing of $2 million in paper bills of credit in the form of Continental dollars, and by November 29, 1777, it had approved and placed more than $241 million in circulation. During this same period, the states issued another $209 million in paper currency.

Unfortunately, neither the U.S. government nor the states had nearly enough hard-money specie to back their paper certificates. They also lacked a taxation process to raise funds to support their monetary system. Despite this financial reality, Congress authorized the Continental Army (7) to pay infantry soldiers $6.67 per month (a little more than $200 in today's money) and to pay cavalry and artillery soldiers $8.33 (about $265 in today's money) per month. This higher pay was supposed to lure more skilled and intelligent recruits into these specialties. Despite their greater exposure to deadly enemy fire, infantrymen ranked as a cheaper commodity.

Early in the war the states authorized payments as high as $36 (a little more than $1,000 in today's money) per month for their militiamen but later changed their pay rates to match that of the Continental Army. The fairness and adequacy of military pay for the Americans in the Revolution is a moot point, for soldiers rarely received any pay at all.

After the value of Continental currency collapsed in 1779, Congress left the responsibility to the states to pay the army. Their financial status was no better than the national treasury, and late in the war the New Hampshire legislature admitted that their troops had "had no pay for nearly twelve months."

Officially, British soldiers earned more than the American rebels, but neither did this mean money in the pockets of the Redcoats. Each soldier had to pay for his own food, shoes, stockings, and even repair of his basic weapon. More payments went to the regimental surgeon, to the paymaster, and to a pension fund. Allotments usually equaled the soldier's pay—meaning that at the end of each payday he was as broke as the day before. This lack of pocket money caused many British soldiers to seek off-duty employment—one of the reasons Bostonians were protesting the Redcoats' taking their jobs when the Boston Massacre (93) occurred in 1770.

Unpaid soldiers could fight, but unfed would not. Colonial America contained vast natural food resources from the forest and the sea, and its lush farmlands produced surpluses of grains, vegetables, and domestic livestock. Most soldiers entered

the Continental Army or their state militias from farms and villages where food was plentiful, and they expected the army to provide adequate nourishment.

Private soldiers in the Continental Army were authorized "one ration," defined as three meals, per day. Congress first prescribed the contents and amount of an army ration on September 12, 1775, and the following November 4 modified it as follows: "Resolved, that a ration consist of the following kind and quantity of provisions: 1 lb. beef, or 3/4 lb. pork or 1 lb. salt fish, per day; 1 lb. bread or flour, per day; 3 pints of peas or beans per week, or vegetable equivalent; 1 half pint of rice, one pint of Indian meal, per man, per week; 1 quart of spruce beer or cider per man per day, or nine gallons of molasses, per company of 100 men per week; 3 lbs. of candles to 100 men per week, for guards; 24 lbs. soft, or 8 lbs. hard soap, for 100 men per week."

One unofficial ration was vinegar that made water secured from nearby creeks, rivers, and lakes more potable and added flavor to food. Vinegar's antiseptic properties also proved beneficial.

British rations were fairly similar. Each day a British soldier was authorized "1 lb beef or 1/2 lb. pork, 1 lb. of bread or flour, 1/3 pint peas, one ounce butter or cheese, 1 oz. of oatmeal, and 1 and 1/2 gills of rum."

Early in the war and during the summer months thereafter, the Americans generally received part, if not all, of their authorized rations. At times, particularly during the long winters at Valley Forge (39) and Morristown, soldiers went hungry to the point where they threatened mutiny and shouted, "No bread, no meat, no soldier." When there were shortages, the deficiencies resulted from producers being unwilling to sell to the army for worthless currency or promises of future payment. Several battles, particularly in the South, might have been better exploited by the rebels if they had not stopped after initial success to raid the British stores and supply trains for food.

British soldiers fared a bit better in receiving their rations. Food was either procured or confiscated locally, or it arrived through the major ports and shipping lanes they controlled along the Atlantic Coast. Much of this food, however, was moldy or rotten before it could actually be delivered to the front lines.

The Continental Army began the war with no standard or authorized uniform. Buckskin jackets and other hunting attire dominated the rebel ranks in the war's early months before Congress recommended brown as the official uniform color. Soldiers dyed their shirts and trousers that color or green because the dye was readily available. Finally, on October 2, 1779, Congress, bowing to popular demand over practicality, reversed itself and adopted blue as the army's official uniform color. In reality, adequate amounts of replacement clothing rarely reached American soldiers during the Revolution. At times, the only item between a soldier and nakedness was a blanket draped around his body and tied with a cord at the waist.

British soldiers fared better in standardization and availability of uniforms. Their army had adopted the red coat that gave their soldiers their nickname in 1660 and would continue the garment until 1882. Different regiments added various attachments and colors of cuffs and collars, but generally the Redcoats were just that.

Both sides offered their soldiers the medical care available at the time, but it was abysmally ill-informed and inadequate. There were no inoculations for diseases at the beginning of the war and "bleeding" was considered the treatment for many ills. John

Adams (51) wrote, "Disease has destroyed ten men for us where the sword of the enemy has killed one." George Washington (1) did take measures in 1777 to inoculate each of his soldiers against smallpox, but there were no protections against typhus, diphtheria, malaria, dysentery, and even childhood diseases such as measles.

A soldier faced amputation of a wounded limb with little care for cleanliness. Dr. Benjamin Rush reported, "Hospitals are the sinks of human life in the army."

Although the British fared a bit better, each side had—at best—only adequate pay, food, uniforms, and medical care during the war. At times, especially among the rebels, adequate was a goal seldom achieved. All in all, however, the soldiers of both sides did their jobs despite shortages and inadequacies, and neither side gained or lost advantage over these supplies. For these reasons, pay, rations, uniforms, and medicine rank in the bottom half of these rankings.

68

JOHN STARK

American General

1728–1822

John Stark, a New Hampshire militiaman, significantly influenced the outcome of the Battle of Bunker Hill (23) and later assisted in the victory at Bennington, Vermont—a win that helped set up the pivotal Battle of Saratoga (3). He left a legacy of remarks and quotations that raised the morale of the soldiers at the time and continues to rouse patriotism among Americans today.

Born on August 28, 1728, in Londonderry, New Hampshire, Stark grew up on the frontier. An Abenaki war party kidnapped the teenage Stark and took him to Canada where they made him a member of their tribe—but only after torturous initiation rituals. A year later a representative of the Massachusetts colony paid a ransom for his safe return to New Hampshire. At the outbreak of the French and Indian War in 1756, Stark joined Rogers's Rangers and fought with that famous unit in operations at Ticonderoga and Crown Point. In 1759 the Rangers received orders to move against the French-allied Abenaki camps. Out of respect for the Native Americans who had spared his life and made him a member of their tribe, Stark left the Rangers and returned home.

Stark spent the next years as a farmer near Derryfield (now Manchester), New Hampshire. When word reached his village about the battles at Lexington and Concord (43), Stark accepted a commission in his local militia on April 23, 1775, and marched at the head of 1,900 volunteers for Boston.

At Breed's and Bunker hills, Stark's regiment prepared their defense on the left flank behind a rail fence near the Mystic River on June 17. Before the first British assault on his position, Stark shouted, "Boys, aim at their waistbands." This order not only encouraged his frightened soldiers, but also it made their shooting with the usually high-firing muskets more accurate. Stark's militiamen repelled three assaults by the British infantry, forcing them to redirect their advance into the stronger American force dug in on Breed's Hill.

Rewarded with promotion to colonel, Stark assisted George Washington (1) in preparing the defenses of New York before departing in the spring of 1776 to march northward to reinforce rebel soldiers invading Canada (84). When that operation failed, he rejoined Washington in time for the much-needed rebel victories at Trenton (8) and Princeton in late 1776 and early 1777.

Stark, always brave and daring in battle, was also occasionally insubordinate to his superiors and consistently headstrong. When he learned that he had been passed over for promotion in favor of several officers with much less combat experience, Stark resigned his commission and returned to New Hampshire on March 23, 1777. His

retirement did not last long. When he heard about John Burgoyne's (33) invasion of New York from Canada, he accepted an appointment as a brigadier general and gathered volunteers to meet the advancing British.

Near Bennington, Vermont, the New Hampshire rebels encountered a British supply base defended by 700 Hessians (37) and 600 British soldiers from Burgoyne's column. Stark paused only long enough to await the arrival of 350 additional troops and then attacked. Before ordering his men forward on August 16, 1777, Stark challenged his men to fight to the death and assured them he would willingly join them as he bellowed, "There are your enemies, the Redcoats and the Hessians. We beat them today or Molly Stark's a widow tonight."

At day's end Molly Stark was not a widow, but more than half the British and Hessians were dead or prisoners. Stark tied the prisoners in pairs and marched them through Bennington while adding hundreds of muskets, four cannons, and four wagons of ammunition to his stores.

When Burgoyne continued his march southward even though he had lost men and supplies at Bennington, Stark followed and blocked the British last avenue of retreat back to Canada. This was a most important tactic because Burgoyne was then left without options when he faced the Americans at Saratoga. Horatio Gates (31) earned the accolades for the American victory at Saratoga that ultimately led to France's recognition of the United States and eventual independence, but had Stark and his New Hampshire men had not prevailed at Bennington, the results might have been quite different.

Stark stayed in uniform for the remainder of the war. He served as commander of the Northern Department and participated in both the Rhode Island operations of 1779 and in New Jersey battles the following year. He finally retired as a brevet major general on September 30, 1783, and returned to New Hampshire. Stark never re-entered public life, preferring to work his farm and raise his large family. When invited to a gathering of Bennington veterans in 1809, the eighty-one-year-old veteran sent a letter to his comrades saying that he was too old to travel while offering his highest regards for their service. In concluding the correspondence, the old soldier showed he still had the gift of originating a well-turned phrase when he wrote, "Live Free or Die. Death is not the worst of evils." A century and a half later, New Hampshire adopted "Live Free or Die" as its official state motto.

Stark died on May 8, 1822, at age ninety-three and is buried in Manchester. He remains today the hero of Bennington known for his pithy statements during and after the war. One in particular continues to pique interest, and that is the ultimatum, "Or Molly Stark's a widow tonight." Historians report that his wife's actual name was Elizabeth, but apparently Stark called the woman with whom he reared eleven children Molly during their long and happy life together.

Whether or not Gates could have prevailed over Burgoyne at Saratoga without Stark's Bennington victory is, of course, unknown. Regardless, it was the high point of a distinguished career of a dedicated patriot. Stark was the kind of commander who performed bravely on the battlefield and had the gift of motivating his troops in trying times.

69

TREATY OF PARIS

September 3, 1783

The Treaty of Paris, signed by representatives of Great Britain and the United States of America on September 3, 1783, brought a formal conclusion to the Revolutionary War. Its provisions acknowledged the independence of the United States from the British and outlined generous boundaries for the new nation that reached westward to the Mississippi River and north to the Great Lakes.

Limited combat between the rebels and the British occurred after the American victory at Yorktown (2) in October 1781. Great Britain finally proclaimed an official end to the hostilities on February 4, 1783, and the American Congress took similar action the following April 11. During the interim months, various negotiations had been ongoing between the British and the Americans as well as with the French, Spanish, and Dutch, the latter three more eager to destroy the British Empire and divide its assets than to aid the independence of the United States.

Congress provided written instructions to its official peace envoys to Europe, declaring that they should seek no separate agreements with the British and that the French should be consulted on all negotiations. After more than a year of talks with the British representatives and with their own allies, three American envoys—Benjamin Franklin (25), John Adams (51), and John Jay—concluded that their allies were focused on their own interests more than those of the United States. This was a time of intrigue and petty bureaucracy. Representatives spent days arguing about credentials and whether "the United States of America" was an authorized term.

Fearing that France was preparing to support Spain's claim for western territories, the three envoys approached London directly with their peace plan in late 1782. British leaders, hard pressed by their countrymen to finalize an agreement and delighted that the Americans were breaking away from their allies, quickly came to terms with their former colonists. The ten-article agreement started with the British formally recognizing the independence of the United States. Article 2 provided the generous boundaries to reach westward to the Mississippi River, north to the Great Lakes, and south to Spanish Florida. Article 3 granted the Americans fishing rights off of Newfoundland, and Article 4 called for the collection of lawful debts to creditors on both sides.

Subsequent articles required concessions on the part of the rebels. Abuse and persecution of those Americans who had remained loyal to the Crown was to stop and Congress was to "earnestly recommend" to state legislatures that property confiscated from Loyalists (34) be returned. Prisoners of war of both sides would be immediately released, and all property seized by the British in America, including slaves, would be returned to rightful owners. Territories captured by the Americans outside their borders, primarily Caribbean islands, were to be handed over to the British without compensation. Both sides agreed to their joint use of the Mississippi River. Finally, they agreed that the treaty would be ratified no later than six months after its signature. No mention of Native Americans (99) or their claims to various lands merited inclusion in the treaty's articles.

On September 3 the two former belligerents made the agreement official. David Hartley, a member of Parliament and representative of King George III (20), signed for Great Britain. Adams, Franklin, and Jay signed in alphabetical order for the United States.

On the same date the British signed separate treaties with the other belligerents. Britain ceded East and West Florida and the island of Minorca to Spain while the Spanish returned the captured islands of the Bahamas and St. Kitts. The Dutch gained the former British possession of Sumatra.

Though it secured little in the negotiations other than the renewal of former treaties with the British and some fishing rights off the Canadian coast, France faced the most consequences. The French were relieved to end the costly war and free themselves from commitments made to Spain in exchange for its support, but the American Revolutionary War planted the seeds of independence among the French who would soon revolt against their king for their own liberty.

The American Congress ratified the Treaty of Paris on January 14, 1784. The British Parliament did likewise on April 9, 1784, with the official documents exchanged by the two countries on May 12.

The Treaty of Paris is remarkable not only for its recognition of the independence of the United States by Great Britain but also for its provisions that greatly expanded inland the borders of the United States far beyond the former Atlantic colonial territories. Other than the minor expedition of George Rogers Clark (55) in 1778, the rebels had done little to lay claim to these territories. Now instead of thirteen states bordering the Atlantic Ocean, the United States reached nearly halfway across the continent. Some Americans were already envisioning a country that would reach "from sea to shining sea."

September 3, 1783, as the official signing date for the Treaty of Paris, slipped quietly into history to be little remembered or marked. The Americans instead chose to focus on July 4 and the *Declaration of Independence* (14) as the centerpiece of their celebrations. The Treaty of Paris was important because of the postwar size and status of the United States that it established. Its direct influence on the Revolution itself was negligible; the fighting was over, the battle won. The Treaty of Paris was a part of the future rather than the past and thusly gains a place only in the latter third of these rankings.

70

WEAPONS AND TACTICS

1775–1783

Weapons and tactics win and lose wars. When the Americans revolted against the British, weapons technology and battlefield tactics had advanced little since the Seven Years' War of a decade earlier. They went essentially unchanged for the duration of the American Revolution. Both sides used the same or similar weapons and employed the same tactics in the field. The smooth-bore flintlock musket with an attached bayonet was the primary individual weapon. Both sides also employed secondary weapons, including rifles, pistols, swords, and other edged implements. Smooth-bore mobile cannons capable of firing 3- to 6-pound projectiles supported ground operations.

By the end of the Seven Years' War in 1763, modern European forces armed their soldiers mostly with muzzle-loading flintlock muskets, the Brown Bess and the Charleville becoming the most popular. The British invented and favored the inexpensive, mass-produced English Long Land Service Musket, better known as the Brown Bess for the color of its wooden stock and barrel. Ten pounds in weight with a 46-inch-long barrel, the sturdily built .75 caliber Brown Bess could sustain the rigors of military field action. Its one-ounce lead ball measured only .71 caliber, so it loaded quickly and easily down the slightly larger barrel.

Another major military power of the eighteenth century, France had developed their own standard military flintlock. Other than having a slightly smaller .69 caliber barrel, the French Charleville closely resembled the British Brown Bess—down to a shared lack of accuracy. Even the most skilled marksman had little control over where his shot landed.

A common military rhyme of the period about both Brown Bess and the Charleville musket shots summed up the situation:

"One went high,
and one went low,
and where in Hell
did the other one go."

At the outbreak of the Revolutionary War, the Brown Bess remained the primary infantry weapon of the Redcoats. The Americans, too, carried the Brown Bess, either from earlier British issue to the militias or from captured stocks. Charlevilles from French supplies also soon appeared in the ranks. In November 1775 the Continental Congress (10) authorized the manufacture of a .75 caliber flintlock known as the Committee of Safety musket, but their numbers never came close to those of the Brown Bess and Charleville. All three of the muskets shared the inaccuracy common to smooth-bore muskets. Early in the war, concerns about the lack of accuracy of the muskets became so acute that Benjamin Franklin (25) even suggested arming the army with bows and arrows.

British ordnance expert and veteran of the campaigns in the South, Major George Hanger, wrote about the accuracy of the muskets used by both sides, stating, "A  soldier's musket will strike the figure of a man at 80 yards; it may even at a hundred, but a soldier must be very unfortunate indeed who shall be wounded by a common musket at 150 yards, provided his antagonist aims at him, and as to firing at a man at 200 yards, with a common musket, you may just as well fire at the moon. No man ever was killed by a musket at 200 yards by the person who aimed at him."

In the years prior to the Revolution, American gun makers had modified European designs to produce smaller-caliber, longer, rifled barrels. Internal groves, or rifles, combined with balls only slightly smaller than the barrels, produced more powerful and accurate shots. Their disadvantage lay in reloading time. An infantryman with a smooth-bore musket could fire about four rounds per minute whereas the rifleman could only produce about half this rate.

The British also fielded their version known as the Ferguson Rifle, but it was never used in sufficient numbers to impact a battle. On the other hand, American riflemen played an important part at Saratoga (3) and during the Southern campaign.

Both the Brown Bess and Charleville were capable of mounting a 14- to 17-inch-long triangular-shaped bayonet. While an unloaded musket was of little use other than as a club, the bayonet-mounted musket proved extremely lethal. Few Revolutionary War battles lasted for more than several volleys of musket fire before the ranks closed to determine the fight's outcome with cold steel. The better-trained and disciplined British were said to often pray for rain before a battle to render the flintlocks useless and leave the outcome at the point of the bayonet.

Cavalry of both sides employed single-shot pistols of various manufacture and sabers of different lengths. Horse soldiers fought with sabers and used them to strike down retreating infantrymen, but cavalry could not stand against bayonet-equipped foot soldiers and avoided combat with them if at all possible. Both foot and mounted troops carried different types of knives and even hatchets, but these were much more useful in camp than on the battlefield.

Both the British and Americans used artillery throughout the war with some success. The British brought their own guns while the Americans relied on pieces captured in combat or those provided by France. Cannons of both sides were generally 3-, 4-, or 6-pounders mounted on wooden carriages with large wheels. Some of the 3-pounders, known as "grasshoppers," had iron legs on which the tube mounted. These cannons fired solid balls or exploding shells to a range of 800 yards and multi-shot or grapeshot to 200 yards.

Popular myths credit much of the American victory in the Revolutionary War to the rebels' use of unconventional tactics copied from the Indians. Hiding and shooting from behind walls and trees at the naïve British who remained in the exposed open—except for the brief aftermath of the Battles of Lexington and Concord (43) and at Kings Mountain (36)—simply did not happen. The Americans, French, and British all employed the linear tactics of warfare that had been in use for decades if not centuries. The two sides formed in lines with various numbers of ranks in the rear. They then marched toward each other, or more often, one attacked the other's defensive position. Both sides fired volleys with their inaccurate muskets to break up the opposition's line. After several volleys the two sides closed to within bayonet range. Prior to assaults, cannon fire reduced an opponent's lines, and in the final assault, an artillery piece could shred an entire attacking company.

Despite the length of the Revolutionary War, few innovations or advances in weapons or tactics occurred. For that reason, weapons and tactics rank in the bottom third in influence on the American Revolution—far below the men who employed them.

71

JOHN SULLIVAN

American General

1740–1795

John Sullivan fought in nearly all the battles in the Northern theater from the Boston Siege (50) through the campaign to neutralize the Native American uprisings in the Wyoming Valley (95). Known for his personal bravery and his popularity with his men, Sullivan nevertheless often quarreled with representatives of the Continental Congress (10) who threatened to relieve him from command and to have him face court-martial.

Born on February 17, 1740, in Somersworth, New Hampshire, as the son of an Irish schoolmaster, Sullivan studied law before opening his first practice in 1760. In 1772, Sullivan accepted an appointment to major in the New Hampshire militia, and in the fall of 1774, his neighbors elected him to the First Continental Congress. In May 1775, he took a seat in the Second Continental Congress only to leave a month later to join the Boston Siege as a brigadier general in the Continental Army (7).

Following the British evacuation of Boston, Sullivan led a relief expedition northward to reinforce the Canada Invasion (84). He reached Saint Johns on June 1, 1776, and assumed command of the Northern Army when General John Thomas died of smallpox. Despite the fact that many of the soldiers also had the disease and that all of them were suffering exhaustion from the long campaign, Sullivan attacked the British garrison at Three Rivers a week later only to be soundly defeated. In danger of being cut off from his supply lines to the south, Sullivan retreated toward Lake Champlain.

General Horatio Gates (31) assumed command of the army when they reached Crown Point. Sullivan protested his being replaced by going to Congress and threatening to resign his commission. Sullivan made no friends with his complaints, but the Congressmen placated him with a promotion to major general. Sullivan joined the Continental Army at Long Island (32) on August 20 only to be captured by the British a week later. Reports from the battlefield claimed Sullivan stood in the midst of the fighting with a pistol in each hand before the British finally overpowered him. As a prisoner, Sullivan delivered a message to Congress for the British proposing a

peace conference. When Congress declined, the British exchanged Sullivan for one of their own captured officers.

Sullivan joined the main army under George Washington (1) on December 20 and led the right wing that cut off the Hessian (37) retreat route at Trenton (8) five days later. He then commanded the main advance against Princeton on January 3, 1777. Sullivan remained with Washington in the winter quarters around Morristown. On August 21–22, 1777, Sullivan led an unsuccessful operation to recapture Staten Island and then hurried southward to rejoin Washington at the Battle of Brandywine Creek (72) on September 11.

Meanwhile Sullivan had made even more enemies in Congress where the politicians thought that he and his fellow generals Nathanael Greene (4) and Henry Knox (12) were attempting to usurp their authority over the military. Congress recommended that Sullivan be removed from command while they investigated his failure at Staten Island, but Washington, who regarded the general as one of his ablest subordinates, refused. Sullivan then led one of the columns against Germantown (48) on October 4 before settling in for the winter with Washington at Valley Forge (39).

In the spring of 1778, Sullivan took command of a joint expedition with the French navy against the British facilities at Newport, Rhode Island (82). When the French fleet withdrew to repair storm damages and with many of his attached militia units deserting, Sullivan had to give up the offensive and assume defensive positions north of Newport. He repelled one British attack before retreating when he learned that Redcoat reinforcements were on their way.

Sullivan withdrew to Providence where he waited out another winter. The following spring, he marched eastward to the Wyoming Valley of Pennsylvania and New York where the British and their Indian allies had committed atrocities against the local residents in previous years. Sullivan, joined by other regulars and militias, swept through the valley in the largest independent operation of the war. With his 4,000 troops, Sullivan burned the crops and destroyed the villages of the Iroquois and their allies. The major Indian stronghold near present Elmira, New York, fell on August 29. The Indians of the region never recovered and for the rest of the war had to look to the British for handouts merely to survive. Sullivan had defeated their will and spirit and negated any further influence by them in the conflict.

Exhausted and ill from the rigors of the campaign, Sullivan resigned his commission on November 30. From all evidence, this was his decision, not influenced by Congress. New Hampshire welcomed him home as a hero and in 1780 returned him to the Congress as a delegate. Lingering resentments brought accusations that he had become a foreign agent by accepting a loan from a French minister. Sullivan resigned his seat in 1781 and again returned home.

Back in New Hampshire, he secured the position of state attorney general where he served until 1786. In 1788 he led the efforts within his state to ratify the Constitution while serving as governor. President Washington named Sullivan a federal judge in the New Hampshire District Court in 1789 where he sat until leaving the bench in 1792 because of illness, likely compounded by his overindulgence in alcohol. He died on January 23, 1794, at Durham, New Hampshire, and is buried there in a family cemetery.

Sullivan earned the respect of his officers and men through his personal leadership and concerns for their welfare, often placing his popularity above more pressing issues. Washington admired him and regarded him as one of his best field commanders, but Sullivan could not get along well with superiors—military or civilian. Arrogant and ambitious, Sullivan served the army and the country well in the major battles of the war's first three years. His advance in command, influence on the war, and ranking on this list might have been even higher if he had learned, or perhaps cared, to be more politically adept with Congress.

72

BRANDYWINE CREEK, PENNSYLVANIA

September 11, 1777

Despite the favorable fighting conditions and familiar territory, the Americans found themselves overwhelmed by the British along Brandywine Creek in the fall of 1777. George Washington (1) operated throughout the battle without accurate information about the terrain or the enemy, resulting in a performance atypical of the leadership he demonstrated in both earlier and later battles. The American defeat at Brandywine cost 10 percent of the Continental Army (7) and opened the way for the British to capture and occupy Philadelphia.

In the summer of 1777, General John Burgoyne (33) launched his offensive south from Canada with the plan that General William Howe (15) would march northward from New York City to meet him in the Hudson River Valley. This offensive would effectively divide the colonies in New England from those in the South, leading to the end of the war. Howe, however, decided instead to move his force southward to capture the rebel capital at Philadelphia, thinking he would have ample time to defeat Washington's army before turning back to joining Burgoyne.

On July 23, Howe embarked his army of 15,000 aboard 260 ships for the Chesapeake Bay. The armada landed at Head of Elk, Maryland, near present-day Elkton on the northern end of the bay on August 25. Instead of making camp and resting his troops from their long sea voyage, Howe immediately marched toward Philadelphia, which lay 50 miles inland.

Howe's quick movement prevented Washington from accurately assessing the British strength, but it was obvious that their objective was the American capital. Washington assembled his army of 10,500 in New Jersey and crossed the Delaware River into Pennsylvania. He chose Brandywine Creek to prepare his defenses for the simple reason that it was of sufficient depth to require the advancing British to use fords to cross the waterway. Unfortunately for the Americans, Washington and his subordinates did not know about all the numerous fords along the creek.

Chadd's Ford on the main road from Baltimore to Philadelphia seemed the most likely place for the British crossing, so Washington chose the high ground overlooking the spot to place his artillery and to prepare his primary defensive line consisting of two divisions led by generals Anthony Wayne (38) and Nathanael Greene (4). To cover his lower or southern flank and to force the British into his primary defenses, the American commander placed a force of 1,000 men under the command of General John Armstrong at Pyle's Ford. General John Sullivan's division covered the area north of Chadd's Ford with Colonel Moses Hazen's brigade responsible for the defense of Buffington's and Wistar's Fords.

Washington was now confident that he had the crossings of the Brandywine to his north and south covered and that the main battle would come at Chadd's Ford. Although he had cavalry to provide reconnaissance of the British advance and had occupied his positions for several days before the British arrival, Washington did not receive correct information about or numbers on the enemy. More importantly, he was not aware that there were many other fords on the Brandywine or that the Loyalists (34) from the area had informed Howe of their locations.

By the time Howe neared the Brandywine, he knew of Washington's dispositions and was more knowledgeable about the creek's fords than the rebels. He had no desire to suffer the probable casualties in a direct attack against the American strength. Instead he deployed 5,000 men—a third of his force under General Wilhelm von Knyphausen—to approach the American center at Chadd's. The rest of the army, commanded by General Charles Cornwallis (22), maneuvered northward to the unde-fended crossing points at Jeffries's and Taylor's Fords north of Wistar's Ford.

Howe began his maneuver early on the morning of September 11. A thick fog con-cealed the initial British movement from American observers. Washington's advance scouts were surprised when they encountered the leading elements of von Knyphausen's force, and they fell back to report the advance. Only after von Knyphausen stopped and began an ineffective cannon barrage did Washington recognize the main attack would not come at Chadd's. His suspicions were confirmed when reports reached him that Cornwallis had crossed to his north and was now sweeping down the northern rebel flank along the creek.

In this position north of Chadd's Ford, Sullivan attempted to adjust his lines to meet the flank attack only to have von Knyphausen now attack his front. Americans abandoned their lines and fled toward Philadelphia. Only the quick deployment of a delaying action by General Greene—along with the approach of darkness—prevented the possible loss of the entire army.

Washington managed to reestablish defenses at Chester between the British and Philadelphia while his army staggered into his new lines in small units and as individu-als during the night. Howe, later criticized for not mounting an active pursuit, camped on the battlefield around Chadd's Ford. British Captain John Andre recorded in his journal, "Night and the fatigue the soldiers had undergone prevented any pursuit."

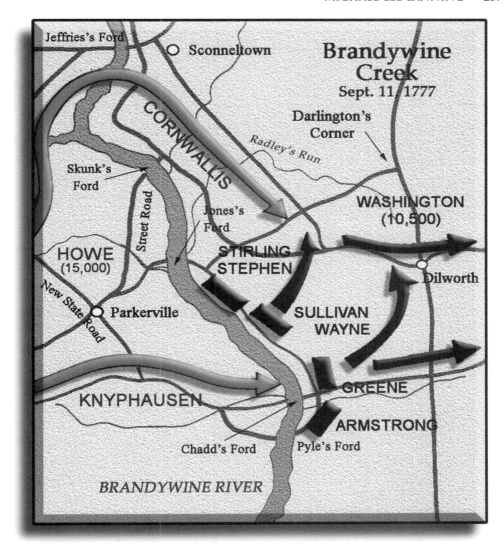

American losses totaled about 1,000 men with 400 of that number taken prisoner. They left eleven cannons behind. British casualties numbered about 600.

In a message to the Continental Congress (10) written "at midnight" after the battle, Washington wrote, "I am sorry to inform you, that in this day's engagement, we have been obliged to leave the enemy masters of the field. Unfortunately the intelligence received of the enemy's advancing up the Brandywine, and crossing at a ford about six miles above us, was uncertain and contradictory, notwithstanding all my pains to get the best." Washington continued with other explanations, and indeed excuses, for his defeat, but he concluded that he was "happy to find the troops in good spirits" and that he hoped to compensate in the future for the loss.

This last claim was more honest that not. Washington's army had fought well under the circumstances of being outflanked by a superior force. He and his subordinates were aware that the defeat was the result of poor intelligence (75) on their part and excellent tactics on the part of the Redcoats.

The Americans were not strong enough to stop Howe and withdrew toward Germantown (48), allowing the British to march into the capital city unopposed on September 26. Time gained along the Brandywine did, however, allow the Continental Congress and many of the military supplies stored in Philadelphia to safely evacuate the city before the arrival of the British. After a one-day stay in Lancaster, the Congress was quickly back in session in York.

Brandywine Creek was only one in a series of American losses in 1776–1777 that left most of New York and Pennsylvania in the hands of the British. However, the American force had survived the battle, and as long as Washington had an army in the field, the revolution survived. Had the British ultimately been successful in defeating the rebellion, Brandywine could have been pivotal. However, the final American victory puts this battle's influence in the bottom third of this ranking.

73

FRANCIS RAWDON

British Lieutenant Colonel

1754–1826

Francis Rawdon fought with bravery and distinction in most of the major battles in both the Northern and Southern theaters of the American Revolutionary War as he advanced in rank from ensign to lieutenant colonel in the British army. Rawdon personally organized and led one of the most efficient Loyalist (34) units and commanded all British forces in the South after Charles Cornwallis (22) retreated to his ultimate defeat and surrender at Yorktown (2).

Born into a noble Irish family at County Down, Ireland, on December 9, 1754, Rawdon studied at Oxford before joining the British army in 1771 and sailing for the American colonies in July 1774. On June 17, 1775, he saw his first combat as a junior officer in the British assaults on the American fortifications on Bunker Hill (23). When his company commander was killed by rebel musket fire, Rawdon took command of the unit and led it forward with conspicuous gallantry.

Rawdon withdrew from Boston with the main British army in March 1776 and then participated in the battles of Long Island (32) in August 1776, White Plains (77) the following October, and Fort Washington (86) a month later in the campaign that secured New York City for the British. During these operations Rawdon penned an often-quoted letter that some claimed showed his ruthlessness while others argue it only displayed his sense of humor. In August 1776, Rawdon wrote from Staten Island, "The fair nymphs of this isle are in wonderful tribulation, as the fresh meat our men have got here has made them as riotous as satyrs. A girl cannot step into the bushes to pluck a rose without running the most imminent risk of being ravished, and they are so little accustomed to these vigorous methods that they don't bear them with the proper resignation, and of consequence we have most entertaining court-martial every day."

Henry Clinton (17), commander of British forces in the former American colonies, cared little about morals or humor, rather judging men by their performance in battle. Clinton promoted Rawdon to lieutenant colonel, appointed him to become his adjutant general, and ordered the young officer to organize a regiment of Irish

Loyalists from Philadelphia who were mostly deserters from the Continental Army (7). Rawdon led the Irish Volunteers at the battle of Monmouth, New Jersey (59), on June 28, 1778, and remained in the Northern theater until joining the expedition against Charleston, South Carolina (47), in the spring of 1780.

Rawdon disagreed with Clinton before his departure, explaining in his letter of resignation as adjutant general on September 3, 1779, that he had "no longer the honor of being upon those terms of mutual confidence in a station whose duties are most irksome to me." Upon his arrival in the South, Rawdon joined the command of Cornwallis and ably led the British left wing in their victory at Camden, South Carolina (65), on August 16, 1780.

Over the next few months, Rawdon advanced with Cornwallis toward North Carolina and then retreated back southward after the rebel victory at Kings Mountain (36) on October 7. After the battle at Cowpens (18) on January 17, 1781, Cornwallis left Rawdon in command of 7,500 troops in the Charleston area while he marched northward to a pyrrhic victory at Guilford Courthouse (26) on March 15 before continuing toward Yorktown. Rawdon now had to not only hold the important port of Charleston, but also he had to defend remote British outposts in South Carolina and Georgia. With his Irish Volunteers in the lead, Rawdon defeated Nathanael Greene (4) in a minor battle at Hobkirk's Hill on April 25 and then conducted a grueling march from Charleston to Ninety-Six (91) to relieve a besieged garrison.

With failing health compounded by the long, hot march to Ninety-Six, Rawdon turned over his command of the region on July 20, 1781, to Colonel Paston Gould and sailed for England. En route, a French privateer captured his vessel, and Rawdon spent the next year as a prisoner at Brest before being exchanged and finally allowed to return home.

Welcomed as a hero, the not-yet-thirty-year-old Rawdon received a promotion and the elevation to the Barony of Hastings. As Francis Rawdon-Hastings he advanced in rank to full general in the Napoleonic Wars while also serving in the House of Commons. Respected by military leaders and subordinates and a friend of the prince of Wales, Rawdon-Hastings became the governor-general and commander in chief of India in 1813. In this position he fought the "Gurkha War" that brought Nepal into the empire in 1814 and negotiated the cession of the strategic island of Singapore to Great Britain in 1819.

After a decade of service on the subcontinent, Rawdon-Hastings assumed the governorship of the island of Malta in 1784. He died aboard the HMS *Revenge* on November 28, 1816, during a visit to Naples. Per his request, his body was returned to Malta for burial, but not before his right hand was amputated for preservation and eventual interment with his wife when she passed away. His requests were honored and his hand rests today with his wife's body at Lowden Kirk.

Aside from an apparently flippant attitude toward the molestation of the women of New York in his 1776 letter, Rawdon enforced a much higher level of discipline than other leaders of Loyalist forces. Unlike his counterpart Banastre Tarleton (44), who often gave no quarter to prisoners, Rawson followed the accepted battlefield practices of the times. From all evidence he was honest in all endeavors and generous to friend and foe alike.

Rawdon's selection by Cornwallis for command in the South is all that more remarkable considering his youth and the fact that several other officers outranked him. Cornwallis not only had respect for the young officer's abilities on the battlefield, but also he had confidence that Rawdon could maintain good relations with other commanders. Rawdon more than met the expectations of his commander. If the British had had more young officers with the fighting, organizational, and leadership abilities displayed by Rawdon, they might have won the war. If they had, Rawdon would have achieved a much higher ranking on this list; however, his position on the losing side relegates him to a place in the latter third of these rankings.

74

WAXHAW CREEK,
SOUTH CAROLINA

May 29, 1780

The Battle of Waxhaw Creek culminated the most successful British cavalry operation of the Revolutionary War with the defeat—many on the rebel side called it a massacre—of retreating Virginia militiamen. In addition to the one-sided casualties on the part of the Americans, the battle elevated the British commander Lieutenant Colonel Banastre Tarleton (44) to the level of hero in England and branded him a murderer within the ranks of the rebels. Ultimately the fight did nothing to assist the British in their effort to end the Rebellion while it converted previously uncommitted colonists to the side of the Rebellion.

When word reached Virginia in early 1780 that British commander Henry Clinton (17) had besieged Charleston (47), regulars and militia units marched south to help defend the port city. Among these were the 380 men of the 3rd Virginia commanded by Colonel Abraham Buford, but they did not reach Charleston before the city fell. The Virginians, accompanied by a few survivors of skirmishes outside Charleston and the state's governor, John Rutledge, retreated back toward North Carolina.

Clinton, anxious to make Rutledge a prisoner and to destroy the Virginia detachment, dispatched Tarleton's cavalry in pursuit. Despite the huge lead by the Americans, Tarleton believed he could catch the rebel foot soldiers with his horse-mounted troops. Riding almost nonstop, the British cavalry covered more than a hundred miles in only fifty-four hours despite the hot weather and horses already tired from the Charleston campaign. By the early morning hours of May 29, 1780, Tarleton had closed to within miles of the Virginians. He stopped for several hours to rest his men and horses and then continued the pursuit.

Buford, aware of the approaching British, dispatched Rutledge and a small escort to make their escape. The American commander then sent his supply wagons and his cannons with his few draft horses to the front of his column while he concentrated his infantry in the rear as they continued their retreat.

In late morning Tarleton caught up with the Americans near Waxhaw Creek, northeast of Lancaster near the North Carolina border, and sent a representative forward to demand their surrender, claiming that he had 700 men with him. According to his own later report, Tarleton hoped that exaggerating the number of his own troops to

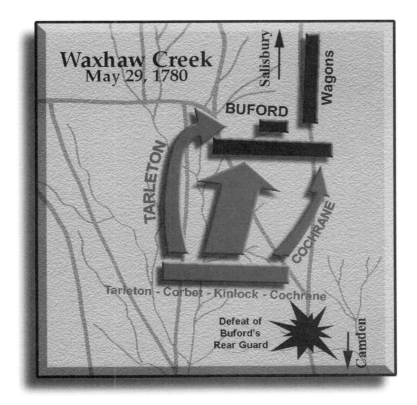

Buford might prevent a fight and "...intimidate him into submission, or at least delay him whilst he deliberated on an answer."

Buford refused the offer, responding, "I reject your proposals, and shall defend myself to the last extremity."

Instead of immediately preparing defenses, the American commander made the mistake of continuing his retreat. When the British cavalry approached at about 3:00 p.m., Buford barely had time to form a line before compounding his previous error by having his troops hold their fire until the horsemen were only yards from their positions. The rebel volley did not even slow the British, who easily broke their line. Buford ordered a white flag of surrender to be raised, but its bearer was cut down, according to reports by Tarleton himself. Tarleton's horse was shot, and word swept the British lines that their commander was dead. The angered Redcoats pushed the attack with sabers and pistols on the outnumbered and now disorganized rebels.

Within minutes, 113 of the Americans lay dead along Waxhaw Creek. Another 150 were wounded so severely they could not be evacuated from the battlefield. Some 53 more, many also wounded, were taken prisoner. Only Buford and a few other mounted rebels escaped to North Carolina. One of Buford's captains, John Stokes, suffered 23 wounds, including a saber thrust that cut off one of his hands and four bayonet wounds that penetrated completely through his body. Miraculously, Stokes, unlike many of his fellow casualties, survived. Word immediately circulated throughout the former colonies about the "Waxhaw Massacre" or "Tarleton's Quarter," names which came to connote any mistreatment of the unarmed or wounded.

The British reported the battle differently. In England the *London Chronicle* of July 18 explained, "Col. Tarleton knew, that having taken a command of the King's troops, the duty he owed to his country directed him to fight and conquer." Previously unknown in Britain, Tarleton was hailed a hero after Charleston and Waxhaw Creek. On the other side, the Americans called him "Bloody Tarleton," and he became the most hated British officer of the war.

In his own writings, Tarleton later admitted that the slaughter went beyond normal bounds. He justified the bloodshed, however, by noting the loss of his own horse, stating, "...a report amongst the cavalry that they had lost their commanding officer stimulated the soldiers to a vindictive asperity not easily restrained."

In the long run, Waxhaw Creek did more to defeat the British in the South and to bring victory to the Americans than it did to assist their efforts to end the Rebellion. Many Southerners, previously sympathetic to the Loyalists (34) or neutral, were so incensed with the news of the massacre that they joined the Revolutionary cause. Included were a group of frontiersmen from what is now Tennessee who "came over the mountains" to join the rebellion and who played an important role in the battle at Kings Mountain (36) the following October.

British victories in the American Revolution get little attention in the history books. The battle—known alternately as Waxhaw Creek, Waxhaws, the Battle of Buford, and Waxhaw Massacre—earns but a few lines in most accounts, and that is usually for its bloody aftermath rather than the brilliant cavalry march that led to it. The British victory alone was not sufficiently influential to earn Waxhaw Creek a place on this list, but the successful postwar propaganda efforts by the Americans to rally those previously undecided merits its inclusion in the latter third of this ranking.

75

INTELLIGENCE

1775–1783

Both the United States and Great Britain lacked information about their opponents throughout the Revolutionary War. Neither had resources to gather or analyze actions by the other when the shooting started. Little verifiable proof of successes or failures by American, Loyalist (34), or British spies exists. Therefore, battlefield commanders had to rely on their own cavalry and foot reconnaissance for information on enemy size, capabilities, and intentions.

Of all the motivations that sparked the colonists to seek independence, the Stamp Act of 1765 (19) was the most unifying and, though at first glance it may appear unrelated, the start of the American intelligence network, such as it was. Earlier British taxes had concentrated on certain regions or specific products; the Stamp Act required a tax stamp to be purchased and placed on every legal and commercial paper in the colonies, including newspapers, pamphlets, and even playing cards. For the first time, levies applied to all colonists at once, regardless of location or stature.

The Stamp Act prompted secret societies to oppose the taxation. One of the larger organizations, the Sons of Liberty, rebelled against the Stamp Act but did not disband when the British repealed the Stamp Act in 1766. Rather, they increased their membership and established communications with similar organizations in other colonies.

The Sons of Liberty gave birth to the more formal yet still secret Committees of Correspondence in 1772, which led to the convening of the First Continental Congress (10) two years later. Since about one-third of the colonists opposed the rebels and remained loyal to the Crown, both the Sons of Liberty and the Committees of Correspondence had difficulties insuring the commitment of their members. Word about many of their activities leaked to British officials, leading to the confiscation early in the Rebellion of several hoards of arms and ammunition.

In response to this infiltration, a small group of prominent colonists—including Samuel Adams, John Hancock, Dr. Joseph Warren, and Dr. Benjamin Church—formed an intelligence organization called the Mechanics. The Mechanics knew that information from their meetings was reaching the British, but they had no idea how or from whom. It was not until two centuries later when Church's papers were opened to the public that it was revealed that the doctor himself had sold out to the British to pay off mounting debts.

To protect the arms and supplies they were storing in Concord in 1775, the Mechanics had several of their men keep a watch on British movements in Boston.

When the British marched toward Concord, Paul Revere (98) made his famous ride to warn the militiamen, resulting in the Battles of Lexington and Concord (43).

After the militias followed the British back to Boston and surrounded the city, the Continental Congress (10) authorized the formation of the Continental Army (7) with George Washington (1) as its commander. Washington knew he needed timely, reliable information, but he had no staff position dedicated to pursuing it. The Continental Congress had not thought to provide for intelligence officers or men. Ultimately, Washington was forced to become his own chief of intelligence.

Most of Washington's early intelligence efforts were failures. The first company of scouts he organized under Captain Thomas Knowlton was annihilated while conducting a reconnaissance of Harlem Heights, New York, on September 16, 1776. A week earlier, a member of Knowlton's command, Nathan Hale, conducted a spy mission in civilian clothes behind enemy lines only to be captured and hanged.

Hale is a good example of the brave but ineffective men dispatched as spies. He was a man taller than the average whose face had been scarred by a childhood explosion. He went behind the British lines with no cover story for his presence and encountered his Loyalist cousin who was a member of the British unit Hale went to spy on.

After the fall of New York, Washington organized the Continental Secret Service under the leadership of Benjamin Tallmadge. Tallmadge formed a system of spies and established the first American system of codes and ciphers. He kept the operations of the Service secret for the remainder of the war, but what little information he gathered usually failed to reach Washington and his front line commanders in a timely manner.

This lack of information about enemy movements led to the capture of Washington's second in command Charles Lee in December 1776 and his defeat at Brandywine Creek (72) the following September. Later, after the American victory at Saratoga (3), a gap in intelligence about the British retreat routes from Philadelphia to New York precluded a decisive rebel victory that might have brought an early end to the war.

When the primary British efforts shifted to the Southern states, American commander Nathanael Greene (4) also suffered from a lack of formal intelligence gathering organization. His best and most timely information came from partisan leaders Francis Marion (60) and Thomas Sumter (83) who had the advantage of growing up in the areas in which they fought.

Back in the North in the fall of 1780, the Americans suffered a major intelligence failure and the most infamous act of American treason with the defection of Benedict Arnold (85) to the British. Arnold's treachery almost cost the rebels their important stronghold at West Point (30). Arnold was never apprehended, but his British contact Major John Andre, caught in civilian clothing, paid the ultimate price on the gallows.

The British fared no better. They rarely had advance information of American locations or movements. The defection of Arnold was one of the high points of British intelligence during the war. Other than successful reconnaissance at Long Island (32) and Brandywine Creek, their intelligence efforts mirrored those of the rebels. Rarely did either have information that influenced a battle or campaign.

Despite the abysmal reality of intelligence failures of the war, the postwar public in both the United States and England doted on tales of spies and espionage. Myths about women and servants who overheard battles plans at dinner abound, but these stories are more often fiction than fact. In reality, neither side trusted the word of spies, the practice considered to be too "ungentlemanly" for the attention of true professional soldiers.

Ultimately, the American Revolution was won by the valor of revolutionary soldiers on the battlefield and sailors at sea and their allies from France and other European powers. Just how many lives could have been saved with timely, accurate intelligence by either side is impossible to calculate. What is known is that during the American Revolution intelligence failures far outnumbered intelligence successes. For these reasons Intelligence rates toward the end of this list.

76

BENJAMIN LINCOLN

American General

1733–1810

Benjamin Lincoln commanded American troops in the field for the entirety of the Revolutionary War with leadership that ranged from superior to dismal. His performances in the Boston Siege (50) and the Battle of Saratoga (3) helped gain early American victories, while his later command actions in the South, particularly at Charleston, South Carolina (47), resulted in some of the worst defeats for the rebels. Resilient to the end, however, it was Lincoln who accepted the British sword of surrender at Yorktown (2) that ensured the independence of the United States.

Born on January 24, 1733, at Hingham, Massachusetts, into a family that had been firmly established in New England for a century, Lincoln received only a basic education before following his father into local politics. He began as a town constable in 1755 and worked his way up to justice of the peace in 1762 while also becoming somewhat successful as a farmer. Lincoln joined his local militia in 1757 and by 1772 had earned promotion to lieutenant colonel. In the years prior to the official outbreak of the Rebellion, he served in the colonial legislature and with his local Committee of Correspondence.

Massachusetts promoted Lincoln to the rank of brigadier general in its militia at the beginning of the war and to major general in May 1776. In August, Lincoln assumed command of all Massachusetts troops participating in the Boston Siege and continued in that position when his militiamen joined in the defense of New York. During this time he met and impressed George Washington (1) who noted in a letter to the Continental Congress (10) in early 1777, "[Lincoln is] an excellent officer and worthy of your notice in the Continental line."

Congress responded by elevating Lincoln from his state militia command to the rank of major general in the regular army on February 19, 1777. Washington dispatched Lincoln to Saratoga in the fall of 1777, where he ably participated in the campaign that defeated John Burgoyne (33). Near the end of the battle, Lincoln suffered a wound to his leg that left him with a permanent limp.

After a ten-month convalescence for his wound, the Congress ordered Lincoln to assume command of the Southern theater, but he arrived too late to influence the British capture of Savannah (80) on December 29, 1778. Lincoln established his headquarters in Charleston only to face a British offensive against the town led by General Henry Clinton (17) in the spring of 1780. Clinton badly "outgeneraled" Lincoln by first cutting off his possible avenues of escape followed by a cannon bombardment of the port city. To prevent the destruction of Charleston and to halt what he thought were unnecessary military and civilian casualties, Lincoln surrendered his army of more than 5,000 after little resistance. With fewer than 300 casualties, the British achieved their greatest victory of the Revolutionary War.

Lincoln remained a prisoner until exchanged for British officers the following November. Although criticized for his failures at Charleston, he was neither court-martialed nor reprimanded. Upon his exchange he began recruiting soldiers in Massachusetts and securing arms and equipment for his new command. In the summer of 1781, Lincoln rejoined the American troops in the vicinity of New York City.

When Washington learned that the British army in the South was withdrawing to a location where the York River emptied into Chesapeake Bay, he sailed and marched toward Virginia with Lincoln as one of his division commanders. When General Charles Cornwallis (22) sent word to Washington that he was ready to surrender after the Battle of Yorktown in October 1781, Lincoln was among the officers who accompanied their commander to the proceedings. At the last minute, Cornwallis claimed to be ill and dispatched his deputy General Charles O'Hara in his stead to formalize the surrender.

While there are many conflicting stories about Cornwallis's excuse, the most often accepted version of the surrender is that O'Hara, who shared his boss's contempt for the rebellious colonists, attempted to hand his sword to the French commander Jean Baptiste de Rochambeau (24), but the Frenchman refused and deferred to the Americans. O'Hara then approached Washington, but the general deferred to Lincoln in accordance with the military protocol of the time that called for officers of equal rank to conduct such transitions. Some later accounts claimed Washington chose Lincoln as his representative because he had been forced to surrender at Charleston, but the general was selected because of his rank, not his past performance or failures.

A month after Yorktown, the Continental Congress appointed Lincoln as secretary of war. He remained in that position for the next two years during the final skirmishes of the conflict. Lincoln returned home to Massachusetts after the Treaty of Paris (69) in 1783 to work on the ratification of the U.S. Constitution. From 1789 to 1809 he served as the collector for the Port of Boston while also acting as a government representative in several disputes with Native Americans (99). He retired from public life a year before his death at Hingham on May 9, 1810. Lincoln is buried in Hingham's Old Ship Church Cemetery.

Described as "portly with loose jowls" and hampered by his limp from the Saratoga wound, Lincoln did not lend himself to any great military presence. His failures as a strategist and as a tactical battlefield leader far overshadowed his superior administrative and organizational abilities. While no one can doubt Lincoln's dedication to the Rebellion and his loyalty to Washington and the Congress, he is an early example of an American officer being promoted beyond his abilities. Most of Lincoln's influence on the Revolution, particularly in the South, was negative. His surrender of Charleston, which remained in British hands for the remainder of the war, seriously threatened the Revolution in the South. His lasting influence and legacy, however, took place when he accepted the British sword of surrender. For that alone he merits a place on this list, but his actual performance limits that ranking to near the end.

77

WHITE PLAINS, NEW YORK

October 28, 1776

At the village of White Plains in Westchester Country in the northern end of Manhattan, the Americans attempted to stand against the British in hopes of defending New York City and preventing it from falling into the hands of the Redcoats. The rebels mounted a determined defense, but the British outmaneuvered them with a flanking movement that forced their retreat. In the battle's aftermath the British failed to exploit their advantages and allowed the majority of the enemy to escape.

Both American General George Washington (1) and British General William Howe (15) recognized the importance of New York City as a center of commerce and communications. When Washington attempted to block Howe's invasion force at the Battle of Long Island (32) on August 27, 1776, the British forced him to fall back to Manhattan where he had established new defenses on Harlem Heights. The British commander then dispatched a reconnaissance force that the rebels repelled after a sharp skirmish that cost each side about one hundred casualties on September 16.

Still reluctant to order frontal assaults after the severe casualties he had sustained at Bunker Hill (23) the previous year, Howe decided to conduct a flanking movement to the east. A victim of a similar tactic at Long Island in August, Washington withdrew his defenses further north. The American commander, while proud of his army's stand at Harlem Heights, was not happy with the overall performance of his forces. On September 21 he corresponded with the Continental Congress (10), noting his displeasure with militia short-term enlistments and the states' units' practice of selecting their officers by popular vote rather than on performance. He used all these reasons to lobby for the creation of a permanent army.

Washington, however, had more immediate problems than could be solved with letters to Congress. His scouts informed him on October 12 that Howe, using his superior naval assets, had moved the bulk of his 14,000-man army up the East River to landing sites at Troug's Neck and Pell's Point. Washington left 2,000 of his best troops at Fort Washington (86) in northwestern Manhattan and deployed the remainder of his 14,000 men to the village of White Plains. Progress was slow. The Americans had few horses and wagons, forcing the soldiers themselves to transport their cannons and supplies. Fortunately for the Americans, Howe advanced at his usual leisurely pace that provided the Americans ample time to prepare their defenses along a 3-mile line.

It took Howe ten days to march his army the short distance of 17 miles from his landing sites to White Plains. He compensated for his pace upon his arrival by using the sound tactic of once again avoiding a frontal attack. Instead he assembled the bulk of his army in an impressive array on a plain to the south, just out of range of the rebel guns. On October 28, he dispatched several Hessian (37) regiments westward across the 14-foot wide Bronx River to occupy Chatterton's Hill, rising 180 feet above White Plains, an ideal place for flanking fire into the American defenses. Washington, however, had manned the hill but with only a few sentries. When he saw the Hessians moving to take that high ground, he ordered his own regiments forward.

Most of the following Battle of White Plains took place not for the village itself but for control of Chatterton's Hill. After several attacks and counterattacks, including bayonet charges, the Hessians dominated and forced the American defenders back to their lines. Howe now held the high ground but did not order a general attack until October 31; he then further postponed it because of strong winds and a heavy rain. By the time the British finally advanced on November 1, the Americans

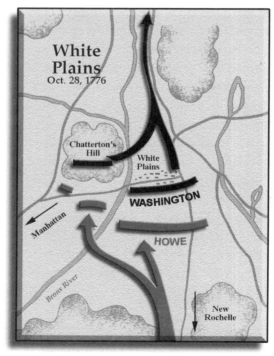

had used the cover of the storm to once again retreat northward. Howe did not pursue, deciding to secure his rear and lines of communications by backtracking to neutralize the rebel defenses at Fort Washington.

British and American casualties each numbered about 300. Some estimates nearly double these numbers while others admit to only a hundred or so on each side, but the total of 600 seems the most probable.

With each side fielding armies of about 14,000, the Americans had the advantage of being on the defensive. Howe took this advantage away by using better generalship to flank the rebel positions. If he had continued his attack after capturing Chatterton's Hill, he might very well have forced Washington's surrender or at least have greatly depleted the rebel army.

The defeat at White Plains undermined the confidence and high morale of the Americans resulting from their defenses of Long Island and their stand at Harlem Heights. Once again, however, the rebel army had escaped along with most of their artillery and supplies. Fort Washington would fall by mid-November, ending any hopes of American control of New York City, but—more importantly—their Revolution, represented by Washington's survivors, lived on.

If Howe had exploited his advantage at White Plains, the American Revolution might have ended in Westchester Country. Since he did not, this battle ranks in the bottom third of this list. While important, it was not pivotal except in continuing the Revolution.

78

FUTURE UNITED STATES PRESIDENTS

1775–1783

Six of the first seven presidents of the United States were active participants in the American Revolutionary War on the field of battle, in the halls of the Continental Congress (10), or as commissioners to secure foreign support. They influenced the outcome of the conflict through contributions large and small and in turn were themselves influenced by the experience of being part of America's fight for independence. The other future president was a child at the time, but as the son of the second president and envoy to Europe, he was also impacted by the Revolution.

George Washington (1) departed the leadership of the Continental Army (7) on December 23, 1783, to return to Mount Vernon in order to restore the property and regain much of his personal wealth that he spent in supporting the Revolution. Washington believed that the *Articles of Confederation* (16) had been adequate during the war but were not comprehensive enough to provide the direction, unity, and defense required by the new country. Soon he was dividing his time between being a planter and a politician as he assisted in disputes between Virginia and Maryland. These meetings evolved into the Annapolis Convention of 1786 and then to the Constitutional Convention of 1787 in Philadelphia.

When the state electors met in February 1789 to select the first president of the United States, there was little consideration for anyone other than Washington. Somewhat reluctantly, he accepted and established many of the traditions and proce-

dures of the office that still exist today. Washington also sought unity by selecting cabinet members from both of the emerging political parties while instilling dignity and decorum into the highest office in the land.

Immensely popular in his first term, Washington planned to retire after four years, but leaders of both parties encouraged him to run again. Delegates unanimously reelected Washington, many echoing the sentiment that "the country could not do without him."

Washington's second term saw increasing division and tensions between the Whigs and Tories, but the first president continued to set the standards of honesty and leadership that would seldom, if ever, be duplicated in the future. Upon his death in 1799 the U.S. Congress passed a resolution submitted by Henry "Light Horse Harry" Lee that proclaimed Washington to be, "A citizen, first in war, first in peace, first in the hearts of his countrymen."

Three years younger than Washington and suffering from poor health, John Adams (51) had no inclination to serve in the military, so he supported the Revolution as a member of the committee that wrote the *Declaration of Independence* (14) in 1776. In late 1777, Adams left Congress to become a commissioner to France to seek their support and recognition of the new country. He then helped negotiate the Treaty of Paris (69) that finally brought the Revolutionary War to a conclusion.

John Adams served as Washington's vice president for both terms, a position he described to his wife as being "the most insignificant office that ever the invention of man contrived or his imagination conceived." In 1796 he advanced to become the second president of the Untied States. His administration, although able and honest, was marked by disputes between the two political parties and emerging problems of a new country with foreign relations. Adams handled the difficulties as best he could under the circumstances but did not earn reelection to a second term. He lived to see his son John Quincy Adams inaugurated as the sixth president in 1824.

Thomas Jefferson (87), another patriot who thought he could better serve the Rebellion as a politician rather than as a soldier, followed Adams in 1800 as the third president of the United States. As the primary author of the *Declaration of Independence*, Jefferson recorded in words the reason behind the Revolution and the spirit and purpose of the liberties it proposed. Remaining in state and national politics after he left the Continental Congress in 1779, Jefferson did much to establish the vision of the country.

Although accused of "inventing the spoils system" by rewarding friends and party members with government positions, Jefferson served his country well as president. His greatest achievements were the vast expansion of U.S. territory via the Louisiana Purchase in 1803 and the dispatching of the Lewis and Clark and Pike expeditions to explore the new lands. He also ordered the U.S. Navy to successfully deploy naval power to deal with the Barbary pirates off the North African coast during his second term in office.

James Madison (1751–1836) became the fourth president with his inauguration in 1808. As a young man, Madison studied for the clergy but turned to law and politics in the years leading to the Revolutionary War. In 1774 he enlisted in his local militia but quickly dropped out because he could not meet the physical strain of military service. He held political offices in his native state of Virginia before advancing to the

Continental Congress in 1780. He then served in the U.S. Congress and back in the Virginia government before becoming the secretary of state under Jefferson in 1801.

As president, Madison faced increasing problems with Great Britain regarding recognition of the rights of the United States and its citizens, a dispute that led to the War of 1812. Poorly prepared, Madison and the United States managed to prevail despite the British capture and burning of the new capitol in Washington, DC.

James Monroe (1758–1831) left college at William and Mary at age seventeen and joined the Virginia militia. Other than Washington, he achieved the most distinguished battle record during the Revolutionary War of all the future presidents. Monroe served as a junior office at Harlem Heights and White Plains (77) in the New York campaign of 1776 and fought with Washington at Trenton (8) where he was wounded at the end of the year. Promoted to major, Monroe returned to fight at Brandywine Creek (72) and Germantown (48) in 1777 and Monmouth (59) in 1778.

When the war shifted to South Carolina in 1780, Monroe left the army to return to Virginia politics, where he held various positions in the war's final years and in the subsequent Constitutional conventions. From 1790 to 1816, Monroe served as a U.S. senator, envoy to France, governor of Virginia, secretary of state, and secretary of war before becoming the fifth president of the United States in 1808. In his two terms as president, he strengthened Atlantic coastal defenses, conducted the first war against the Seminole Indians in Florida, secured the passage of the Missouri Compromise, and instituted the Monroe Doctrine.

John Quincy Adams (1767–1848), who became the sixth president in 1824, did not participate in the American Revolution other than to accompany his father's diplomatic mission to France as a ten-year-old boy.

Adams's replacement, and seventh president of the United States when inaugurated in 1828, had a more direct role in the war. Andrew Jackson (1767–1845) at age thirteen joined the Continental Army as a courier. There is no evidence that Jackson saw much combat, but he did manage to be taken prisoner in April 1781. When a British officer ordered the youthful Jackson to clean his boots, the future president refused, earning a sword strike that badly cut his hand.

Nurturing his wound and a lifelong hatred of the British, Jackson returned home to briefly teach school before entering politics in Tennessee and to advance in rank to a militia major general. Joining the regular army in the same rank in 1812, he fought against the Native Americans in the Creek War and earned national fame for his defeat of the British in the Battle of New Orleans in 1815. Before and during his time as president, Jackson was known as a sincere friend and a fierce enemy. Jackson rewarded his friends with "spoils" of his election, placing them in cabinet and other high positions. He evicted Indians from their native lands and relocated them in order to open new territory for white settlements. Jackson did away with the National Bank and advocated power of the Federal government over that of the states.

Presidents who succeeded Jackson were born after the war or were mere children while it was fought. Of all the Revolutionary War soldiers who became president, none was a professional soldier, and only Washington had any great military influence on the conflict's outcome. Adams and Jefferson—and to a lesser degree, Madison— influenced the political war and risked the hangman's noose as traitors if the Rebellion failed. Monroe saw enough combat to understand the risks and results of warfare, while Jackson experienced only enough to develop a lasting dislike of the British.

Regardless of their varying personal impacts on the outcome of the Revolution, all six future presidents were influenced by what they saw and felt during the war. Their presidencies and future lives were influenced by the war as much as they influenced the conflict itself.

79

CHARLES LEE

American General

1731–1782

Charles Lee joined the rebels as the most experienced military officer in the Continental Army (7) and quickly became its second highest ranking officer. Despite his exalted status, Lee resented being subordinate to George Washington (1), a resentment he could never overcome. Combined with his negative demeanor and failure on the battlefield, the attitude finally led to his court-martial and dismissal from the service. As a soldier who often appeared more interested in money than in the cause he served, Lee may well have been a traitor to the Revolution.

Lee was born on February 6, 1731, in Dernhall, Cheshire, England, and joined his father's infantry regiment while still in his teens, gaining a commission at age twenty. In 1755 Lee fought in several of the primary battles of the French and Indian War in North America where he served with future American leaders, including Washington and Horatio Gates (31). Lee rose to the rank of major despite a serious wound. During his stay in North America, Lee befriended the Mohawks who adopted him into their tribe. He also took the daughter of a Seneca chief as his "wife"—at least for the duration of his stay in America.

Lee returned to England and joined General John Burgoyne (33) for operations in Portugal in 1762 and again fought with distinction, earning promotion to lieutenant colonel. At the conclusion of the Seven Years' War in 1763, Lee's regiment was disbanded, and he was retired on half-pay. Between 1765 and 1770, Lee acted as a military aide and advisor to the King of Poland. In the latter year he received a general's commission and fought with the Poles against the Turks.

With sufficient funds in his coffers from his time as a soldier of fortune and suffering from illness, Lee returned to England. In 1773 he sailed to the American colonies where he purchased land in Virginia. Although still drawing his retirement pay as a British officer, Lee supported those who backed independence. When the Revolution began in 1775, Lee offered his services to the Continental Congress (10)—but only after sending a letter to London resigning his commission and giving up his retirement pay. In volunteering for the Continental Army, Lee noted this loss of income and the likelihood that his property in England would be seized and asked the Congress for compensation. Only after he received assurance that he would receive this payment did he accept a commission as major general on June 17, 1775.

Lee's commission made him subordinate only to Washington and Artemas Ward, who would soon resign his position and leave the former British officer as the second highest ranking general in the American army. This did not satisfy Lee. Not only did he dislike Washington personally, but also he felt that, as the most experienced general, he should be in overall command.

After brief service in the Southern theater, Lee returned to Philadelphia where he received a "Thanks of Congress" for his actions at Charleston, South Carolina. Lee joined Washington's army at White Plains (77) near the conclusion of the unsuccessful New York campaign. When Washington retreated into New Jersey, he left Lee in charge of the rear guard. Washington then called for Lee to rejoin the army, but the general was slow in following the order. The rear guard reached Washington in mid-December 1776, but Lee was not with them, having become the highest-ranking American officer ever to become a prisoner of war.

Exact details about the general's capture on December 13 are not clear, but apparently Lee, confident that the British were nowhere near, decided to spend the night at a tavern near Morristown, New Jersey. Some accounts claim that Lee was at the establishment to meet a woman and remained there through the next morning to take care of correspondence. He did have a small security detachment, but it proved no match for the British cavalry patrol that took him captive.

Some British officials, including Secretary of State George Germain (9) wanted Lee returned to England for trial as a traitor. Others, led by General William Howe (15), believed that Lee had honorably resigned his British commission and was not subject to British orders. Lee remained a British prisoner in New York until April 1778 when he was exchanged for General Richard Prescott.

Lee rejoined the Continental Army just before the Battle of Monmouth (59) on June 27, 1778. He was initially opposed to Washington's plan to attack the British and refused to assume command, but when he learned that fully one half of the army would attack the British rear, he reconsidered and accepted the job. With no ground or map reconnaissance, he advanced against the retreating British only to hastily withdraw when the British turned to fight. Washington's personal leadership in rallying and reorganizing the force saved the day.

When Washington relieved him from command and harshly criticized his actions, Lee responded with profanity and insubordination, leading to his court-martial and suspension from command for a year. Lee passed this time by corresponding with members of the Continental Congress, requesting his court-martial be overturned. When this failed, he added to earlier correspondence disparaging the military abilities of Washington. Lee soon lost what little favor he had in the army and the Congress. Colonel John Laurens, an aide to Washington, became so angry with Lee's comments that he challenged the general to a duel and wounded him in the side. Lee recovered from the wound only to be dismissed from the service on January 10, 1780. He settled in Philadelphia where he died on October 2, 1782.

Profane, slovenly, and mercenary are just a few of the uncomplimentary descriptions provided by those who knew Lee. Even worse for his already tattered reputation was the discovery many years after the war of his possible treasonous acts. In 1858 a researcher discovered a document among the papers of the British Howe brothers in Lee's handwriting dated March 29, 1777, that he had prepared while a captive in New York. The letter offered a plan by which the British could crush the Rebellion by gaining control of the middle colonies of Maryland, Pennsylvania, and Virginia.

There is no evidence that the British responded to the recommendations, nor is there proof that Lee's treachery directly influenced his poor performance. Whatever his loyalties or abilities, Lee and his influence were minimal and negative, causing his ranking to fall near the end of this list.

80

SAVANNAH, GEORGIA (FIRST SAVANNAH)

December 29, 1778

The First Battle of Savannah in the final days of 1778 initiated the British strategy of defeating the American Rebellion by shifting their focus from the North to the South. In a brief, nearly bloodless fight, the Redcoats, using their superior numbers and intelligence about the American defenses, defeated the rebels and occupied the port city. Savannah remained in British hands for the remainder of the war, allowing them access to the interior of Georgia and an invasion route into South Carolina.

After their defeat at Saratoga (3) in October 1777, British commanders realized that their chances of defeating the rebels in the North were greatly reduced. To increase their opportunities of victory and curb the mounting casualties, the British commander General Henry Clinton (17) decided to redirect his efforts to the South. In the fall of 1778, Clinton concentrated the majority of his Northern army around New York City and dispatched other parts to the South.

On November 27, Clinton ordered Lieutenant Colonel Archibald Campbell and 3,500 troops to sail from New York southward, escorted by a convoy commanded by Commodore Hyde Parker, to capture Savannah. Clinton also sent instructions for General Augustine Prevost, commander of British forces in East Florida, to march northward to join the invasion force.

Soon after the British fleet from New York arrived off Tybee Island at the mouth of the Savannah River, Campbell sent a reconnaissance party ashore. During their search of the countryside, the reconnaissance group detained two men who, according to Campbell's later report, provided "the most satisfactory intelligence concerning the state of matters at Savannah."

Campbell now knew that the American commander in the area, General Robert Howe, had only 800 regular Continental soldiers and an additional 150 militiamen—and they were located at the village of Sunbury about 30 miles south of Savannah rather than at the port itself. Campbell decided that he did not need to wait for the reinforcements from Florida to attack the rebels. The main British force came ashore on December 27 and marched eastward toward Savannah.

Meanwhile Howe and the Americans, aware of the British maneuver, arrived in Savannah from Sunbury to find defenses in such poor condition that they were of

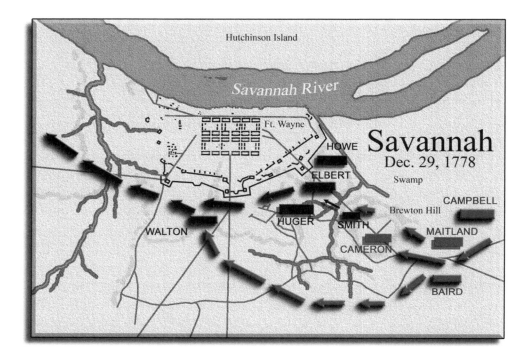

little use in protecting the town. Knowing he was badly outnumbered, Howe still decided to make a stand. He concentrated his army on the road he thought was the most likely avenue of approach. About a half-mile outside Savannah, Howe had his troops dig trenches to block the road and to tie in with what he thought were impassable swamps on each flank.

On December 29, with clear skies and unseasonably warm weather in the low 60s, Campbell approached the American defenses. He stopped several hundred yards short of the rebel positions and arrayed his infantry and artillery on line. He did not immediately attack, however, but rather took advantage of additional intelligence provided by an African American slave. The black man told the British commander about a path through the swamp that would take them behind the American right wing.

Campbell dispatched several hundred soldiers into the swamp about the same time, around 3:00 p.m., that Howe opened artillery fire on the main British line. The British held their fire until the force in the swamp broke out and attacked the American rear. Only then did Campbell begin his cannon barrage. With enemy infantry to their rear and British artillery pounding their front, the American lines collapsed. A disorganized retreat quickly turned into a rout with Americans leaving wounded soldiers and artillery pieces behind.

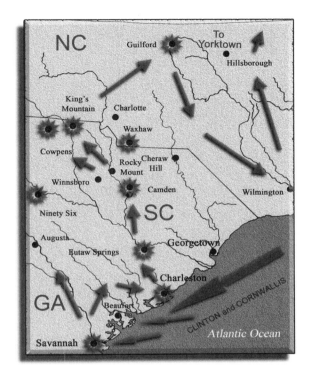

Only the several hundred Redcoats who approached through the swamp and the hundred or so rebels who initially opposed them in the rear actually participated directly in the fight. A total of eighty-three Americans either died in the brief battle or drowned fleeing across the swamp in its aftermath. Another 483, including thirty-eight officers, became prisoners. The British also captured forty-eight cannons, twenty-three mortars, and fourteen naval and river vessels of various sizes. British casualties totaled only three dead and ten wounded.

Howe was among those who escaped. He eventually reorganized his surviving army and retreated across the river to join the American force at Charleston, South Carolina.

The British rewarded Campbell with promotion to full colonel and the governorship of Jamaica. His organization of a Jamaican black militia proved so successful that it deterred any French efforts to capture the Caribbean island.

For his part in the battle, Howe later faced a court of inquiry questioning why he had stood against a much larger force rather than retreating with his army intact. He was also questioned about why he had not opposed the British landing rather than taking up positions along their likely avenue of approach, which then allowed his rear to be so easily compromised. In the end, Howe was cleared of any malfeasance but never again held a field command.

The British occupation of Savannah gave the Redcoats control of nearly all of Georgia and removed that state's agricultural production from support of the Revolution. Except for the allied efforts to recapture Savannah in late 1779, the town and the state remained securely British for the remainder of the conflict. When the British captured Charleston (47) in May 1780 and won the Battle of Camden (65) the following August, the focus of war switched to South Carolina and then on to operations that eventually led to Yorktown (2).

The First Battle of Savannah was important because it allowed the British to control a great deal of the South and reinforced their belief that they could end the Rebellion by focusing on that area. The war's final outcome, however, calls for the battle to be ranked in the bottom quarter of this list.

81

JAMES GRANT

British General

1720–1806

James Grant proved to be one of the most capable military planners among the British senior officers in the Revolutionary War. His strategies as the primary tactician for the New York campaign and subsequent battles in Pennsylvania and New Jersey led to the series of British victories in the Northern theater. On the other hand, he also designed the defense policies at Trenton (8) and Princeton where he was the overall commander of the region when George Washington (1) made his successful attacks. If the British had followed his tyrannical scorched-earth ideas, the war might very well have ended differently.

Born in 1720 at his family's estate of Ballindalloch in Banffshire in northeastern Scotland, Grant studied law before purchasing a commission in the Royal Scots on October 24, 1744. Less than a year later he saw his first combat at the Battle of Fontenoy in the southern Netherlands during the War of Austrian Succession. In February 1757, he accompanied the 77th Highlanders to North America as a major to fight in the French and Indian War.

In 1758, Grant joined the expedition to capture Fort Duquesne, Pennsylvania. The French and Indians ambushed the British-American column, leaving almost half of them killed, wounded, or captured. Among the prisoners was Grant, who blamed much of the debacle on the lack of discipline and poor fighting abilities of the Americans.

During the ill-fated expedition it is likely that Grant met George Washington and many of the future American rebel leaders. His letters home did not mention Washington per se, but he did write about his unrelentingly low opinion of the American militiamen as soldiers. By the time he left for further duty in the West Indies, including combat against the Spanish in Cuba, Grant had become extremely anti-American.

The end of the French and Indian War left the British in control of Florida, and when they divided it into two colonies, Grant became the governor of East Florida. He remained in that position from 1764 to 1771, administering affairs from his capital in St. Augustine. One of the first to believe that the future of the region lay in a plantation economy supported by African slaves, Grant quickly had the colony producing exports of cotton, indigo, timber, and cochineal—this latter product being the primary ingredient of the red dye used to color the distinctive British uniform jackets.

As colonial governor Grant invested much of his own money and accrued a small fortune by the time he sailed home in 1771. Reportedly he returned so that he could

recover from a "bilious fever," but it may have been that he was simply exhausted from the excesses of food, drink, and female companionship he enjoyed almost nightly.

In 1773, Grant's fellow Scots elected him to Parliament where he spoke out against the Americans, calling for military action to keep them in line. He made clear his continued distain for the colonial militias on February 2, 1775, when he stated that "the Americans could not fight" and that he could "march from one end of the continent to the other with five thousand men."

Six months later Grant returned to active service as a colonel with orders for North America. Upon his arrival in Boston, he moved into the confiscated home of John Hancock. He advised General Thomas Gage, to no avail, to abandon Boston and move the army to New York where they would have more room to maneuver against the rebels. Grant advanced to brigadier general in command of the 55th Regiment of Foot in December 1775. When the Americans forced the British to evacuate Boston in March 1776, Grant advocated burning the town as well as ports along their route to Canada—a policy he supported for the remainder of his tenure in North America.

William Howe (15), who had replaced Gage, did not follow the advice of his subordinate but did look to him for operational planning in upcoming campaigns. When the British left Canada for New York, they followed Grant's battle plans that yielded victories at Long Island (32) and White Plains (77). Grant led his regiment, contributing to the outcome.

Now a major general, Grant took command of the wide-spread British and Hessian (37) outposts in New Jersey during the winter of 1776–1777. His most controversial and disastrous battles took place during this time when the Americans launched surprise attacks and achieved victories at Trenton and Princeton. Grant's distracters blamed the defeats on the general's contempt for his opponents and his assumption that the Americans could not mount a winter offensive. Grant claimed he had intelligence about the offensive and warned the Hessian commander at Trenton about the attack. The truth of what happened died with the Hessian commander who took no preparatory measures to defend himself and his soldiers.

Despite the debacles in New Jersey, Grant's superiors maintained confidence in him, and he again prepared the British plans for the Battle of Brandywine Creek (72) in September 1777 and fought well in the Battle of Germantown (48) the following October. However, at the Battle of Barren's Hill near Philadelphia on May 20, 1778, Grant allowed Marquis de Lafayette (46) and his army to escape once more, earning him additional criticism.

Never censured for his actions at Barren's Hill, Grant was nevertheless transferred to the West Indies (45). He performed well in the Caribbean, capturing the French island of St. Lucia on December 12, 1778. On August 1, 1779, Grant returned home.

Over the next decades, Grant served additional terms in Parliament while advancing in military rank to full general in command of forces in Scotland. Though corpulent from his love of food, he managed to command troops in the field. He finally resigned from the army in 1805 and, despite his decadent lifestyle, lived to the age of eighty-six before he died at his family estate on April 13, 1806.

If the British had followed Grant's recommendation of a merciless scorched-earth policy, they might very well have ended the Rebellion in its early years. They did not, and even Grant finally admitted about the Americans, "They may from compulsion become dutiful subjects for a time, but they will never be cordial and affectionate." He is most worthy of inclusion on this list for no other reason than his being the most superior British battle planner of the Rebellion.

82

NEWPORT, RHODE ISLAND

July 29–August 31, 1778

The joint American-French effort to capture Newport, Rhode Island, in the summer of 1778 failed miserably. More importantly it strained relations between the two countries, the United States and France, threatening their very alliance. The battle also exposed the lack of leadership ability and diplomatic skills of American General John Sullivan (71) as he commanded troops and dealt with French commander Charles d'Estaing (92).

During the final month of his successful campaign to capture New York in December 1776, British commander General William Howe (15) dispatched General Henry Clinton (17) and 6,000 troops to occupy the town and naval facilities at Newport, Rhode Island. Over the next eighteen months, the British held Newport uncontested as their strength dwindled to 3,000 men under the command of General Robert Pigot.

With the entry of France into the war on the side of the Americans in early 1778, General George Washington (1) initiated operations with his new ally. In July, he dispatched General Sullivan and 1,000 troops to Rhode Island where that state's militia expanded his army to 10,000 men. Washington, not entirely confident in Sullivan's abilities, dispatched Generals Nathanael Greene (4) and Marquis de Lafayette (46) to assist in the operation.

Meanwhile, the French fleet under d'Estaing had arrived off the Virginia coast, sailed north to New York—where they discovered the British fleet taking advantage of the protected harbor and its shallow reefs—and then sailed to Rhode Island to join Sullivan against Newport. While Sullivan besieged the British garrison from the land approach, d'Estaing and his fleet of warships and infantry transports took up positions outside the Newport harbor.

General Pigot prepared his defenses by digging trenches to the northwest of Newport and by moving livestock and other foodstuffs within his lines. He also leveled houses, orchards, and other barriers to his fields of fire in front of his positions. The British navy came to their support with eight vessels commanded by Admiral Richard Howe (90), brother of William Howe.

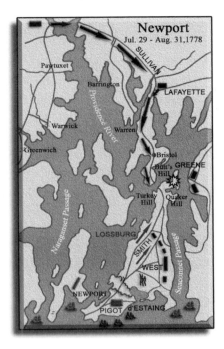

The Americans dug ditches parallel to those of the British while the two fleets maneuvered offshore for superior positioning. On August 11, before the French and British ships had actually engaged in combat, a violent storm swept the sea, damaging both fleets. Howe sailed for New York to make repairs while d'Estaing limped to Boston to refit his ships.

American troops on the mainland were cold and wet from the storm, but their commander was angry, and his ire inflamed his compatriots. Sullivan dispatched a letter that claimed that d'Estaing had deserted the operation, declaring that the actions "stain the honor of France, are contrary to the interests of His Most Christian Majesty, are most pernicious to the prosperity to the United States, and an outrageous offense upon the alliance between the two nations."

Sullivan spoke out so harshly against d'Estaing that he and the young French-born General Lafayette almost dueled. Instead, Sullivan dispatched Lafayette to Boston in an attempt to convince d'Estaing to return to Rhode Island. Lafayette found the citizens of Boston about as angry at the French as those in Rhode Island. Stories reached him that American and French sailors were rioting against each other in ports from Boston to the Carolinas. Lafayette wrote to Washington on August 25, stating, "I am more upon a warlike footing in the American lines than when I came near the British lines at Newport."

The Americans continued their siege of Newport for several more weeks. Sullivan was already plagued by massive desertions from the Rhode Island militia units and aware that d'Estaing would not be returning. He withdrew his remaining army under the cover of darkness on the night of August 28. When dawn of August 29 revealed that Sullivan had pulled back from his defenses, Pigot came out of Newport to pursue the withdrawing Americans. The rebels, often under heavy artillery fire, managed to defend their route of retreat until the majority of the army was safely inside defenses at Bristol and Tiverton. American losses in the campaign totaled 30 dead, 137 wounded, and 44 missing or captured. British causalities numbered 38 killed, 210 wounded, and 12 missing or captured.

While the Americans were retreating from Newport, d'Estaing departed Boston harbor and sailed for Martinique. Although d'Estaing left many enemies behind in North America, his sailing to the West Indies (45) forced the British to transfer 5,000 soldiers to the Caribbean—thus effectively removing those troops from the war against the rebels.

Washington, always the proficient diplomat, moved immediately to bind the wounds between France and the United States. He ordered his own officers to cease their criticisms of this most-needed ally and wrote to Lafayette to thank him for his efforts during the campaign. In another missive, Washington expressed to d'Estaing his continued confidence.

Fortunately for the Americans and their Revolution, the French did not waver in their commitment. As the war shifted to the Southern states, the French navy and army significantly contributed directly to the combat while arms and supplies from France supported the Continental Army.

Newport itself was not so important strategically as to be overly influential in the Revolution. However, if France had withdrawn its support of the Americans after the Newport incident, the hopes of the Rebellion might very well have gone with them. French support was critical to the Americans for their future success in maintaining their independence and ultimately winning the war.

Because these rankings are based on what did occur rather that what might have happened, the Battle of Newport ranks in the lower quarter. The battle's outcome and complications with France did display once again Washington's diplomatic skills, validating his ranking as the war's most influential figure.

83

THOMAS SUMTER

American General and Partisan

1734–1832

A rebel among rebels, Thomas Sumter fought by his own rules, using bold and imaginative actions on the battlefield that sometimes were eclipsed by his poor tactical decisions and his insubordination. Despite his shortfalls, Sumter and his partisans—along with those of Francis "Swamp Fox" Marion (60)—stood virtually alone against the British in South Carolina after the fall of Charleston (47) in May 1780. Their presence and their harassment of the British outposts laid the ground-work for the eventual victories by General Nathanael Greene (4) that led to the Yorktown (2) surrender of the British.

Born on August 14, 1734, near Charlottesville, Virginia, Sumter received little formal schooling, but he read and studied his way to an adequate self-education. As a youth he first fought against the Cherokees as a militia sergeant and then later lived among the Indians on the western frontier. In 1762 he accompanied a Cherokee delegation to England as an interpreter in peace negotiations. Upon his return he was arrested for indebtedness, something he had problems with for most of his life.

In 1765 Sumter escaped debtors' jail and made his way to Eutaw Springs, South Carolina, where he established a crossroads store and developed a plantation worked by slaves. The following year he became a local justice of the peace and over the next decade served in the South Carolina Provincial Congresses. At the outbreak of the American Revolution, he accepted a captain's commission in a mounted ranger unit. By March 1776, he had advanced to lieutenant colonel in command of an infantry regiment that fought against both the Cherokees and the South Carolina Loyalists (34).

In the summer of 1778, Sumter transferred from his state's militia to the Continental Army (7) as a full colonel, but he became so disenchanted with following orders of regular officers that he resigned his commission on September 19. Loyalists burned Sumter's plantation when the British successfully occupied Charleston and pushed inland in May 1780. Sumter fled to Charlotte, North Carolina, and recruited partisans to renew the fight in his home state. Over the next year, he led raids against his former Loyalist neighbors and British outposts, earning the nickname "Carolina Gamecock."

On October 6, 1780, the governor of South Carolina appointed Sumter the senior brigadier general in the state's militia. Sumter ordered fellow partisan Francis Marion to join him in operations against the British, but the Swamp Fox avoided joint actions as much as possible because he believed Sumter often neglected to properly plan for battles and attacked even when the odds were against him. Since

partisans did their best work by avoiding large-scale battles and thrived on "hit and run" tactics, Marion was cautious. Sumter, unlike Marion, never shied from a fight or broke contact until absolutely necessary. Regardless of their differences, Sumter and Marion provided the only viable rebel resistance to the British and Loyalists in the South for the six months between the fall of Charleston and the arrival of Greene from the North.

When Greene planned to push the British out of the interior of South Carolina and Georgia, he found Sumter a reluctant subordinate. The Carolina Gamecock did not want to join the Continental Army in conventional operations, preferring to continue his own guerilla tactics. When Sumter finally agreed to join Greene, his maneuver blunders contributed to the American defeat at Ninety-Six (91) in the early summer of 1781.

Sumter's superiors often ignored his arrogant independence because of the service he had rendered during the months after the occupation of Charleston. The enemy took a very different view of him. Sumter became one of the American officers most hated by the British and particularly by the Loyalists. Usually out of contact with higher authorities, Sumter recruited his men with promises that their pay would be "all that they could plunder from the Loyalists." What became known as "Sumter's Law" meant a partisan could kill a Loyalist soldier and then freely pilfer his home or other possessions. In many ways Sumter and his partisans fought a civil war against the local Loyalists of his own state rather than a revolution for national independence and liberty.

When the American civil government of South Carolina finally returned to the state on August 2, 1781, one of the first acts by Governor John Rutledge was to issue a proclamation banning "Sumter's Law." With the war in the South mostly won, with promises of plunder eliminated from his efforts to recruit, and with wounds and fatigue from extended campaigning, Sumter retired to North Carolina where he officially resigned his commission on January 8, 1782.

Sumter returned to South Carolina after the war to raise cotton, tobacco, silk worms, and race horses on land grants totaling 150,000 acres. With assistance of old friends, he won court cases brought against him by Loyalists seeking damages for losses to "Sumter's Law." The Carolina Gamecock served in the South Carolina legislature from 1785 until 1801 when he was elected to the U.S. Congress. He remained in the Congress and then the Senate until his retirement in 1810.

Sumter fought for two great causes after the war. His first battle was financial. He spent a great deal of time fending off creditors from failed business dealings. Finally, in 1827 the South Carolina legislature granted him a lifetime moratorium from his note holders. Sumter's other fight was for "States' Rights"—a factor that contributed to the eventual civil war between North and South that began at a fort named for Sumter in Charleston Harbor. He died on June 1, 1832, at age 97 at his family estate of South Mont and is buried on the plantation's grounds. Before his death, he was the last surviving general officer of the American Revolution.

Sumter was difficult to get along with both on the battlefield and in business, making him a much better partisan than a regular army leader. His tactics and recruiting practices were questionable; his results were not. Sumter and Marion set the stage for Greene's successful operations that led to forcing the British to retreat to their ultimate surrender at Yorktown.

The more famous Marion, who was more successful on the battlefield without allowing general plunder, ranks above the Carolina Gamecock, but both are worthy of places on this list. All in all, Sumter was not really a "nice" or "good" man, but these characteristics are not requirements in time of war—particularly in the ranks of partisan leaders.

84

CANADA INVASION

August 1775–October 1776

In their first major offensive of the Revolution, the Americans marched northward in two columns with the clear objective of making eastern Canada their "fourteenth state." The new freedom fighters, however, were indecisive and unprepared for their campaign. They delayed; they miscalculated. In the end, they arrived and found the French Canadians lacking the desire to revolt against the English. They returned to their home colonies, and the British preserved its claim on Canada. The foray north was not without its consequences, for it opened the war for the British invasion of the rebel colonies down the Hudson River that led to the Battle of Saratoga (3).

The capture of Fort Ticonderoga (52) in May 1775 gained the rebels much-needed artillery and had presented the opportunity for an invasion of Canada. Most of the British soldiers stationed in eastern Canada had been dispatched to Boston before the city was surrounded by the rebels, leaving few to assist General Guy Carleton (49) in defending the major cities of Montreal and Quebec. The Americans believed that the 80,000 French Canadians, who had lived under the British flag only since the end of the French and Indian War a dozen years earlier, would readily join their revolt. In addition to adding a fourteenth state, the capture of Canada would deprive the British of a safe haven from which to attack the rebellious colonists.

Many Americans favored an immediate invasion, but others opposed any offensive actions, hoping still that the British would redress their grievances rather than force the issues. The Continental Congress (10) resolved on June 1, 1775, that no invasion plans should be undertaken. However, the bloody Battle of Bunker Hill (23) on June 17 dimmed hopes for a peaceful solution and, on June 27, Congress authorized an offensive against Montreal and Quebec, an act that further eroded chances of a diplomatic solution.

Congress placed Philip Schuyler in charge of the Montreal column, but the general proved to be a better logistician than a tactician. Instead of immediately marching his 2,000 men from New York and Connecticut to reach Canada before the British had time to prepare, Schuyler spent months gathering supplies and preparing his supply trains. By the time he was ready to begin his attack in September, he became disabled with rheumatic gout and turned over his command to General Richard Montgomery.

Montgomery's column captured forts Saint Johns and Chambly north of Lake Champlain in October and early November. An initial attack by a small force led by Ethan Allen against Montreal in September failed, but Montgomery took the city with little further bloodshed on November 13.

The British resistance, particularly at Saint Johns, provided Carleton time to assemble the widespread British regulars into the defense of Quebec and to seek additional man power. Carleton was concerned to find French-Canadians had no interest in joining his fight against the American rebels, but he was relieved to discover that neither did they have the desire to join the Americans. When urged by his superiors in Boston and London to enlist Native Americans (99) in the fight, Carleton refused, stating his contempt for the undisciplined Indians whom he believed were prone to run from a fight or to commit atrocities.

Carleton escaped Montreal with 300 troops before its occupation and moved down river to reinforce the defenders of Quebec. Meanwhile the second American column under the command of Benedict Arnold (85) had conducted a grueling march through 350 miles of Maine wilderness to the St. Lawrence River. Plagued by food shortages, illnesses, and desertions, Arnold's force had dwindled to only 600 soldiers by the time they reached the Plains of Abraham outside the Quebec fortress on November 13. With neither cannons nor siege gear, Arnold recognized that an attack against the Quebec walls would be fruitless. After unsuccessful efforts to negotiate a British surrender, he withdrew his army on November 19 in fear of a counterattack. Carleton arrived on December 2 to take over command of Quebec.

Arnold established a camp 20 miles up the St. Lawrence to await reinforcements. Montgomery arrived on December 2 with 300 men and much-needed blankets and food captured at Montreal. Two days later the Americans moved back to the Plains of Abraham outside the Quebec defenses. With fewer than a thousand men, the combined forces of Arnold and Montgomery faced nearly twice that many under Carleton. Furthermore, the British had the advantage of walls and blockhouses to protect them.

Montgomery, as the senior commander, knew that a direct attack would be foolish. To enhance his dim chances, he decided to attack at night under the cover of bad weather. Offering little chance of success, the plan was the only offensive option available to the Americans, who were increasingly weakened by disease and desertions.

A snowstorm early on the morning of December 31 finally provided the desired conditions, and at 4:00 a.m. the Americans moved forward with a feint against the city's wall that faced the Plains of Abraham. Their major attack by two columns was directed against what they thought would be the weakly defended lower town. Carleton had anticipated both the ruse and the main attack, and had maneuvered his larger force along his defenses accordingly. By 9:00 a.m. the battle was over. Nearly half the Americans were prisoners while another sixty, including Montgomery, lay dead or wounded. British casualties totaled a mere five dead and thirteen wounded.

The remainder of the American army withdrew but remained near Quebec. General John Thomas of Massachusetts joined them in March to assume command. Thomas found the force further weakened by smallpox and the harsh Canadian winter. When he learned about the arrival of British reinforcements in Quebec, he ordered a withdrawal toward Montreal. Along the way, on June 2, Thomas died of smallpox and General John Sullivan (71) assumed command. A week later the Americans turned to unsuccessfully counterattack the pursuing British force. Sullivan then ordered his surviving army to march south toward Lake Champlain. By July there were no longer any rebel Americans—at least living ones—on Canadian soil.

Carleton pursued the retreating rebels until Arnold delayed him at the Battle of Valcour Island (28) on October 11–13. Arnold then fell back to Fort Ticonderoga while Carlton stopped to reorganize and await reinforcements. It would be a year

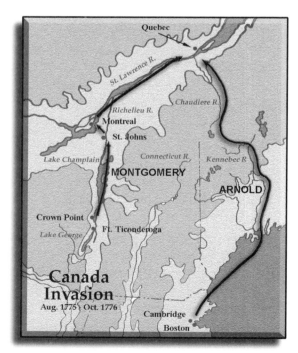

before the British under General John Burgoyne (33) would attempt to split the colonies into two sections along the Hudson River only to be defeated at Saratoga.

Although later criticized as a waste of men and resources, particularly for the loss of the excellent General Montgomery, the invasion of Canada was a bold stoke that only narrowly failed. If the Americans had not delayed the invasion because of politics and had not chosen the methodically slow Schuyler as a leader, the invasion might very well have succeeded before Carleton could rally his meager force and defend Quebec—a feat for which he earned his knighthood.

The American invasion of Canada was a critical milestone in the Revolution. The colonists had yet to proclaim their independence. Once Montgomery and Arnold crossed the Canadian border, there was no longer any chance of peaceful resolution between the colonists and Great Britain. When the invasion failed, Washington initiated planning for the occupation of Dorchester Heights to force the British out of Boston. It was plain to all on both sides that the Revolution could now only be settled by military means.

Like any other pursuit, the invasion of Canada might have proven a pivotal action. However, the venture failed, and, as a result, it becomes a footnote rather than a major subject of the war. For that reason it ranks in the lower rather than the upper quarter of battles.

85

BENEDICT ARNOLD

American General and Traitor

1741–1801

Even today the words *Benedict Arnold* and *traitor* are synonymous. However, in the early years of the American Revolution, Benedict Arnold was a respected officer in the Continental Army (7) who advanced in rank to major general as a result of his performance during the Canada Invasion (84) and the battles of Valcour Island (28) and Saratoga (3). By war's end he became the most disdained man in America because of his attempt to hand over the key Hudson River defenses at West Point (30) to the British and his leadership of enemy forces against his former friends and soldiers.

Born on January 14, 1741, in Norwich, Connecticut, into a prominent family that included a grandfather who had been governor of Rhode Island, Arnold quit school at age fourteen when his father suffered financial setbacks. Two years later Arnold left home to serve with the colonial militia in the French and Indian War, but he quickly tired of military service and deserted. In March 1760 he again enlisted only to desert once more.

After returning home Arnold studied under a local druggist until 1762 when he moved to New Haven, Connecticut, to establish a drug and book store. Arnold found being a merchant much more to his liking than soldiering and soon expanded into shipping goods to Canada and the West Indies. By the end of 1774, his community considered him such an outstanding citizen that they elected him captain of the local militia company.

Hearing about the battles of Lexington and Concord (43) in April 1775, Arnold joined the revolutionaries at the Boston Siege (50). There he proposed an expedition against the British fort at Ticonderoga (52). En route he joined the command of Ethan Allen, and the combined force captured the fort's cannons. They continued the march up Lake Champlain to capture Saint Johns, Quebec. Arnold returned to Connecticut and then convinced George Washington (1) to provide 1,100 men for an expedition against Quebec City. He set off in September 1775 on a grueling march that led to the death of 200 of his soldiers and the desertion of 200 more.

By the time Arnold's column reached Quebec on November 8, they were too weak to attack the fortifications. On December 2, a second force of 300 led by General Richard Montgomery brought reinforcements to join Arnold. On December 31 the combined armies attacked. In the subsequent battle, Montgomery was killed and Arnold suffered a serious wound.

The Americans fell back to besiege Quebec as Arnold recovered from his injury and accepted promotion to brigadier general from the Continental Congress. When British reinforcements closed on Quebec City in the spring of 1776, Arnold retreated southward with the British in pursuit. On Lake Champlain, Arnold seized and built boats until he had a sufficient flotilla to defeat the British at Valcour Island (28) in mid-October and to prevent them from occupying New York City.

Arnold spent the winter of 1776–1777 at home and threatened to resign his commission when Congress selected five officers junior to him for promotion to major general. Only a visit by Washington convinced Arnold to remain in uniform. In April he rode to Danbury, Connecticut, to take command of local militias and successfully resisted a British attack. Congress rewarded Arnold with promotion to major general, but he again threatened to resign because his seniority was not back-dated. Once more, Washington intervened to placate Arnold.

In July Arnold marched northward to block Barry St. Leger's (64) invasion column from Canada at Fort Stanwix. He then hurried to Saratoga to join Horatio Gates (31) in the battle against John Burgoyne (33). Arnold commanded the rebel left flank at Freeman's Farm on September 19 and was in the thick of the fight at Bemis Heights on October 7 when he was again wounded. Congress rewarded Arnold by restoring his seniority in rank and placing him in command of Philadelphia in June 1778 after the British evacuated the city.

Arnold enjoyed his status as commander of the city, hosting elaborate parties and participating in the Philadelphia social scene to a level beyond what his military salary could support. Soon in debt and involved in what some thought were disreputable business practices, Arnold's enemies in Congress investigated his financial accounts at the urging of a former officer he had relieved from command in the Ticonderoga campaign. Court-martial proceedings were initiated against Arnold on June 1, 1779. Arnold, whose left leg had never properly mended from his wound at Saratoga, wrote to Washington, "Having become a cripple in the service to my country, I little expected to meet such ungrateful returns."

Crippled or not, the social Arnold had managed to marry nineteen-year-old Margaret (Peggy) Shippen, the daughter of a prominent Loyalist (34) sympathizer and the previous lady friend of British Major John Andre. Whether influenced by his

wife, the pending court-martial ordeal, or his own character flaws, Arnold initiated secret correspondence with General Henry Clinton (17), the British commander in New York, revealing information about American activities and plans in exchange for money. Arnold ceased this treasonous letter-writing after only a few months when he was led to believe that the pending charges against him over his financial discrepancies were to be dropped.

When the court-martial was actually held in December, the major charges were indeed nullified, but he was mildly reprimanded for minor financial accounting malfeasance. Arnold, angered by the rebuke, renewed his contacts with Clinton. Over the next months Arnold provided the British details on American defenses and intentions. After he transferred to assume command of the important defenses of the Hudson Valley at West Point in June 1780, he dispatched a message in September offering to turn the fort over to the British. An American patrol captured his courier, who was none other than his wife's former suitor Major Andre, with papers in Arnold's handwriting detailing the betrayal. The Americans hung Andre, caught in civilian clothes, as a spy. Arnold escaped West Point aboard a British warship on the Hudson River only minutes before officials arrived to arrest him.

In New York the British rewarded Arnold with a commission as a brigadier general. Two months later he commanded Loyalists in operations in Virginia and then, in September 1781, in his old home state of Connecticut. At New London he burned the town of his former neighbors and friends, inflaming the rebel Americans' hatred of the former hero. The following December, Arnold sailed for England where he retired on a modest pension. His later attempts to renew his old trade relationships with Canada and the West Indies failed. Peggy remained with him, but the American traitor had few friends on either side of the Atlantic Ocean. He died in London on June 14, 1801, and is buried in St. Mary's Church.

From his early days as a teenager, Arnold displayed his character. He deserted the army not once, but twice. He lived beyond his means. He cavorted with the enemy. He mishandled government funds. He manipulated Washington. Then he simply sold out to the highest bidder, betraying his fellow soldiers and country. In every instance of betrayal, Arnold asked for and received cash rewards from the British.

If Arnold had remained loyal to the new American republic, he would have secured a ranking in the upper half of this list if for nothing else than his performances at Valcour Island and Saratoga. If this were a list of American traitors, he would rank at the top. But it is not, so he stands, in odious memory, near the end, only because he is the country's most infamous traitor.

86

FORT WASHINGTON, NEW YORK

November 16, 1776

The British victory at Fort Washington on November 16, 1776, left New York City and the lower Hudson River in the hands of the Redcoats. This achievement by the Crown weakened the already sagging morale of the Americans when the rebels witnessed the capture of their veteran infantrymen, muskets, munitions, and other supplies. The battle also once again proved, at least temporarily, the superiority of the generalship of William Howe (15) over George Washington (1) and Nathanael Greene (4).

After Howe defeated the Americans at White Plains (77) on October 28, 1776, he decided to solidify his hold on Manhattan Island and New York City rather than pursue the retreating rebel commander and his main army. He turned his attention to the last significant rebel threats against New York City at Fort Washington—located at present Washington Heights in Fort Tyron Park at the far northwestern end of Manhattan Island along the Hudson River—and Fort Lee, immediately across the river in New Jersey, where rebels guarded against boat traffic moving northward. Greene was in overall command of both forts with Colonel Robert Magaw, who was in charge of Fort Washington.

Built the previous July, Fort Washington contained a pentagon earthwork on a 230-foot-high hill that ran for a mile along the river. High cliffs protected the fort on the river side, but the landward approach had no ditches or other defenses. The inside of the fort lacked barracks or bomb shelters and had no internal drinking water source. Outer defenses along the hillside amounted to little more than shallow trenches.

When Washington learned that the British were doubling back to attack the Hudson forts, he wrote Greene, "I am inclined to think it will not be prudent to hazard men and stores, but as you are on the spot, I leave it to you to give such orders as to evacuating Mount Washington as you judge best."

Greene responded that he thought that the forts were valuable in restricting traffic on the Hudson River and for maintaining communications between the Southern and Northern states. Washington's second in command, Charles Lee (79), expressed concerns and recommended evacuation, but the commanding general followed the military axiom of allowing "the man on the ground" to make the decision and left it to Greene to determine the course of action. Greene decided to stay and fight.

British General Howe apparently agreed with Greene's analysis of Fort Washington's importance by planning to capture it. His decision was reinforced with the defection of a member of Colonel Magaw's staff who delivered the complete plans of the fort's defenses to the British.

Howe moved Hessian (37) troops under the command of General Wilhelm von Knyphausen and British regulars led by General Charles Cornwallis (22) toward Fort Washington on November 4. By mid-month more than 8,000 Hessian and British soldiers covered the land approaches to the fort and its 2,900 defenders. On November 15, a British officer approached the fortification under a flag of truce and demanded the American's surrender. Magaw refused.

The next morning, in a light snowstorm blown by 20–30 knot winds, the British attacked in three columns from the north, east, and south. Over the next hours the Americans fell back from their trenches into Fort Washington itself as British artillery shelled its dirt berms. Hessian Colonel Johann G. Rall, who would play an important role in the battle for Trenton (8) only six weeks later, was among the first to reach the fort's walls. In midafternoon the British again demanded surrender, and Magaw ageed, fearing the annihilation of his command from the artillery and an infantry assault.

The battle had been brief but bloody. Nearly 100 Americans were wounded, and 53 lay dead. Among the rebel wounded was Margaret Cochran Corbin, a Pennsylvania woman in her midtwenties who had joined her cannon-gunner husband at the fort as a camp follower. When her spouse was hit in the battle, she took his place on his gun until she, too, was seriously wounded.

Magaw and his soldiers fought well, but their surrender was a disaster for the rebels' cause, sending 2,818 Americans into captivity. While the 100 or so American officers were paroled back to their communities, the British confined the enlisted personnel on prison ships in New York City harbor under extremely austere conditions. Many did not survive the war. Not only did the Americans lose so many veteran soldiers, but also Magaw surrendered 146 cannons and 2,800 muskets along with stores of shot, shell, gunpowder, tents, food, and other supplies—all of which were in short supply in the Continental Army (7). In their state of devastation, the Americans could only abandon Fort Lee. The British had taken control of both forts at the cost of 78 dead and 374 wounded.

Back in England those who opposed Howe once again criticized him first for not pursuing the rebels and then for accepting the surrender of Fort Washington. They believed that if the British had overrun the fort and killed most of its defenders, the surviving rebels in the colonies would have capitulated and ended the Rebellion.

Whatever his reasons, Howe allowed Washington and the remainder of his army to escape, which, in effect, permitted the American commander to represent a viable United States. Howe enjoyed the comforts of New York City during the long winter

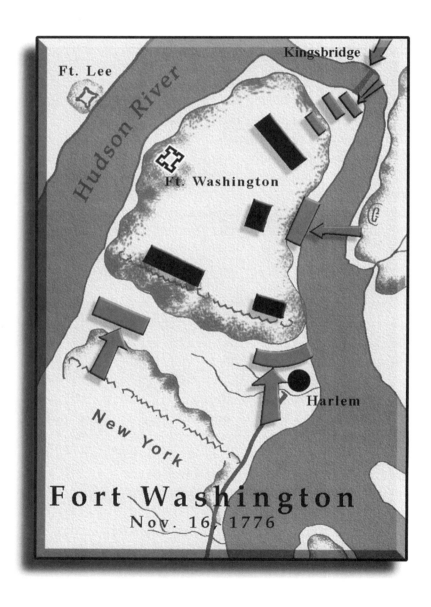

months before beginning his campaign against Philadelphia the next spring. While both Greene and Washington had failed to make good decisions at Fort Washington, ultimately they would become the most influential leaders of the conflict. Washington used the winter to recruit new soldiers and to successfully attack British and Hessian outposts at Trenton and Princeton, New Jersey, that restored American morale and revitalized the Revolution. Greene would go on to lead the successful defense of the Southern colonies that led to the final victory at Yorktown (2).

The fall of Fort Washington and the abandonment of Fort Lee left all of Manhattan, Long Island, and the lower Hudson River Valley under British control. It opened the way for the offensive from Canada the next year that attempted to divide the rebel Southern colonies from those in New England. If the Battle of Saratoga (3) had not stopped that effort and Washington had not gained his winter victories in New Jersey, the future of the Rebellion would have been in doubt. But the rebels did win at Saratoga, and Washington's winter victories reinvigorated the morale of the rebels. For these reasons Fort Washington ranks near the end of this list and below the more influential battles of Long Island (32) and White Plains that led to the British occupation of New York City.

87

THOMAS JEFFERSON

American Statesman

1743–1826

Thomas Jefferson promoted separation from Great Britain from the first clash between the Empire and its North American colonies. As an early Revolutionary leader and primary author of the *Declaration of Independence* (14), he provided the contents of the most famous document in American political history. Jefferson's subsequent service as wartime governor of Virginia was not as distinguished, but his later performance as secretary of state and president of the United States elevated him to the ranks of the most famous and influential Americans.

Born on April 13, 1743, at Shadwell, Virginia, into a family dating back to the founding of the colony, Jefferson attended William and Mary for two years before beginning his study of law. Although Jefferson's family was affluent, they were not members of the coastal planter elites or of the titled British officials and land owners. Jefferson began construction on Monticello near Charlottesville on land inherited from his father a year after entering the Virginia House of Burgesses in 1769. Jefferson, never an effective speaker or debater, honed his skills as a writer to express his opinions, and by the time he joined the House of Burgesses, he had begun to focus his writings on opposing British rule and aristocracy of any kind. In 1774 he published a pamphlet titled *A Summary View of the Rights of British America* in which he claimed that colonial allegiance to the Crown was voluntary and that "the God who gave us life, gave us liberty at the same time."

The pamphlet positioned Jefferson as one of the best-known and most thoughtful supporters of independence. It also brought him to the Second Continental Congress (10) in June 1775 as a representative of Virginia. Jefferson drafted several papers in his early months in Congress, but his fellow representatives, many of whom still hoped for a peaceful reconciliation with the Crown, rejected them as too "anti-British." By the end of 1775, Congress had concluded a peaceful settlement with the British was impossible. On June 11, Jefferson joined a committee to draft a declaration of independence.

Other distinguished Americans, including Benjamin Franklin (25) and John Adams (51), met with Jefferson on the committee, but they quickly acquiesced to the ideas and particularly the writing talents of the young Virginian. His fellow committee members and Congress made minor stylistic alterations to the final product, but it remained Jefferson's document. Jefferson later explained that "it was intended to be an expression of the American mind."

Although of military age, Jefferson had no desire, nor the talent, to defend his declaration on the battlefield. He recognized that he lacked direct leadership abilities and "had no stomach for physical combat." Instead of donning a uniform, Jefferson returned to Virginia in late 1776 to become a delegate to the General Assembly established by the newly declared state's constitution. As such he proposed bills that granted power based on ability rather than birth or wealth. He also supported measures assuring religious liberties.

In June 1779, the citizens of Virginia elected Jefferson to be their governor. He moved the vulnerable coastal capital at Williamsburg to a safer inland location at Richmond. He governed well except for his lack of attention to military matters that left the state's militia poorly prepared for the British attack against Richmond in the spring of 1781. Jefferson and the state government fled to Charlottesville on May 24. The British continued their pursuit, and Jefferson just barely evacuated his family from Monticello and avoided capture by a raid led by British Lieutenant Colonel Banastre Tarleton (44). During their retreat Jefferson fell from his horse and injured himself.

Virginia elected a new governor in June 1781 when political enemies accused Jefferson of personal cowardice in his retreat from Richmond and Monticello. While no evidence exists to prove this, Jefferson's prestige, especially in Virginia, suffered. At the close of the war, Jefferson—still not yet forty years old—retired to Monticello to rebuild his lands and fortune.

Jefferson's retirement did not last long. Virginia elected him to Congress in 1783 where he reformed the American monetary system and wrote what would become the Ordinance of 1787 that outlined the country's expansion westward. From 1784 until 1789, Jefferson served as an ambassador to Europe, where he negotiated treaties and agreements for the new nation. Upon his return to the United States, he became the first secretary of state under the administration of President George Washington (1). In this position Jefferson disagreed with some of his fellow cabinet members on many issues, yet his thoughts and ideas strongly influenced how the United States would govern itself and how it would conduct its business.

Jefferson resigned his position in 1793 to again retire to Monticello where he worked on his library and agricultural experiments. In 1796 he returned to politics

as the vice president to John Adams. Four years later he became the third president of the United States and the first president to be inaugurated in Washington, DC. In this office for two terms, he shaped the future of the United States.

Declining to run for a third term, Jefferson returned to Monticello where he stayed during the final seventeen years of his life, never again venturing more than a few miles from home. In 1815 he sold his books to the U.S. government—a collection that eventually formed the nucleus of the Library of Congress. In 1819 he established the University of Virginia.

Jefferson died at Monticello on July 4, 1826—the fiftieth anniversary of the *Declaration of Independence* and a few hours before the death of John Adams. He is buried on the grounds of Monticello under a marker that lists those things for which he wanted to be remembered—the *Declaration of Independence*, the Virginia statute for religious freedom, and the establishment of the University of Virginia.

The majestic words of Jefferson's *Declaration of Independence* inspired Americans as well as future revolutions around the world. It ranks as possibly the most famous document in history. It alone gains Jefferson a place on this list. His long career greatly influenced the future of the United States, but his direct impact on the American Revolution is mostly limited to the writing of the Declaration. For that reason he ranks near the end of this list, exceeded by the combat commanders, battles, and his fellow civilian leaders including Franklin and Adams.

88

STONY POINT, NEW YORK

July 16, 1779

The successful night attack by the Americans against the British fort at Stony Point on New York's Hudson River in the summer of 1779 had little strategic influence on the outcome of the Revolution, but it did provide a boost to sagging rebel morale. In combination with the Battle of Monmouth (59) fought a year earlier, the outcome at Stony Point encouraged the British to move their offensive operation into the Southern states. Furthermore, Stony Point solidified the reputation of Anthony Wayne (38) as one of the Continental Army's (7) most formidable commanders.

After wintering most of his army in New York City, British Commander Henry Clinton (17) took little action in the spring until pressured to do so by authorities in London. To secure his New York headquarters and to open the way for a possible attack on the rebel stronghold at West Point (30), a British expedition sailed northward on May 28, 1779. Four days later they occupied the abandoned rebel camp at Stony Point located on the western side of the Hudson, 35 miles north of New York City and 11 miles south of West Point. They then defeated a small garrison of rebels on the river's east bank at Verplanks Point.

Stony Point and Verplanks Point were important ferry crossings on the Hudson for moving men and supplies. George Washington (1) feared the British might use Stony Point as a staging area for an attack on the crucial fort at West Point that controlled the upper Hudson. In anticipation of this British attack northward, Washington moved the bulk of his army near West Point. When he determined the British had decided to halt at Stony Point to complete its defenses, the American commander decided to take the offensive.

In mid-June Washington gathered information on the British positions from military scouts and civilian spies. On June 28, Washington ordered General Wayne to attack Stony Point. Wayne, often called "Mad Anthony," is reputed to have responded, "Issue the orders, sir, and I will lay siege to Hell."

"Hell" might very well have been an apt description of Stony Point. Built on a 150-foot rise above the river and surrounded by water on three sides, the semi-enclosed fort stood on the highest ground surrounded by abatis containing seven batteries of artillery. An additional abatis and fortified outposts stood 200 yards west to provide early warning of an approaching enemy. Even the land route to this fort, covered by a marsh, was impassable when high tide pushed up the river. Lieutenant Colonel Henry Johnson stood in overall command of the British defenders, who numbered about 650.

Wayne, with his army of 1,350, knew that an ordinary frontal attack would fail, or at best prove extremely costly. Instead, he planned a night attack using a diversionary feint in the center with main advances from columns on the north and south. He gathered as much information as possible on the British defenses and then, to ensure that surprise was not compromised by an accidental gunshot, Wayne ordered his men into battle with muskets unloaded and bayonets fixed. To further maintain secrecy, Wayne cleared civilians from the line of march and sent them to the rear. He killed local dogs to prevent their barking and alerting British sentries.

Wayne's columns neared the fort undetected shortly after midnight on July 16. The center column loaded their muskets and fired, an action which drew British artillery fire as well as an assault column that charged from the defenses to meet the advance. Meanwhile the other two rebel columns charged past the outer defenses into the fort itself with lunging bayonets, slashing swords, and musket butts used as clubs. Wayne fell with a head wound early in the fight but revived to continue the assault. Some accounts credit the aggressiveness of the rebel attackers on their patriotism and "love of freedom." Others note that Wayne had promised cash bonuses of $100 to $500 for the first five soldiers to enter the British fort.

Whatever their motivation, Wayne's men performed extremely well. After a brutal fight, the surviving Redcoats laid down their arms. At this stage of the war victors usually gave no quarter, but the rebels exercised the discipline demanded by Wayne and did not harm their prisoners. A British officer, Commodore George Collier, later noted the American valor and honor in his journal, writing, "The rebels had made the attack with a bravery never before exhibited, and they showed at this moment a generosity and clemency which during the course of the rebellion had no parallel."

British losses included 63 dead, 70 wounded, and 472 captured. American casualties totaled 15 killed and 83 wounded. The captured British guns, powder, and other supplies went to West Point and Washington's always needy army.

Initial plans called for a subsequent assault against Verplanks Point across the river, but news that Clinton's main army was approaching forced the end of that plan and the evacuation of the captured Stony Point as well. After only two days, mostly spent destroying the British fortifications and removing captured material, Wayne evacuated Stony Point and rejoined Washington's main force. Clinton reoccupied

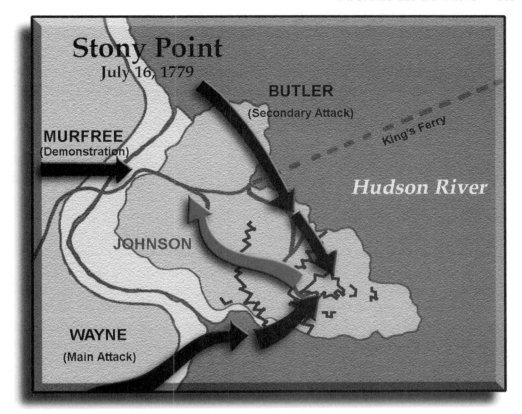

Stony Point the next day and rebuilt its defenses but later abandoned the fortifications as well. No longer willing to endure casualties received in the Northern theater, the British turned their efforts to the Southern states where they believed they would have a greater amount of support from the numerous native Loyalists (34).

Wayne's attack on Stony Point marked one of the war's best planned, prepared, and executed attacks. News of the battle's success swept across the remainder of the army as well as all thirteen states and greatly reinvigorated the ever-threatened morale of the rebels. Wayne received recognition from Washington, a medal from Congress, and praise as a hero from his fellow revolutionaries.

While good for the morale of the Americans and excellent for the career of Wayne, Stony Point had little other importance in the outcome of the Revolution. Clinton had already decided not to attack West Point and the British were preparing to move the primary war efforts to the South. These facts relegate it to near the end of these rankings.

89

NEWBURGH ADDRESSES

March 10 and 12, 1783

The Newburgh Addresses of March 10 and 12, 1783, outlined the many griev-ances the Continental Army (7) officers had at the end of the American Revolution. Their complaints about the failure of the Continental Congress (10) to reward their service and to secure their future were the initial steps of what could have led to a military insurrection against civilian rule of the United States. Once again George Washington (1) displayed his tremendous leadership in responding to the addresses and regaining the support and loyalty of the army.

After the surrender of Charles Cornwallis (22) at Yorktown (2) in October 1781, the bulk of the Continental Army encamped at Newburgh, New York, just north of West Point. As they awaited the signing of the Treaty of Paris (69) to officially end the war, many of the army's officers believed that the American government and civilian population did not sufficiently appreciate their long service and sacrifices. They also complained that they were due back pay and claims for food and cloth-ing allowances. The fact that Congress had offered no pensions or medical care also angered the officers.

Two groups within the Continental Army moved to force Congress to take action. The first of these, led by Generals Henry Knox (12) and Alexander McDougall, feared that Congress would ignore their grievances once peace became official. The Knox-McDougall faction, while still remaining loyal to Washington, delivered a petition to Congress in January 1783, stating, "We have borne all that men can bear, our property is expended, our private resources are at an end." The petition concluded with a warn-ing that failure on the part of Congress to act might lead to serious consequences.

The second group centered on General Horatio Gates (31) whom many in Congress and the army had long supported as a replacement for Washington. These men sup-ported more immediate and more extreme actions, including potentially taking over the government. On March 10, 1783, Gates's aide-de-camp, Major John Armstrong, Jr., wrote an unsigned letter urging officers to refuse to disband at the end of the war if their demands were not met. The letter further stated that if the war continued and their demands were not fulfilled, they should "retire to some unsettled country" and leave Congress without an army. The First Newburgh Address, as the letter became known, went on to call for a meeting the next day to discuss future actions.

Washington was, of course, not happy about the unrest among his officers, their letter, or the scheduled meeting. On March 11, he issued a general order denouncing the "irregular invitation" and the "disorderly proceedings" and called for his own meeting of officers on March 15 "to attain the just and important object in view."

The meeting sought in the First Newburgh Address did not take place, but the next day Armstrong and his friends issued another letter. This Second Newburgh Address suggested that Washington's General Order showed that his loyalties were more with Congress than with the army, making him a part of their complaints.

Washington realized that his future, as well as that of the army and possibly the nation, depended on his actions at the March 15 meeting. The commanding general began his remarks by condemning the First and Second Newburgh Addresses for implying the Congress was guilty of "premeditated injustice." Washington then encouraged his officers not to take "any measures which, viewed in the calm light of reason, will lessen the dignity and sully the glory you have hitherto maintained." He concluded by saying, "…you will, by the dignity of your conduct, afford occasion for posterity to say, when speaking of the glorious example you have exhibited to mankind, 'had this day been wanting, the world had never seen the last state of perfection to which human nature is capable of attaining.'"

After his prepared remarks, not sure of how his words had been received, Washington paused. He started to read a letter written to the Continental Congress from Joseph Jones, a delegate from Virginia, about the financial problems the country faced before it could meet the claims of the officers. Before he could continue, Washington retrieved a pair of glasses from his pocket. The officers, never having seen their commander wear spectacles, were surprised when he did this. Noting their interest, Washington put on the glasses as he remarked, "Gentlemen, you must pardon me. I have grown gray in your service and now find myself growing blind."

Washington's words, dignity, and obvious affection for his soldiers brought many of his officers to tears. Thoughts of actions against Congress or out-and-out rebellion ended with Washington's remarks. A few minutes later, the officers agreed unanimously to place their confidence in Congress to take appropriate actions in their benefit. They also repudiated the Newburgh Addresses as "infamous propositions."

Washington never knew exactly who was responsible for the Newburgh Addresses or the complicity of Gates in the actions. Armstrong attempted to revive the unrest the following month but, finding little support and fearing that Washington might become aware of his actions, abandoned his plans.

The Newburgh Addresses serve as written proof that factions within the Continental Army were not always in agreement. More importantly, the resolution to the letters once again demonstrated the magnificent leadership and humanism of Washington. His admonishment to "not sully the glory" they had previous attained moved his men. Whether or not he really needed his glasses, this display of personal vulnerability to his soldiers appealed to their emotions and united them again in a shared cause.

Without the single leadership of Washington, the Newburgh Addresses might very well have escalated into a military coup. Because of Washington's response to the Newburgh Addresses, the letters and incident had little impact at the time or on the future of the United States. Had Washington not, however, ended the uprising in its initial stages, the outcome of the Revolution and the country's government might have been vastly different. For what they actually became rather than what they might have been, the Newburgh Addresses rank in the bottom quarter of this list.

90

RICHARD HOWE

British Admiral

1726–1799

Richard Howe commanded the British naval forces in North America while his brother William Howe (15) commanded the land forces there in the early years of the American Revolutionary War. Both brothers favored a nonmilitary settlement with the rebellious colonists and attempted to negotiate a peaceful end to the conflict. Without a resolution, Richard Howe's ships evacuated the Boston garrison, assisted in the campaign that captured New York City, and resisted the French fleet at Sandy Hook and Newport.

Born into a titled family in London on March 8, 1726, Richard Howe went to sea at age fourteen with Admiral George Anson who was attempting to sail around the world until storms at Cape Horn forced him to turn back. In 1744 Howe joined the fleet in the West Indies and over the next thirty years he served in the North Sea, off the West African coast, and in his home waters. Howe's abilities and family connections advanced him to the rank of vice admiral by the outbreak of the American Revolution. In addition to that rank, he had inherited the title of viscount when his elder brother George was killed near Ticonderoga on July 6, 1758, during the French and Indian War.

In February 1776, the British government and crown agreed to dispatch Admiral Howe to command the naval forces off North America. Howe, an acquaintance of Benjamin Franklin (25) and sympathetic to the complaints of the colonists, insisted that he and his brother, as commanders of sea and land forces in the rebellious colonies, be given the authority to negotiate a peace settlement with the Americans. King George III (20) and members of Parliament thought that any offers of peace might be seen by the rebels as weakness on the part of the British and limited the Howe brothers to little more than individual pardon authority.

Admiral Howe arrived in America in time to assist his brother's evacuation of Boston. In the late summer of 1776, Admiral Howe's sailors transported and supported General Howe's soldiers during the New York campaign that captured the city after decisive victories over the rebels. In September 1776, the Howes sent emissaries to the Continental Congress (10) in efforts to end the war, but neither that nor later efforts produced results. Admiral Howe became even more frustrated when the British Parliament dispatched its own peace commissioners. Although they, too, met with no success, Howe resigned his command and prepared to return to England in the summer of 1778.

Before he departed, Admiral Howe learned the French fleet, commanded by Charles d'Estaing (92), was approaching and resumed the leadership of the British naval forces. Howe withdrew his smaller fleet into New York harbor and waited for a French attack at Sandy Hook. Instead of attacking, d'Estaing sailed northward to

support the first joint Franco-American land and sea operations against Newport, Rhode Island (82), in late July.

Howe followed the French fleet, which turned to meet the British off Rhode Island on August 10. The two flotillas were nearing each other in what would have become the largest naval engagement of the war up to that time when a severe storm became the enemy of both Howe and d'Estaing. The tempest so damaged and scattered the ships of the two adversaries that both were forced to seek sheltered harbors for repairs. D'Estaing put in at Boston while Howe returned to New York.

When Admiral John Bryon arrived with reinforcements from England in September, Admiral Howe returned home. Back in England he joined his brother William, who had left command of the land force the previous May, in defending accusations that they had mismanaged the war in America. Although criticized in the press and by members of Parliament, neither Howe brother was formally censured. Richard Howe nevertheless refused to serve further under the current government and did not again go to sea until a change of leadership occurred.

In 1782 Richard Howe took command of the British fleet in the English Channel and executed the difficult relief of Gibraltar that kept that key Mediterranean entrance in British hands. He advanced to the senior naval position, First Lord of the Admiralty, in 1783 and remained in that post for the next five years. In 1793 at age sixty-seven he resumed command at sea against the French in the War of the First Coalition. After a brief retirement, he died on August 5, 1799, and is buried in the family vault at Langer.

Known as a tough but just disciplinarian who demanded and received well-trained crews, Howe was popular with his sailors, who called him "Black Dick" because of his swarthy complexion. Despite his affection for the Americans and sympathy for their cause, Howe was a formidable adversary who performed as well as anyone could have considering the limited support he received from England. His training methods and the mentoring of junior officers who served Britain in future campaigns were admirable.

Howe's transportation and support of his brother's army in the war's early years resulted in the capture of the port of New York City that remained in British hands for the remainder of the war. The Howe brothers coordinated land and sea forces in a superior manner without the conflicts that usually mark such ventures between soldier and sailor. Richard Howe's ranking near the end of this list is more the result of his shortened tenure in North America and the eventual loss of the war by his country rather than his personal performance and accomplishments.

91

NINETY-SIX, SOUTH CAROLINA

May 22–June 19, 1781

Ninety-Six, South Carolina, a Loyalist (34) garrison, was one of the last British outposts in the South to offer resistance to the determined—and, in this case, somewhat misguided—American revolutionaries. In the early summer of 1781, the Loyalists withstood a rebel siege and attack at Ninety-Six that finally ended with a defeat for the American rebels. However, the battle there never should have happened at all since the Loyalists would have abandoned the fort imminently anyway.

For nearly a century before the Revolutionary War, merchants from Charleston had been trading with Indian settlements in the foothills of the Blue Ridge Mountains. Along the path between the two places, they frequently camped at a spot they thought was 96 miles from their objective. Although they eventually figured out that the campsite was only about two-thirds of that distance, the name stuck. A permanent settlement sprung up at the site in 1751, and by the outbreak of the Revolutionary War, it had grown into a prosperous community of more than a dozen houses and one hundred residents.

Both the Loyalists and the rebels realized the importance to controlling Ninety-Six and its inland trail. The two sides clashed in an inconclusive fight on November 19–21, 1775, but it was not until the British redirected their main offensive from the North to the South in the summer of 1780 that the Loyalists took a firm hold on the village. It remained in their hands even after the battles at Kings Mountain (36), Cowpens (18), and Guilford Court House (26) had forced General Charles Cornwallis (22) to move his main British army toward the Virginia coast.

Lieutenant Colonel Francis Rawdon (73), commander of British forces in the region, ordered all outpost defenders to withdraw to Charleston in the spring of 1781, but the word failed to reach Ninety-Six, leaving the Loyalist garrison of 550 men on their own. As commander, Lieutenant Colonel John Cruger strengthened the village stockade in anticipation of a rebel attack. On the east end of his defenses Cruger built a star-shaped redoubt surrounded by a ditch and abatis, and then he connected this Star Redoubt, as it was known, to a covered trench on the west side of the village where a reinforced stockade named Fort Holmes protected the fort's water source. As veterans of the Long Island campaign (32) and of counter-partisan operations in the South, the Loyalists at Ninety-Six were capable soldiers. They were highly motivated, believing that the rebels would imprison or massacre them and their families if the fort fell.

Meanwhile American rebel General Nathanael Greene (4), unaware of the British outposts' recall, headed toward South Carolina to eliminate the remaining British strongholds. Greene, with about 1,000 troops, reached Ninety-Six on May 22, 1781, and focused not on the lightly defended water source protected by Fort Holmes but on the Loyalists' strongest defenses at the Star Redoubt. The rebels dug a series of paralleling trenches against the fortifications, but progress was slowed by Loyalist artillery fire and small raiding forces that ventured from the fort to attack the rebel workers.

On June 8, American Colonel Henry "Light Horse Harry" Lee arrived with reinforcements from his recent victory at Augusta, Georgia. He held prisoners from that fight whom the Loyalists later claimed he "paraded" near their defenses to demoralize and humiliate the defenders. Lee rebutted the story, saying that the prisoners had been near the fort because one of his subordinates had taken a wrong trail. Whatever the truth, the incident strengthened the defenders' fighting resolve.

Lee's troops concentrated to the north of Fort Holmes, while Greene's main force advanced against the Star Redoubt. On June 11, Greene learned that Rawdon was on his way from Charleston with 2,000 British regulars to relieve Cruger's forces. Greene dispatched his cavalry and called on other rebel units in the area to delay Rawdon while he tightened the siege on the Loyalists.

At noon on June 18, Greene ordered a coordinated attack against Fort Holmes and the Star Redoubt. Lee's men quickly captured Fort Holmes while Greene's men, equipped with long hooks to pull down the sandbag-and-log walls of the Star Redoubt, were delayed by musket fire. A Loyalist counterattack wounded several of the rebel leaders, forcing the Americans to retreat.

With Rawdon nearing the area, Greene had no choice but to withdraw toward Charlotte. American losses totaled 185 killed, wounded, or missing, while Loyalist casualties totaled about 90. Another 50 British soldiers in Rawdon's command died of sunstroke in the summer heat in their rapid march to reinforce the Loyalists' stronghold. Rawdon pursued Greene, but his exhausted troops could not close the distance separating the two armies. He turned back to Ninety-Six to prepare its troops for evacuation to Charleston.

The British had won the battle, but the Americans had achieved a greater victory. Rawdon and the Loyalists departed their fort, burning everything flammable, and left the interior of South Carolina to the rebels. Greene had accomplished his objective of ridding the state of the Loyalist fort, but the bloodshed had been in vain. Had he

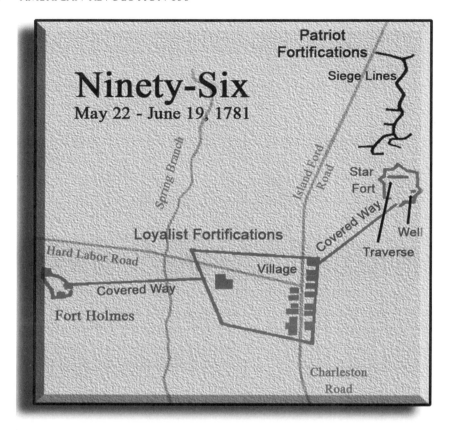

waited several weeks before attacking Ninety-Six, the Loyalists would have finally received their orders and abandoned the fort without a fight.

Ninety-Six was not Greene's finest hour as a field commander. First, he did not have to fight this fight. Second, his decision to focus on the Star Redoubt was a mistake. If he had attacked Fort Holmes upon his arrival, he would have cut off the enemy water source and possibly forced their surrender without further fighting.

Greene's advance on Ninety-Six and his subsequent operations at Eutaw Springs, South Carolina (63), the following September received little attention at the time because the Americans were concentrating their forces to surround Cornwallis at Yorktown (2). Their siege and battle have been included in subsequent histories as little more than footnotes in the American Revolution. Ninety-Six was not as influential as Eutaw Springs, and both rank in the latter half of this list. They do merit inclusion, however, because they firmly established American control over the South, and by the time of the Treaty of Paris (69), the British were encircled at Charleston.

92

CHARLES HECTOR D'ESTAING

French Admiral

1729–1794

Charles Hector d'Estaing, first the hope and then the despair of the American Revolution, led the initial military support operation provided directly by the French. As a career-soldier-recently-turned-sailor, d'Estaing proved inept at sea, failing to defeat the British along the New England coast, in the West Indies, and at Savannah, Georgia. D'Estaing's ineptness greatly damaged the morale of the Americans who had looked to the French for assistance and salvation in their fight for independence.

Born at Chateau de Ravel in Auvergne, France, on November 24, 1729, d'Estaing used the influence of his wealthy, aristocratic family to secure a commission in the French army as a full colonel of infantry at the mere age of sixteen. In 1757, d'Estaing, now a brigadier general, served in the East Indies during the Seven Years' War where the British captured him during the siege of Madras in 1759. Paroled on the condition he would return to France and not resume the fight, d'Estaing ignored the agreement and joined the French East Indian Company. Taking command of two warships, he attacked and destroyed British trading facilities in Sumatra and the Persian Gulf.

On his way back to France in 1760, d'Estaing once again encountered the British, who charged him with violation of his original parole. He faced a long imprisonment at Portsmouth but was soon released when the charges could not be fully substantiated, likely the result of communications between the French and English royals on his behalf.

D'Estaing emerged from prison with a hatred for the English that exceeded that of even the normal Frenchman. The comment by the British Commander in Chief in India that he would "chain him upon the quarterdeck and treat him like a baboon" if he again captured d'Estaing did not further endear the relationship.

In 1763 France awarded d'Estaing the unusual rank of lieutenant general in the navy. He advanced in rank to the more traditional rank of vice admiral in 1777 and the next year assumed command of the first French fleet preparing to assist the Americans against the British. D'Estaing sailed from Toulon harbor on April 13, 1778, with twelve ships of the line and fourteen frigates. His crossing took an extraordinary eighty-seven days, a month longer than normal to span the Atlantic. As a result, he missed the chance to catch the British fleet in Chesapeake Bay before it sailed northward. Discovering this, d'Estaing followed the British to New York where he blockaded them at Sandy Hook from July 11–22. Although d'Estaing had vastly superior numbers, he did not attack.

D'Estaing sailed from New York to Newport, Rhode Island (82), for the first joint operation between the American army and the French navy. Before d'Estaing could influence the land battle, he put out to sea to meet the approaching British fleet. As the two flotillas neared each other, a violent storm damaged and scattered both belligerents. D'Estaing gathered his ships and sailed to Boston for repairs.

Since the danger of the annual Gulf hurricane season was now past, d'Estaing sailed for the Caribbean on November 4. He made a feeble, unsuccessful attack to

retake St. Lucia and then failed to capture the lightly defended islands of St. Vincent and Grenada. On July 6, 1779, the French met the British fleet and forced them to retire to St. Christopher. Although he outnumbered the British, d'Estaing did not attack them in their port.

On October 9, 1779, d'Estaing joined another Franco-American operation in the attempt to recapture Savannah. The operation failed with great casualties, including the severely wounded d'Estaing. He recovered sufficiently to return to France in 1780 to find that his failures in America had cost him many of his influential friends in court. He did, however, lobby for the deployment of the expedition of General Jean Baptiste de Rochambeau (24) that would significantly influence the American victory at Yorktown (2). It took d'Estaing three years to regain personal support, and in 1783 he was preparing a Franco-Spanish fleet to sail from Cadiz for North America when news of the Treaty of Paris (69) reached him.

D'Estaing returned to France and left military service to devote his time to politics. After a brief period as a representative to Spain, he won election to the Assembly of Notables. At the outbreak of the French Revolution, d'Estaing spoke out for national reforms even though he expressed loyalty to the deposed royal family. The revolutionary government overlooked his feeling toward the Crown and rewarded him with the appointment at the commandant of the National Guard in 1787. Three years later he accepted a promotion to admiral and returned to the navy.

The admiral still remained loyal to the royal family and in 1783 testified on behalf of Marie Antoinette. This testimony, combined with the revelation of correspondence between him and Antoinette, precipitated charges against him as "a reactionary." D'Estaing, who had served the revolution in America, fell victim to another in his own country. Convicted, he died by the guillotine on April 28, 1794.

D'Estaing enjoyed little success during the American Revolution, and the influence he did exert on it was more negative than positive. His failures, especially at Newport, left the Americans demoralized and doubting the value of their French allies. While personally brave, d'Estaing simply did not have the naval leadership skills to accomplish his difficult missions. The very fact that he led the first French fleet to America is difficult to understand because since the beginnings of time armies and navies—soldiers and sailors—simply have not gotten along. Placing a soldier, especially a general, in command of a fleet was asking for failure. Naval officers in his command who had been passed over for the position could not be expected to fully commit themselves to a former soldier.

D'Estaing tried to be both a soldier and a sailor as well as both a revolutionary and a loyal court follower simultaneously. In America he—and the rebels—paid for his inadequacies with casualties and failure. Back home in France, his attempts to please both sides cost him his head.

D'Estaing makes this list simply for being first. Any effort, no matter how poor, to show the Americans that the French were indeed going to assist the Revolution was immensely influential. By no means, however, does he outrank fellow Frenchmen Rochambeau or the Marquis de Lafayette (46) on this list.

93

BOSTON MASSACRE

March 5, 1770

The Boston Massacre that left five dead and six wounded was the inevitable result of conflict between radical rebel elements in the city and the British soldiers stationed there to keep order. While it was more a minor skirmish than a real massacre, the bloody incident and its legal aftermath fueled the unrest in the colonies.

The Boston Massacre was precipitated by the 1767 Townshend Acts (19) passed by the British Parliament to generate revenue to pay their military expenses in the American colonies and to fund the salaries of royal officers. The colonists so resented the taxes the Acts levied on glass, lead, tea, painters' colors, and paper that they organized a boycott of the products. In turn, British customs officials requested additional troops as a show of force to assure colonial compliance. Soldiers began to arrive in late 1768, and soon in Boston alone 4,000 Redcoats, a number equal to a quarter of the city's total population, were present.

The people of Boston resented the occupation by what they considered foreign troops, but there were other problems as well. British soldiers were so poorly paid that they often sought part-time work when off duty, competing with the local labor force for scarce jobs. The Bostonians taunted the British soldiers when they were on duty and argued with them on the streets. Tensions came to a head on March 5, 1770. One account says a British soldier refused to pay for a haircut and then struck the barber when he demanded his money. Other accounts cite an argument between citizens and off-duty soldiers seeking work at a local rope-making plant.

While there is disagreement on what sparked the flare between the two groups, it is a fact that by nine o'clock that evening a crowd of about sixty angry colonists had gathered outside the British Customs House on King Street. The crowd pelted the single sentry with stones, ice, coal, and oyster shells. Reinforcements, including a corporal and six privates led by Captain Thomas Preston of the 29th Regiment of Foot, soon arrived only to be also struck by stones and other projectiles hurled by the colonists. The ranks of the rioters swelled with the arrival of dock workers and sailors, including an escaped slave named Crispus Attucks.

Several accounts say that Attucks became the mob's leader and struck either Captain Preston or a British soldier with a piece of firewood. This action caused

one of the soldiers to drop his musket into the icy slush. Attucks may have grabbed for the musket, or the soldier may have been humiliated enough to pull the trigger; regardless, the weapon fired. A volley from the British followed. Preston called for a cease-fire, but three Americans, including Attucks, lay dead in the street. Two others were mortally wounded, and six more had non-life-threatening injuries.

British officials acted immediately to placate the angry Bostonians. The next day they moved the entire military command onto Castle Island in Boston Harbor, but colonists who were already supporting independence from Great Britain propagandized the event. Samuel Adams fanned the patriotic flame in speech and writings, while Paul Revere (98) published an engraving incorrectly showing Preston ordering his men to fire on the unarmed colonists. Revere also published a poem,

"Unhappy Boston! see thy sons deplore
Thy hallowed walks besmear'd with guiltless gore."

A few days after the massacre, a crowd of 10,000 attended a joint funeral for the slain. Massacre Day became a great patriotic holiday celebrated annually on its anniversary until the more glorious and appropriate Fourth of July replaced it in 1776.

British officials, as well as moderate colonists who favored the Crown, wanted to resolve the incident with no further bloodshed. In addition to relocating the soldiers to Castle Island, the officials agreed to a trial of Captain Preston and his men. As a gesture of fairness, Samuel Adams's second cousin John agreed to act as defense council to the accused. Jurors were selected from towns outside Boston to reduce bias.

Preston faced a trial separate from his command. No evidence was presented that he had ever given an order to fire, and testimony was offered commending his efforts to control his troops and quell the riot.

Adams argued at the trial of the soldiers that they felt their lives were in danger from the crowd, and, at most, they were guilty of manslaughter rather than murder. The jury agreed that the soldiers had every right to feel threatened and acquitted six. They did convict two soldiers of manslaughter and sentenced them with branding on their thumbs—a severe but relatively minor punishment for the time.

Boston remained calm for several more years. The so-called massacre only briefly fanned the flames of revolution and, despite later claims, did little to promote the eventual armed conflict. While history books still cite the incident in Boston as playing an important role in sparking the Revolution, it was a minor skirmish more famous than influential.

In 1887 the Massachusetts Legislature, in response to public demands, authorized a memorial to the massacred dead. The Massachusetts Historical Society disagreed with the decision and published its own opinion, stating, "While greatly applauding the sentiment which erects memorials to the heroes and martyrs of our annals, the members of the Society believe that nothing but a misapprehension of the event styled the 'Boston massacre' can lead to classifying these persons with those entitled to grateful recognition at the public expense."

The Boston Massacre remains one of the most well-known incidents of the American Revolution era. For its fame rather than its true significance, it is included in this list. For its real influence on future events, it ranks near the bottom.

94

PATRICK FERGUSON

British Major

1744–1780

Patrick Ferguson fought the rebels in both the Northern and Southern theaters. He was an example of the professional British officers who served their king and country well throughout the Revolutionary War. Major Ferguson distinguished himself by inventing a breech-loading rifle and then fielding a company of marksmen with this weapon early in the war. These accomplishments aside, Ferguson is more widely known—and deserving of a place on this list—for something he refrained from doing. During the Battle of Brandywine Creek (72), he had the opportunity to shoot George Washington (1)—but the shot would have been into the back of the American leader, and Ferguson believed that taking such an act was not the gentlemanly thing to do.

Born in Edinburgh, Scotland, on June 4, 1744, into a family of judges and literary patrons, Ferguson began his military career at age fourteen. He served briefly on the Continent in 1761 during the Seven Years' War but left the war zone with a leg ailment likely caused by tuberculosis. Ferguson regained his health, albeit with a slight limp, to serve with the 70th Foot Regiment to help quell a slave uprising on the West Indian island of Tobago in 1768.

In 1772 Ferguson returned to London where he broadened his interest in rifle manufacture and marksmanship. Using his own funds, he adapted a breech-loading system from a sporting gun to fit a military rifle. This adaptation decreased the loading time and increased the rate of fire of traditional muskets. Just as significant, the Ferguson Rifle proved more reliable in damp weather and safer in combat, allowing the soldier to reload in the prone position rather than a standing position.

In 1776 Ferguson demonstrated his rifle to senior British generals and King George III (20). At a range of 300 yards, Ferguson accurately fired four rounds per minute and at 100 yards increased his accurate fire to six rounds per minute. Ferguson's demonstration so impressed King George that the monarch dispatched him to North America with orders to form a "Sharp Shooters Corps" armed with the new rifles. Ferguson armed, trained, and fielded 150 riflemen, mostly Loyalist (34) frontiersmen, in his "Corps" before their first significant battle.

The Sharp Shooters performed well in the Battle of Brandywine Creek on September 11, 1777, but it was an incident a few days before the fight that established Ferguson's lasting legacy. Early on the foggy morning of September 4, Ferguson, several riflemen, and a local guide went forward of the British lines hoping to gather intelligence. While there is no consensus, the most accurate account of what hap-

pened next appears to be that General Washington and a "brilliantly clad Hussar officer" rode out of the mist. Ferguson had never met the American commander and had no idea what he looked like. In his own account written shortly after the incident, he described the American only as appearing to be a "senior officer." Another account claims the civilian guide identified the possible target as Washington. Based on American records, Washington and the Polish Kazimierz Pulaski (96), who wore the uniform of a French Hussar, did make a mounted reconnaissance of the area that day.

In a letter to a relative a few days later, Ferguson wrote of the incident, saying that his initial reaction was to shoot the riders from their saddles. He ordered his riflemen "to steal near to them and fire at them," but quickly changed his mind because he found that shooting men from concealment "disgusting."

Instead Ferguson stepped from his hiding place and ordered the Hussar to step down from his mount. The soldier shouted an alarm, and he and the American officer whirled their horses and sped away. Of this Ferguson wrote, "As I was with the distance, at which in the quickest firing, I could have lodged a half dozen balls in or about him before he was out of my reach, but it was not pleasant to fire at the back of an unoffending individual who was acquitting himself coolly of his duty, and so I let him go."

Four days later, in the primary Battle of Brandywine Creek, Ferguson suffered a musket ball through his right elbow. While in the hospital, he talked with a captured American officer who related that Washington and a fellow officer dressed as a Hussar had indeed ridden beyond their lines several days previously. Ferguson, writing with his uninjured left hand, alluded to this being the first instance in which he was sure that the man he had not shot was the commander of the American army.

Ferguson recovered to rejoin his regiment and learned to reload his rifle using only one arm. His Rifle Corps, however, saw no more service after Brandywine. British Commander General William Howe (15) apparently resented a mere major inventing a superior weapon. This attitude and the complaint that the stock of the Ferguson Rifle easily broke, rendering it useless, justified Howe in the disbanding of the Sharp Shooter Corps and ordering the remaining rifles into storage.

Ferguson led a successful raid against a New Jersey privateer (61) port at Little Egg Harbor in October 1778 before going south to join the siege of Charleston. In South Carolina he recruited Loyalists into units to fight the remaining rebels. During this time he differed with the "no quarter" policy of fellow officer Banastre Tarleton (44) and even threatened to court-martial some of his rival's soldiers for killing prisoners.

On October 7, 1780, Ferguson led an expedition into the western Carolinas to protect the British flank. At Kings Mountain (36) a group of rebel militiamen, many armed with rifles rather than muskets, surrounded and killed or captured most of the Loyalist force. Among the dead, with at least eight rifle bullets in his body, lay Ferguson. According to later reports, he was buried on the battlefield in an unmarked grave, either with some of his soldiers or alongside his mistress and camp follower, known only as Virginia Sal, who was also killed in the battle.

Ferguson, known as "Bulldog" for his tenacity, was so short and thin as to appear elf-like. His letters and papers show a gentleman of great sophistication and intellect. Ferguson spent twenty-one of his brief thirty-six years in uniform and, as a professional soldier, believed in putting what he considered right above all other expediencies. His gentlemanly behavior of not shooting a man in the back likely saved the life of George Washington and perhaps the Revolution as well.

Ferguson invented a rifle his commander would not let his troops use; he led a tactically significant Sharp Shooter Corp that was disbanded; he refrained from shooting George Washington in the back. For all these reversals, Ferguson ranks near the end of this list as an afterthought in the American Revolution. Despite what he did not accomplish, he is the kind of man whom soldiers desired to follow and one whom his fellow officers and citizens could and did hold in respect.

95

WYOMING VALLEY, PENNSYLVANIA

July 3–4, 1778

The Battle of Wyoming Valley and the massacre that followed inflamed the hatred between rebels on the one hand and Loyalists (34) and their Native American (99) allies on the other, strengthening the resolve of the rebels and reminding them of their fate if independence failed. The battle illustrates the strong feelings that divided American factions and displays the ruthlessness of the Indians. It was also a clash that was confusing, with the leaders of both sides named Butler.

After the American victory at Saratoga (3) in October 1777, Loyalists and their Indian allies in upstate New York no longer operated from a position of strength. Unable to take back control of the region, they withdrew to the area of Fort Niagara from which they limited their operations to guerrilla attacks against isolated farms and villages.

Major John Butler, a Connecticut-born Loyalist veteran of the French and Indian War in command of the 300 Loyalists at Niagara, wanted to take the fight deeper into rebel territory. In May 1778, he recruited additional individual volunteers and a detachment called the Royal Greens to bring the strength of his unit to about 400 men. In June he marched southward with what he designated as his "Rangers," gathering 500 Native Americans from the Seneca and Cayuga tribes into his column with the objective of attacking rebels in Pennsylvania's Wyoming Valley.

The Wyoming Valley, a fertile 25-mile stretch of land along the Susquehanna River that now includes modern Wilkes-Barre, was home to both rebel and Loyalist families—the rebel ones being somewhat in the majority. The area, named for a Delaware Indian phrase meaning "upon a great plain" and claimed by both the colonies of Connecticut and Pennsylvania when it was first settled in 1753, was a thriving community until the Revolution began. At that time, many of the Loyalists fled to Canada while the rebels dispatched two companies of eighty-two men each to join George Washington's (1) army.

Major Butler had obtained British permission to attack the rebel stronghold in the valley by implying the purpose was to safeguard families of Loyalists left behind. Butler's Rangers and their Indian allies marched 200 miles through dense forest and neared the valley without being detected. Butler, somewhat elderly for a field commander at age fifty-seven, entered the region in late June and occupied the farm of a Loyalist named Wintermoot in the northern edge of the valley.

The residents, living in about 1,000 homes, had a series of rudimentary defensive positions in villages along the river that they called forts, though none merited the title. Between 40 and 60 regular soldiers, commanded by Captain Detrick Hewett, were its only formal defenders. When news of the approaching Loyalists reached the valley, Colonel Zebulon Butler, a Continental Army (7) officer home on leave, stepped forward and assumed overall command of the area, calling for volunteers and militiamen to join Hewett at Forty Fort, just above current Wilkes-Barre. Many residents, fearful for the safety of their families, remained at home to protect them. Colonel Butler assembled what militiamen and volunteers he could find with Hewett's regulars at Forty Fort. With only about 360 men and no chance for reinforcements to arrive from the east, Butler made the foolish decision to attack rather than remain in the defensive position of Forty Fort. He had almost succeeded in surprising the Loyalists, when Indian scouts detected his advance July 3, 1778, and alerted the main force.

Colonel Butler deployed the rebels with Hewett's company in the center with his own force anchoring the right flank and more militiamen on the left. At a range of 200 yards, they opened fire on the Loyalists whom Major Butler had arrayed with his regulars on the left flank, the greens in the center, and the Indians on his right flank. The outcome of the battle resulted from simple arithmetic. An attacking force of only 360 men has no chance against an enemy that numbers more than a 1,000.

After a half-hour of fierce musket fire, the rebels' ranks broke. There are conflicting stories of a Loyalist envelopment, misunderstood orders to retreat, panic on the part of inexperienced militiamen, and general confusion. Whatever the real cause, when the rebel ranks fell apart, discipline and order collapsed with them. Men fled the battlefield as fast as they could run. Unfortunately for them, the Indians proved faster, killing or capturing many. Colonel Butler, on horseback, escaped back to Forty Fort, but of the 360 rebels who had advanced with him against the Loyalists, only 60 escaped. Loyalists' casualties totaled a mere three dead and fewer than a dozen wounded.

No accurate accounts exist about the fate of the 300 rebels. Many died in battle, some were tortured, and others were executed in its aftermath. A popular story of the time claimed that Hewett and several officers were tossed into a fire by the Indians and held there with pitchforks until they burned to death. Another story claimed that Ester Montour, a mixed-race woman, led or encouraged the torture of prisoners, earning her the title of "Queen Ester, the fiend of Wyoming."

Wyoming Valley
July 3 - 4, 1778

PENNSYLVANIA

Forty Fort

Wyoming Valley

Lackawanna R.

Susquehanna River

The tribulations of the Wyoming Valley rebels were not at an end. Major Butler approached Forty Fort on July 4 and called for its surrender. He also demanded the return of confiscated Loyalist property and a promise that valley residents would no longer take up arms against the Crown. When Major Butler assured the rebels that their lives and property would be protected, they agreed to the terms. Once again accounts differ on what followed. Some claim that the Indians immediately killed and looted, while others, including several reports from militia officers, state that Major Butler maintained control and honored the agreement. It is fact, and admitted by Butler, that his force destroyed a thousand homes and confiscated more than that number of cattle, horses, and other livestock.

Butler and his army started back to Niagara on July 8. Several groups of Indians stayed behind, and only after October 22 could the Americans reoccupy the valley to gather and bury their dead in a common grave.

Major Butler's official report claimed his Indians carried back 227 scalps. A hundred years after the battle, the Wyoming Commemorative Commission could only gather 178 names of battle dead for their monument. Whatever the actual number of casualties, the Battle of Wyoming Valley served as a great propaganda tool for both sides. British officials hailed the close cooperation between Loyalists and Native Americans. The rebels called the fight the Wyoming Valley Massacre and embellished the factual stories of murder and torture with more mayhem. In 1779 the rebels used the excuse of the Wyoming Massacre to destroy forty Indian villages in upstate New York.

Except for those immediately involved who lost their lives and property, the Battle of Wyoming Valley had little direct influence on the war. What the battle did accomplish was to exacerbate the already extreme hostilities between Loyalists and rebels and to deepen the overall resentments by the eventual victors against the Native Americans. Wyoming Valley earns its place on this list as an example of these strong polarities and the resulting bloodshed that occurred with little or no honor. Because of its lack of overall impact, it ranks near the end of the battles that influenced the final outcome of the Revolution.

96

KAZIMIERZ PULASKI

American General

1747–1779

Kazimierz (also written Casimir) Pulaski employed the military skills he learned in fighting the Russians in his home country of Poland to organize the first formal horse mounted units in the Continental Army (7). As the "Father of American Cavalry" he became the most famous Pole to fight in the Revolutionary War and remains today the most popular Polish hero in the United States.

Born into a family of landed gentry in Winiary, Mazovia, Poland, on March 4, 1747, Pulaski entered the military at age nineteen. The next year he joined his father in fighting the Russians who were encroaching on Polish territories. Pulaski's leadership in the defense of Czestochowa in 1770–1771 brought him fame throughout his home country as well as across Europe. In 1772, however, Prussia and Austria joined Russia against Poland, forcing the young Pulaski into exile, first in Turkey and then in France.

In late 1775, Pulaski met Benjamin Franklin (25) and Silas Deane in Paris, where they suggested he join the Americans in their fight against the British. With funds provided by Deane and a letter of introduction from Franklin that proclaimed Pulaski as "famous throughout Europe for his bravery and conduct in the defense of liberties of his country," the Polish officer arrived in America in July 1777. He joined George Washington (1) prior to the Battle of Brandywine Creek (72) on September 11 where he served as the general's volunteer aide.

At this time the Continental Army had no formal cavalry organization. Officers and couriers were usually mounted, but the fledgling army had neither the assets to procure horses and their feed nor expertise to use them for tactical advantage. Both the Continental Congress (10) and Continental Army officers recognized the need for cavalry troops and formed four regiments of dragoons.

Washington, impressed with the bearing and cavalry experience of the young Pole, recommended to the Continental Congress that Pulaski be appointed brigadier general as "the Commander of the Horse." With Congressional approval, Pulaski

formed a cavalry detachment that saw limited action at Germantown (48) in October 1777 before wintering at Valley Forge (39).

Pulaski's Legion, as they were now known, took the field to conduct guerilla operations against the British in Pennsylvania and New Jersey in the spring. None of the operations was particularly successful, and neither was Pulaski himself. While he may have understood cavalry tactics, he had few social skills where subordinates and superiors were concerned. Not only did he not speak English, but also he displayed a superior attitude. Pulaski demanded that he outrank all foreign officers with the exception of Marquis de Lafayette (46). He accepted that he was subordinate to Washington but refused to follow orders from anyone else except the Congress that appointed him to his rank. In May 1778, Pulaski resigned his commission in protest over the acquittal of a subordinate in a court-martial that he had recommended.

Congress placated the Polish nobleman with a larger command. He performed poorly in defending against a raid on Little Egg Harbor, New Jersey, on October 5, 1778. In response to a threat from Native Americans (99)—or possibly to just get him out of the way of the real war—Congress ordered Pulaski to defend the Delaware River Valley the following month. Again, Pulaski was unhappy, writing Congress on November 26 that he could find "nothing but bears to fight."

The dejected Pulaski decided to return to Europe but instead accepted orders to join the operations in the Southern theater. He arrived in time to be badly beaten again by the British in the defense of Charleston in May 1779. In a letter to Congress,

Pulaski complained about his treatment by other officers while also emphasizing that he remained devoted to the cause of independence.

On October 9, 1779, Pulaski led his cavalry in a charge at Savannah, Georgia, that many called needless and others labeled foolhardy. Pulaski's objective was to relieve pressure on an allied French unit, but he was hit by a grape shot to the loin. Aboard the warship *Wasp* in Savannah harbor, surgeons were unable to remove the shot, and Pulaski died two days later on October 11. According to several witnesses, including his own aide, they buried Pulaski at sea. Later unsubstantiated reports say Pulaski was buried either on St. Helena's Island about 50 miles off the Georgia coast or at Greenwich Plantation just outside Savannah.

At no time during the war did Pulaski lead more than 250 horse soldiers, and their failures far exceeded their successes. Although he was not able to successfully practice his ideas on organizing, training, and using cavalry, the principles he tried to apply remained after his death and were eventually adopted as doctrine. Most importantly, he was first to command units of mounted United States soldiers, thus earning the title of "Father of American Cavalry."

This title, as well as his fame among Polish immigrants, is more symbolic than representative of his actual performance. Pulaski never understood the democracy Americans were seeking, believing his noble birth still meant privilege even though he was exiled and thousands of miles from Poland. In fact, had he not died in a cavalry charge at age thirty-four, he might not have become famous at all. But he was brave and he did die as a result of his combat wounds. Today he remains a hero to Polish-Americans. Pulaski never achieved the influence on the Revolution as did other allied officers like Lafayette or Friedrich von Steuben (62), who both outrank him on this list.

97

RAMSEUR'S MILL, NORTH CAROLINA

June 20, 1780

The Battle of Ramseur's Mill was an extremely bloody engagement between North Carolina Loyalists (34) and rebels. This fight between neighbors—and even relatives—over loyalty to King George III (20) produced appalling casualty rates considering the numbers involved. The outcome prevented the British from expanding their occupation of the Southern states into North Carolina.

After they captured Charleston (47) in May 1780, the British deployed inland to establish outposts from which to control the interior of South Carolina and Georgia. When word reached Loyalists in North Carolina about the British occupation, they renewed their resolve to reassume control of their state. The rebels had secured the region with their victory at Moores Creek Bridge (57) on February 27, 1776. For four years the state's Loyalists had been offering no resistance to the rebel government, but now they hoped Charles Cornwallis (22) would expand his occupation northward to where they lived.

Cornwallis did indeed have plans for occupying North Carolina in a fall invasion. He specifically asked the North Carolinians to forego any action until the end of summer so that crops could be harvested and warehoused to provide provisions for his army. But the Loyalists were impatient. When Colonel John Moore, a North Carolinian who had served with Cornwallis in the early operations in South Carolina, returned home in June, he called a meeting of Loyalist leaders at this father's home at Ramseur's Mill in present-day Lincoln County.

Moore informed the forty Loyalists who attended the June 10 meeting about Cornwallis's plans to invade the state. He neglected to tell them that the British general wanted them to delay any overt actions until September. During the meeting Moore learned that nearby rebel militia units had heard about the Loyalist gathering and were marching toward them. The small band of Loyalists engaged the rebels in an indecisive skirmish, after which Moore called for all able-bodied Loyalists to assemble at Ramseur's Mill. By June 20 more than 1,300 had answered his call, but few possessed uniforms and a full third had no weapons other than clubs and farm tools.

When North Carolina Governor Griffith Rutherford learned of the Loyalist resistance, he ordered his state's militia units to assemble near Charlotte. Rutherford planned to personally lead the 800 militiamen against the Loyalists, but Colonel Francis Locke had already gathered 400 soldiers at Mountain Creek much nearer Moore's camp. On June 19, Locke marched toward Ramseur's Mill with three small horse-mounted units in the lead followed by two files of infantry.

Locke's force, like Moore's, wore mostly civilian clothes and carried an assortment of arms. Neither side boasted any degree of combat experience or organization and discipline. What both sides shared was a belief in their cause—and opportunity to settle long-held political differences with their neighbors and kin.

Moore's camp occupied a hill about 300 meters from Ramseur's Mill and a half mile north of the present town of Lincolnton. The rebel horsemen quickly forced a small Loyalist detachment posted 600 meters forward to retreat back to their main camp. Unarmed Loyalists fled the camp while those with muskets took up positions at the base of the hill. Then, in a remarkable maneuver considering their inexperience, the Loyalists withdrew to the reverse slope of the high ground. Although outnumbered by a ratio of about two to one, the attacking rebels flanked both ends of the enemy line quickly, forcing the Loyalists to fight hand to hand. Neither side had the advantage of possessing bayonets, so most of the close fighting continued with musket stocks, clubs, and fists. In the midst of the brawl where neither side had uniforms, it was difficult for the combatants to distinguish between enemy and ally.

The Loyalists held their ground until several of their captains were downed by rebel musket shots or club strokes. Moore rallied the retreating Loyalists at a creek at the base of the hill from where he dispatched a flag of truce with a proposal for a cease-fire to care for the wounded and bury the dead. Though only able to assemble about 110 effective combatants, Locke demanded the Loyalists surrender while he sent a mounted courier urging Rutherford to come forward as quickly as possible.

Moore refused to surrender and hastily withdrew toward Camden to rejoin Cornwallis. By the time he arrived, he had only thirty men accompanying him. Cornwallis, furious that Moore had not followed his orders to delay action until fall, arrested the Loyalist officer and threatened him with a court-martial for disobedience. When Cornwallis cooled down a bit, he released Moore and dropped judicial action.

Personal narratives of the battle that later circulated related that Locke's men were motivated by spirits they consumed at Dellinger's Tavern on the way to the battlefield. These stories also reflect just how personal this fight was between neighbors and former friends. One account claimed that in the thickest of the fighting a young Loyalist spotted an acquaintance on the other side. He said, "How do you do, Billy? I have known you since you was a little boy, and never knew no harm to you except you was a rebel." Billy, who had already fired his musket but not reloaded it, attempted to use

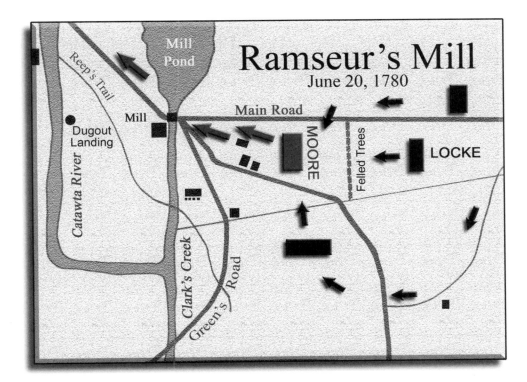

it as a club against his Loyalist friend. The Loyalist dodged and shouted, "Stop! Stop! I am not going to stand still and be killed like a damn fool neither." He then attempted to club Billy with his own musket. A companion of Billy's heard the exchange and took his musket, which was loaded, and shot the Loyalist dead.

In the actual battle never more than 400 of Locke's militiamen were engaged, but 150 were either killed or wounded. When the fight began, Moore had about 700 combatants and his casualties about equaled that of the rebels. Moore, however, lost more than dead and wounded soldiers. He lost North Carolina. Had he followed Cornwallis's orders and delayed the fight until the fall when the main British army would have marched northward—or even waited for 2,000 reinforcements commanded by Patrick Ferguson (94) on their way from Charleston—the outcome would have been different. But that did not happen, and North Carolina remained under rebel control for the remainder of the war. When Cornwallis marched toward the Virginia coast and Yorktown (2) a year later, he hoped to add to his army by recruiting North Carolina Loyalists. Instead, his numbers were actually depleted as more men deserted than volunteered.

Little known outside North Carolina, the Battle of Ramseur's Mill helped set the stage for the eventual rebel victory in the South and Cornwallis's surrender at Yorktown. While not nearly as influential as the battles of Camden (65), Cowpens (18), Guilford Court House (26), and Ninety-Six (91), it nonetheless merits inclusion in the latter quarter of these rankings.

98

PAUL REVERE

American Lieutenant Colonel

1735–1818

Paul Revere, made famous by a poem written nearly a century after the end of the Revolutionary War, earned his place in history for his nighttime ride to warn the militia and American leaders at Lexington and Concord (43) about the approach of the British. Revere also contributed to the war effort first as a producer of propaganda engravings and then as a courier between the early Committees of Correspondence and battlefield leaders.

Born in 1735 in Boston to a French immigrant silversmith Apollos Rivoire, Paul Revere assumed his family's Americanized name at birth. As a young man he joined his father's trade before becoming an artillery lieutenant in the colonial militia during the French and Indian War in which he participated in the unsuccessful British attack against Crown Point in 1756. Upon leaving the army, he returned to Boston to take over his father's silversmith business.

By 1765, Revere had become an advocate and an instigator of more rights, if not outright independence, for the American colonies. He befriended many of the early leaders, including Dr. Joseph Warren, Samuel Adams, and John Hancock. Revere's somewhat fanciful engraved rendition of the Boston Massacre (93) in 1770 did much to rally the colonists to the cause of rebellion. Rumor says he participated in the Boston Tea Party; fact shows that soon after the event he became a horse courier, carrying messages about political unrest from Boston to New York and Philadelphia. By 1774, Revere had relinquished most of this silversmith shop to his own son while he worked full time for the Massachusetts Committee of Correspondence.

In the spring of 1775, the Committee learned that the British were planning to seize arms and other military supplies stored at Concord and to capture the rebel leaders Hancock and John Adams (51). In order to warn fellow rebels about British whereabouts, Revere arranged for a friend at the Old North Church to provide the final bit of intelligence. If the British crossed the Charles River, Newman would hang two lanterns in the church tower; if they marched on the land route of Charleston Neck, he would hang a single lantern. Revere was to cross the Charles River to

Charlestown and then ride to Lexington with the warning about the British approach while his compatriot William Dawes would ride the long way around Boston Neck to warn Lexington and Concord.

When two lanterns appeared in the tower on the night of April 18, Revere rode toward Lexington and legend. Popular history has Revere shouting, "The British are coming, the British are coming!" along his route, but this is most doubtful. He would not have wanted to come to the attention of British patrols in the area or alert the many colonists who considered themselves Loyalists (34). According to his own

later account, he quietly warned those in need of the information along his route via Somerville, Arlington, and Medford that "the regulars are coming."

Revere reached Lexington a little after midnight with Dawes arriving about a half-hour later. With Adams, Hancock, and the local militia alerted, Revere and Dawes, joined by Dr. Samuel Prescott, rode toward Concord to continue the alert. At Lincoln a British roadblock stopped the three riders. Prescott jumped a wall on his horse and continued toward Concord while the British managed to detain Dawes and Revere. Dawes escaped a short time later but was thrown from his mount and was unable to finish his ride. Near dawn, the British, unaware of Revere's mission, released him but confiscated his horse. Revere walked back to Lexington, arriving in time to observe the skirmish on Lexington Green.

After his return to Boston, Revere assumed the management of a gunpowder mill in Canton, Massachusetts. From 1778 to 1779 as a lieutenant colonel, he commanded a fortification in Boston Harbor known as Castle William. During this time he took part in the unsuccessful offensive against Newport, Rhode Island (82), and in the disastrous Penobscot Expedition that failed to take a British base in Maine. Most of the officers in this latter expedition, including Revere, were court-martialed, but he was acquitted of all charges.

During and after the war, Revere continued his engravings. He designed and printed the first Continental currency and opened a foundry that cast cannons. He also produced the first official seal for the Continental Congress (10) and the seal for the State of Massachusetts that is still in use.

After the war, Revere resumed his silver business and produced quality silverware that was in much demand then and remains so today. He also continued in the production of cannons as well as in casting church and ships' bells. His work with copper and brass led him to develop rolled copper sheets that could be used for roofing buildings as well as plating for early naval vessels.

For the remainder of his life, Revere displayed his pride and belief in America by wearing his Revolutionary War uniform. He died at his Boston home on May 10, 1818.

Revere was virtually unknown outside of Boston until Henry Wadsworth Longfellow published his poem "Paul Revere's Ride" in 1863. Its opening lines, "Listen my children, and you shall hear, of the midnight ride of Paul Revere," are some of the best known and most memorized words by American school children. It is unknown if Longfellow knew of Dawes and Prescott, or if "Revere" simply offered a better rhyming pattern. Whatever his intentions, Longfellow elevated a relatively minor player in the American Revolution to that of one of its most famous.

Without Longfellow, Revere would be obscure and surely not on this list. However, no history of the Revolutionary War is complete without inclusion of the man and his midnight ride. He does earn a place on this ranking, if not for his accomplishments, then for his fame.

99

NATIVE AMERICANS

1775–1783

Native Americans participated in the Revolutionary War not to assist the rebel colonists or the British but rather to protect their own land claims. Most ended up siding with the British, who made promises of preserving Indian territory west of the Appalachian Mountains from further encroachment by American pioneers. Ultimately, the Native Americans made little impact on the war and, in the treaty that ended the conflict, lost all their lands west to the Mississippi River.

When the Europeans arrived in the New World, more than a million Indians occupied America north of Mexico. Of these, about a quarter million lived in the areas of the Atlantic seaboard where English and French settlers made their homes. Initially receiving the colonists in peace, the Indians soon rose up against what they considered intruders on their lands. Despite their superior numbers and skills and bravery as individual warriors, Indian tribes had no history of formal military organization or tactics; most were limited to bows and arrows, spears, and hatchets for weapons. As a result they fought as unorganized bands where their success usually depended upon superior numbers and surprise. While they could destroy an isolated farm or a small unsuspecting village, they were not able to defeat the musket-armed colonial militiamen. By the 1760s, the English colonies had mostly neutralized the Indian tribes along the coastal regions.

When the Seven Years' War between Britain and France extended into North America, both sides sought the assistance of Native Americans. The French, who had developed strong trading relationships with the Indians in Canada and the colonial Northwest, used gifts of rum, tobacco, and weapons to draw the Native Americans to their side. Indian support for France was so significant that the war in North America became known as the French and Indian War. The only major tribe to side with the British, the Iroquois, was still nursing resentments from the killing of several of their chiefs more than a century earlier by the French explorer Samuel de Champlain.

As differences between the colonists and the British grew in the 1760s, the British secured the favor of the Native Americas by the Proclamation of 1763 that declared lands west of the Appalachians to be "reserved" for the Indians and not open to colonial settlers. The act may have pleased the Indians, but it joined the long list of factors that were encouraging the Americans to rebel against Britain. It is noteworthy that the colonists, who believed the lands to the west belonged to them, conducted the Boston Tea Party disguised as Indians.

When hostilities finally broke out between the colonists and the British, neither side initially formally attempted to enlist Native American support. The Continental Congress (10) in July 1775 went so far as to issue this statement: "This is a family quarrel between us and Old England. You Indians are not concerned in it. We don't wish you to take up the hatchet against the king's troops. We desire you to remain at home, and not join either side, but keep the hatchet buried deep."

Not everyone in the rebel forces supported Indian neutrality. Ethan Allen in Vermont solicited Iroquois warriors to "ambush the Regulars" in exchange for blankets, tomahawks, and knives. British agents likewise sought support from the Iroquois, inviting them "to feast on a Bostonian and drink his blood."

Ultimately the Americans were the first to successfully recruit Indians when the Massachusetts provincial government formed a company from the Stockbridge tribe. The British also sought assistance by taking Mohawk leader Joseph Brant on a tour of England. By the time he returned, Brant was convinced that the best future for his people lay with the British. He convinced his fellow Mohawks, and three of the other five tribes that made up the Iroquois Nation, to take up arms against the rebel colonists.

By the time the Americans issued their *Declaration of Independence* (14) on July 4, 1776, protests against raids by Indians against mostly nonmilitary targets, including women and children, merited inclusion in the document. Near the end is the statement, "He [British King George III] has endeavored to bring on the inhabitants of our frontiers the merciless Indian savages, whose known rule of warfare is an undistinguished destruction of all ages, sexes, and conditions."

Over the next years additional tribes joined the British in the North, but their actual numbers of warriors in the field probably never exceeded more than a thousand. While Indian raids and ambushes continued to shed the blood of rebel and noncombatant alike, they never significantly contributed to major battles. In 1778 and 1779, American troops led by General John Sullivan (71) conducted offensives in the Iroquois lands and destroyed villages and fields, ending most Indian resistance in the North.

Indian tribes, encouraged by gifts of alcohol, blankets, and arms in the South, also joined the British side with about 14,000 warriors from the Cherokee, Choctaw, and Creek tribes opposing the rebels. Cherokee raids on American settlers so angered Thomas Jefferson (87) that he wrote, "I hope that the Cherokees will now be driven beyond the Mississippi and that this in the future will be declared to the Indians the invariable consequence of their beginning a war. Our contest with Britain is too serious and too great to permit any possibility of avocation from the Indians."

American militiamen quickly answered Jefferson's call and easily defeated the Cherokees. British officials discovered their Indian allies avoided direct combat with regulars and preferred the gifts from England over battlefield duties. The demise of the Cherokees discouraged most of the Creeks from further action, but a few from the tribe joined the Choctaws in one of their better battlefield performances in the British loss to Spanish General Bernardo de Galvez (40) at Pensacola in 1781.

When the war finally came to an end, the British had little use or respect for their Native American allies. In the Treaty of Paris (69) in 1783 the British surrendered to the United States all its territory east of the Mississippi River, south of the Great Lakes, and north of Florida. In later negotiations with the Indians the Americans stated that the Native Americans had lost all their land claims because they had fought on the losing side.

The Northwest Ordinance of 1787 took a somewhat more conciliatory attitude by asserting good faith toward the Indians and held that "their land and property shall never be taken from them without their consent," and that various laws would be made time-to-time "for preserving the peace and friendship with them."

Over the next century "peace and friendship" proved rare as American settlers continued their move westward. For decades Americans in search of land referenced Indian atrocities and their support of the British. Treaties were made, treaties were broken, and blood was shed by both sides.

Other than a few skirmishes and raids, Native Americans had little influence on direct combat in the Revolutionary War, but they remained on the minds of Redcoats and rebels alike. Behind the scenes both the Americans and British expended resources to secure their support or at least their neutrality. The British gained the favor of the Indians, but it did little to defeat the Rebellion. The few tribes that supported the Americans fared little better in the postwar period than those who fought with the British, but even before the war the Indian way of life was doomed because of their lack of numbers, unity, and military resources to oppose the white movement west. Their inclusion on this list is more from their perceived threat to both sides rather than any real influence.

JAMES WILKINSON

American General

1757–1825

James Wilkinson serves as the leading example of those Americans who favored their own self-interests and desires over the needs of the Revolution and the future of the United States. Duplicitous, scheming, and dishonest are but a few of the accurate descriptions of Wilkinson; traitor would be added during his postwar career. Wilkinson's negative influence on the Revolutionary War, along with his overall character flaws, secure for him the very last entry on this list.

Born on March 24, 1757, to a wealthy merchant-planter in Benedict, Maryland, Wilkinson studied under a private tutor before going to medical school in Philadelphia. Although still a teenager, he left school to join a Pennsylvania militia unit at the beginning of the Revolution. His education and family background quickly led to his appointment as an officer and he served in the Boston Siege (50) before joining Benedict Arnold's (85) expedition to Quebec in the fall of 1775.

In early 1776, Wilkinson advanced in rank to captain and by the end of the year was a major and aide to Horatio Gates (31). Wilkinson then joined George Washington (1) for the assaults on Trenton (8) and Princeton in late 1776 and early 1777 before rejoining Gates for the Saratoga campaign (3) in the fall as a lieutenant colonel. Up to this time Wilkinson's service had been honorable if not distinguished, but his actions at Saratoga revealed his true character. Just before the pivotal second Battle of Bemis Heights on October 7, 1777, Lieutenant Colonel John Hardin scouted the British positions and learned critical information that he asked Wilkinson to carry to Gates. Wilkinson did so but took credit for obtaining the intelligence himself. When the information helped win the Battle of Saratoga, Gates rewarded Wilkinson by asking him to deliver the news of the victory to the Continental Congress (10) at York, Pennsylvania. In the news dispatches to Congress on October 17 about the British surrender, Gates recommended Wilkinson be promoted to brigadier general.

The journey from Saratoga to York was only a few days' ride, but Wilkinson did not arrive until October 31 and then did not make his report to Congress until November 3. Along the way Wilkinson had stopped at Reading, Pennsylvania, to court a young lady and then called on the headquarters of General William Alexander to encourage a group of officers who were conspiring to replace Washington with Gates as the commander of the Continental Army.

Congress, already aware of the victory at Saratoga from unofficial sources, was not pleased with the delay and lack of respect they perceived on the part of the young Wilkinson. They were especially unhappy with Gates's request for the promotion of the tardy messenger but reluctantly approved the order making him a brigadier general. Wilkinson's fellow officers, now aware of his misrepresentations and self-interests, protested the promotion with a letter signed by forty-seven colonels. Gates felt so betrayed that he and Wilkinson almost fought a duel.

Throughout all this controversy, Wilkinson maintained important friendships, particularly with representatives from New England who favored replacing Washington, who was from Virginia, with one of their own generals. Instead of returning Wilkinson to the field, Congress appointed him to the Board of War, a vague predecessor to the War Department. Wilkinson served as the board's secretary until leaks about his cooperation with those seeking to replace Washington forced him to resign on March 29, 1778. In his letter of resignation he was so abusive of Gates that Congress refused to include the correspondence in their official records.

For the next several months, Wilkinson did little but imbibe alcohol, apparently his favorite pastime. On July 24, 1779, he accepted an appointment of clothier general of the army. In this position he demonstrated that thievery was another of his character flaws as he diverted funds meant for supplies for the army in the field into his own pockets. Reconciliations of his accounts never fully revealed the extent of his theft, but audits indicated sufficient irregularities to force his resignation on March 27, 1781.

Wilkinson settled in Bucks County, Pennsylvania, where he still had friends who appointed him as a brigadier general in the militia and elected him to the state legislature in 1783. In 1784 he moved to the Kentucky frontier and joined the movement to separate that territory from Virginia to become its own state. Three years later, he traveled down the Mississippi River to New Orleans to meet with the Spanish governor. Wilkinson now added treason to his long list of vices when he signed a paper promising his allegiance to Spain in exchange for exclusive trade rights. In addition to the lucrative trade profits, Wilkinson was to receive an annual payment from the Spanish government.

Wilkinson returned home to rejoin the regular army in operations against the Indians in the 1790s. In the extremely small armed force of the period, he rapidly rose in rank until he was the U.S. Army's senior officer in 1796. He held this position for about eighteen months before Congress placed Alexander Hamilton over him.

Upon the expiration of Hamilton's commission, Wilkinson once again became the army's ranking officer on June 15, 1800.

Over the next fifteen years Wilkinson held the position of governor of the Louisiana Territory, became involved with the Aaron Burr conspiracy trials, performed with unusual ineptness even for him in several battles of the War of 1812, and survived two courts-martial before accepting an honorable discharge in 1815. The next year he published his three-volume memoirs in which he presented his views of his exploits. He lived in New Orleans until 1821 when he went to Mexico City to pursue a Texas land grant. Delays kept him there as he increased his alcohol consumption and added opium to his list of personal indulgences. He died on December 28, 1825, and is buried in Mexico City.

At the trial of Aaron Burr, John Randolph of an old-line, prestigious Virginia family, said, "Wilkinson is the only man I ever saw who is from the bark to the core a villain."

Wilkinson's personal treason was not revealed until 1854 with the publication of the correspondence of the Spanish governor of New Orleans. He remains today the highest ranking American military officer ever to betray his country. While Benedict Arnold's treachery during the Revolution is much better known and had a much greater influence at the time, Wilkinson easily earns the title of one of the most treacherous officers and scoundrels in American military history.

Except for Wilkinson's first few months as a junior officer, his entire service in the Revolution is marked by deceit, double-cross, and out-and-out theft. His negative influence secures his this ranking at number 100 to show that not all of Washington's and the army's difficulties came from the British and Loyalists. Wilkinson and other lesser known internal malcontents made the final American victory all that much more remarkable.

BIBLIOGRAPHY

Allen, Gardner W. *A Naval History of the American Revolution.* 2 vols. Boston: Houghton Mifflin, 1913.

Arwood, Rodney. *The Hessians: Mercenaries from Hessan-Kassal in the American Revolution.* Cambridge, UK: Cambridge University Press, 1980.

Babits, Lawrence E. *A Devil of a Whipping: The Battle of Cowpens.* Chapel Hill: University of North Carolina Press, 2000.

Bailey, Thomas A. *The American Pageant: A History of the Republic.* Boston: D. C. Heath, 1956.

Bailyn, Bernard. *The Faces of Revolution: Personalities and Themes in the Struggle of Independence.* New York: Knopf, 1990.

Bakeless, John. *Background to Glory: The Life of George Rogers Clark.* Lincoln: University of Nebraska Press, 1957.

Barthelmas, Della G. *The Signers of the Declaration of Independence: A Biographical and Genealogical Reference.* Jefferson, NC: McFarland, 2003.

Bass, Robert. *Gamecock: The Life and Campaigns of Thomas Sumter.* New York: Holt, Rinehart and Wilson, 1961.

Bearss, Edwin C. *Battle of Cowpens: A Documented Narrative.* Johnson City, TN: Overmountain Press, 1993.

Berg, Fred A. *Encyclopedia of Continental Army Units: Battalions, Regiments, and Independent Corps.* Harrisburg, PA: Stackpole, 1972.

Bernstein, R. B. *Thomas Jefferson.* New York: Oxford University Press, 2003.

Bicheno, Hugh. *Rebels and Redcoats: The American Revolutionary War.* London: HarperCollins, 2003.

Bill, Alfred. *New Jersey and the Revolutionary War.* New Brunswick, NJ: Rutgers University Press, 1964.

Bird, Harrison. *Attack on Quebec.* New York: Oxford University Press, 1968.

Birnbaum, Louis. *Red Dawn at Lexington.* Boston: Houghton Mifflin, 1986.

Black, Jeremy. *George III: America's Last King.* New Haven, CT: Yale University Press, 2006.

———, *War for America: The Fight for Independence, 1775–1783.* New York: St. Martin's, 1991.

Boatner, Mark M. III. *Encyclopedia of the American Revolution.* New York: David McKay, 1966.

———. *Landmarks of the American Revolution.* Harrisburg, PA: Stackpole, 1973.

Bobrick, Benson. *Angel in the Whirlwind: The Triumph of the American Revolution.* New York: Simon & Schuster, 1997.

Bodle, Wayne. *The Valley Forge Winter.* University Park: Pennsylvania State University Press, 2002.

Bonwick, Colin. *The American Revolution.* London: MacMillan Co., 1991.

Borick, Carl P. *A Gallant Defense: The Siege of Charleston, 1780.* Columbia: University of South Carolina Press, 2003.

Boudinot, Elias. *Journal of Events in the American Revolution.* New York: New York Times/Arno Press, 1968.

Boyle, Lee. *Writings From the Valley Forge Encampment of the Continental Army.* Bowie, MD: Heritage Books, 2001.

Boynton, Edward C. *History of West Point and Its Military Importance During the American Revolution.* Whitefish, MT: Kessinger, 2006.

Brands, H. W. *The First American: The Life and Times of Benjamin Franklin.* New York: Doubleday, 2000.

Brecher, Frank W. *Securing American Independence: John Jay and the French Alliance.* Westport, CN: Praeger, 2003.

Brooks, Nora. *Henry Knox: A Soldier of the Revolution.* New York: Da Capo Press, 1974.

Buchanan, John. *The Road to Guilford Court House: The American Revolution in the Carolinas.* New York: John Wiley and Sons, 1997.

Calhoon, Robert M. *Loyalists in Revolutionary America.* New York: Harcourt, 1973.

Callahan, North. *Daniel Morgan: Ranger of the Rebellion.* New York: Holt, Rinehart, and Wilson, 1961.

———. *Henry Knox: General Washington's General.* New York: A. S Barnes, 1958.

Calloway, Colin G. *The American Revolution in Indian Country.* Cambridge U.K.: Cambridge University Press, 1995.

Carp, E. Wayne. *To Starve the Army at Pleasure: Continental Army Administration and American Political Culture 1775–1783.* Chapel Hill: University of North Carolina Press, 1990.

Carstens, Kenneth C. and Nancy Carstens. *The Life of George Rogers Clark, 1752–1818: Triumpts and Tragedies.* Westport, CT: Praeger, 2004.

Caughey, John Walton. *Bernardo de Galvez in Louisiana, 1776–1783.* Gretna, Louisiana: Pelican Press, 1972.

Chadwick, Bruce. *George Washington's War: The Forging of a Revolutionary Leader and the American Presidency.* Naperville, IL: Sourcebooks, 2004.

———. *The First American Army: The Untold Story of George Washington and the Men Behind America's First Fight for Freedom.* Naperville, IL: Sourcebooks, 2005.

Chidley, Donald Barr. *The American Privateers.* New York: Dodd, Mead, & Co., 1962.

Collines, Varnum. *A Brief Narrative of the Ravages of the British and Hessians at Princeton in 1776–1777.* New York: New York Times/Arno, 1968.

Cook, Don. *The Long Fuse: How England Lost the American Colonies, 1760–1785.* New York: Atlantic Monthly Press, 1996.

Cook, Fred J. *The Privateers of Seventy-Six.* Indianapolis: Bobbs-Merrill, 1976.

Cox, Caroline. *Sense of Honor: Service and Sacrifice in George Washington's Army.* Chapel Hill: University of North Carolina Press, 2004.

Cragg, Dan. *Generals in Muddy Boots: A Concise History of Combat Commanders.* New York: Berkley, 1996.

Damient, Lincoln. *Chaining the Hudson: The Fight for the River in the American Revolution.* New York: Carol Publishing, 1989.

Davidson, Philip. *Propaganda and the American Revolution 1763–1783.* Chapel Hill: University of North Carolina Press, 1941.

Davis, Burke. *Cowpens-Guilford Courthouse Campaign.* Philadelphia: University of Pennsylvania Press, 2002.

Davis, David B. *The Problem of Slavery in the Age of Revolution.* Ithaca, NY: Cornell University Press, 1965.

Desjardin, Thomas A. *Through a Howling Wilderness: Benedict Arnold's March to Quebec in 1775.* New York: St. Martin's, 2006.

Dupuy, Ernest, and Trevor Dupuy. *The Compact History of the Revolutionary War.* New York: Hawthorn, 1963.

Edgar, Walter. *Partisans and Redcoats: The Southern Conflict That Turned the Tide of the American Revolution.* New York: Harper Perennial, 2003.

Eggenberger, David. *An Encyclopedia of Battles.* New York: Dover, 1985.

Egnal, Marc. *A Mighty Empire: The Origins of the American Revolution.* Ithaca, NY: Cornell University Press, 1988.

Elting, John. *American Army Life.* New York: Charles Scribner's Sons, 1982.

Fischer, David Hackett. *Paul Revere's Ride.* New York: Oxford University Press, 1994.

———. *Washington's Crossing.* New York: Oxford University Press, 2004.

Fleming, Thomas. *First in Their Hearts: A Biography of George Washington.* New York: W. W. Norton, 1968.

Fowler, William M. Jr. *Rebels Under Sail: The American Navy During the Revolution.* New York: Scribner's, 1976.

French, Allen. *The Siege of Boston, and of the Battles of Lexington, Concord, and Bunker Hill.* New York: Macmillian, 1911.

Frothingham, Richard. *History of the Siege of Boston and of the Battles of Lexington, Concord, and Bunker Hill.* New York: Da Capo Press, 1970.

———. *The Taking of Ticonderoga in 1775.* Cambridge, MA: Harvard University Press, 1928.

Furneaux, Rupert. *The Battle of Saratoga.* New York: Stein and Day, 1983.

Gallagher, John. *The Battle of Brooklyn.* New York: Castle Books, 2002.

Galvin, John R. *The Minutemen: Myths and Realties of the American Revolution.* Washington, D. C.: Brassey's, 1989.

Gilchrist, M. M. *Patrick Ferguson: A Man of Some Genius.* Edinburgh, UK: National Museum of Scotland, 2003.

Golway, Terry. *Washington's General: Nathanael Greene and the Triumph of the American Revolution.* New York: Henry Holt, 2005.

Gould, Dudley C. *Times of Brother Jonathan: What He Ate, Drank, Wore, Believed In, and Used for Medicine during the War of Independence.* Middleton, CT: Southfarm Press, 2001.

Graymont, Barbara. *The Iroquois in the American Revolution.* Syracuse, NY: Syracuse University Press, 1972.

Greene, George W. *The Life of Nathanael Greene, Major-General in the Army of the Revolution.* New York: Books for Libraries Press, 1972.

Gruber, Ira. *Howe Brothers and the American Revolution.* New York: W. W. Norton, 1975.

Hairr, John. *Guilford Courthouse: Nathanael Greene's Victory in Defeat, March 15, 1781.* Cambridge, MA: Da Capo Press, 2002.

Harvey, Robert. *A Few Bloody Noses: The Realities and Mythologies of the American Revolution.* New York: Overlook Press, 2003.

Hatch, Robert M. *Thrust for Canada: The American Attempt on Quebec in 1775–1776.* Boston: Houghton Mifflin, 1979.

Heinl, Robert Debs, Jr. *Dictionary of Military Quotations.* Annapolis, MD: United States Naval Institute, 1967.

Heusser, Albert. *George Washington's Map Maker.* New Brunswick, NJ: Rutgers University Press, 1966.

Hibbert, Christopher. *George III: A Personal History.* London: Viking, 1998.

————. *Rebels and Redcoats: The American Revolution through British Eyes.* London: Penguin, 2001.

Higginbotham, Don. *Daniel Morgan: Revolutionary Rifleman.* Chapel Hill: University of North Carolina Press, 1979.

————. *George Washington and the American Tradition.* Athens: University of Georgia Press, 1985.

Hoffert, Robert W. *A Politics of Tensions: The Articles of Confederation and American Political Ideas.* Boulder: University Press of Colorado, 1992.

Hyma, Albert. *Sir Henry Clinton and the American Revolution.* Ann Arbor: University of Michigan Press, 1957.

Ingaro, Charles W. *The Hessian Mercenary State: Ideas, Institutions, and Reform Under Frederick II, 1760–1785.* New York: Cambridge University, 1987.

Isaacson, Walter. *Benjamin Franklin: An American Life.* New York: Simon & Schuster, 2003.

Jackson, John. *Valley Forge: Pinnacle of Courage.* Gettysburg, PA: Thomas Publications, 1999.

Jaffe, Irma B. *John Trumbull: Portrait-Artist of the American Revolution.* Boston: New York Graphic Society, 1975.

Jensen, Merrill. *The Articles of Confederation: An Interpretation of Social-Constitutional History of the American Revolution, 1774–1781.* Madison: University of Wisconsin Press, 1976.

Kail, Jerry, et al., editors. *Who Was Who During the American Revolution.* Indianapolis, IN: Bobbs-Merrill, 1976.

Ketchum, Richard M. *Decisive Day: The Battle for Bunker Hill.* New York: Henry Holt, 1999.

————. *Saratoga: Turning Point of America's Revolution.* New York: Henry Holt, 1997.

————. *Victory at Yorktown: The Campaign That Won the Revolution.* New York: Henry Holt, 2004.

————. *The Winter Soldiers: The Battles for Trenton and Princeton.* New York: Owl Books, 1999.

Kaye, Harvey J. *Thomas Paine and the Promise of America.* New York: Hill and Wang, 2005.

Lands, Edward. *The Hessian and Other German Auxiliaries of Great Britain in the Revolutionary War.* New York: Harper and Brothers, 1884.

Lanning, Michael Lee. *Defenders of Liberty: African Americans in the Revolutionary War.* New York: Kensington, 2000.

———. *Mercenaries: Soldiers of Fortune, from Ancient Greece to Today's Private Military Companies.* New York: Ballantine, 2005.

———. *Senseless Secrets: The Failures of Military Intelligence from George Washington to the Present.* New York: Birch Lane Press, 1996.

———. *The African American Soldier: From Crispus Attucks to Colin Powell.* New York: Birch Lane, 1997.

———. *The Battle 100: The Stories behind History's Most Influential Battles.* Naperville, IL: Sourcebooks, 2003.

———. *The Military 100: A Ranking of the Most Influential Military Leaders of All Time.* New York: Citadel Press, 1996.

Leckie, Robert. *George Washington's War: The Saga of the American Revolution.* New York: Harper Collins, 1992.

Lengel, Edward G. *George Washington: A Military Life.* New York: Random House, 2005.

Lumpkin, Henry. *From Savannah to Yorktown.* New York: Paragon, 1987.

Lundeberg, Philip K. *The Gunboat Philadelphia and the Defense of Lake Champlain in 1776.* Basin Harbor, VT: Lake Champlain Maritime Museum, 1995.

Martin, David G. *The Philadelphia Campaign: June 1777–July 1778.* Cambridge, MA: Da Capo, 2003.

Mattern, David. *Benjamin Lincoln and the American Revolution.* New York: Columbia University Press, 1995.

McCullough, David. *John Adams.* New York: Simon & Schuster, 2001.

———. *1776.* New York: Simon & Schuster, 2005.

McGuire, Thomas J. *The Philadelphia Campaign: Volume One: Brandywine and the Fall of Philadelphia.* Mechanicsburg, PA: Stackpole, 2006.

McHenry, Robert, editor. *Webster's American Military Biographies.* Springfield, MA: G.&C. Merriam, 1978.

Middlekauff, Robert. *The Glorious Cause: The American Revolution, 1763–1789.* New York: Oxford University Press, 1982.

Miller, Nathan. *Sea of Glory: A Naval History of the American Revolution.* New York: D. McKay, 1974.

Milsop, John. *The Continental Infantryman of the American Revolution.* Oxford, U.K., Osprey, 2004.

Mintz, Max W. *Generals of Saratoga: John Burgoyne and Horatio Gates.* New Haven, CT: Yale University Press, 1992.

Mitchell, Joseph B. *Discipline and Bayonets: The Armies and Leaders in the War of the American Revolution.* New York: Putnam, 1967.

Moore, George H. *The Treason of Charles Lee: Major General, Second in Command in the American Army of the Revolution.* Kennikat Press, Port Washington, NY: 1970.

Morrissey, Brendan. *Boston 1775: The Shot Heard Around the World.* Oxford, UK, Osprey, 1995.

———, *Monmouth Courthouse 1778: The Last Great Battle in the North.* Oxford, UK: Osprey, 2004.

———, *Quebec, 1775: The American Invasion of Canada.* Oxford, UK: Osprey, 2003.

———, *Saratoga 1777: Turning Point of the Revolution.* Oxford, UK: Osprey, 2000.

Moss, Bobby Gilmer. *The Patriots at the Cowpens.* Blacksburg, SC: Scotia Press, 1985.

Nelson, Craig. *Thomas Paine: Enlightenment, Revolution, and the Birth of Modern Nations.* New York: Viking, 2006.

Nelson, Paul David. *General James Grant, Scottish Soldier and Royal Governor of East Florida.* Gainesville: University Press of Florida, 1993.

———, *General Sir Guy Carleton, Lord Dorchester: Soldier, Statesman of Early Canada.* Madison, NJ: Fairleigh Davidson University Press, 2000.

Nelson, William. *The American Tory.* Boston: Beacon Press, 1961.

O'Donnell, James H. III. *Southern Indians in the American Revolution.* Knoxville: University of Tennessee Press, 1973.

Paine, Thomas. *Common Sense, The Rights of Man, and Other Essential Writings of Thomas Paine.* New York: Signet Classics, 2003.

Palmer, Dave R. *George Washington and Benedict Arnold: A Tale of Two Patriots.* Washington, D.C.: Regnery, 2006.

Peterson, Harold. *The Guns of the Continental Soldier.* Harrisburg, PA: Stackpole Books, 1968.

Pettengill, Ray W. *Letters from America, 1776–1779: Being Letters of Brunswick, Hessian, and Waldeck Officers with the British Armies during the Revolution.* Boston: Houghton Mifflin, 1924.

Quarles, Benjamin. *The Negro in the American Revolution.* Chapel Hill: University of North Carolina Press, 1961.

Rakove, Jack N. *The Beginnings of National Politics: An Interpretive History of the Continental Congress.* New York: Knopf, 1979.

Randall, Willard S. *Benedict Arnold: Patriot and Traitor.* New York: William Morrow, 1990.

———. *George Washington: A Life.* New York: Henry Holt, 1997.

———. *Thomas Jefferson: A Life.* New York: Henry Holt, 1993.

Raphael, Ray. *A People's History of the American Revolution.* New York: Harper Perennial, 2002.

Reiss, Oscar. *Medicine and the American Revolution: How Diseases and Their Treatments Affected the Colonial Army.* Jefferson, NC: McFarland, 1998.

Rice, Howard C., and Ann S.K. Brown, editors. *The American Campaigns of Rochambeau's Army: 1780, 1781, 1782, 1783.* Princeton, NJ: Princeton-Brown, 1972.

Risch, Erna. *Supplying Washington's Army.* Washington, D.C.: U.S. Army Center of Military History, 1981.

Roberts, Kenneth. *The Battle of Cowpens.* New York: Eastern Acorn Press, 1989.

Royster, Charles. *A Revolutionary People at War.* Chapel Hill: University of North Carolina Press, 1979.

Schecter, Barnet. *The Battle for New York: The City at the Heart of the Revolution.* New York: Penguin, 2002.

Selby, John. *The Road to Yorktown.* New York: St. Martin's, 1976.

Shelton, Hal T. *General Richard Montgomery and the American Revolution: From Redcoat to Rebel.* New York: New York University Press, 1994.

Stephenson, Michael. *Patriot Battles: How the War of Independence Was Fought.* New York: HarperCollins, 2007.

Steuben, Friedrich Wilhelm von. *Baron von Steuben's Revolutionary War Drill Manual: A Facsimile Reprint of the 1794 Edition.* Mineola, NY: Dover, 1985.

Still, Charles J. *Major General Anthony Wayne and the Pennsylvania Line in the Continental Army.* Cranbury, NJ: Scholar's Bookshelf, 2005.

Stryker, William S. *The Battle of Monmouth.* Whitefish, MT: Kessinger, 2006.

Tebbel, John. *Turning the World Upside Down: Inside the American Revolution.* New York: Orion Books, 1993.

Thayer, Theodore. *Nathanael Greene: Strategist of the American Revolution.* New York: Twayne, 1960.

Thomas, Evan. *John Paul Jones: Sailor, Hero, Father of the American Navy.* New York: Simon and Schuster, 2003.

Triber, Jayne E. *A True Republican: The Life of Paul Revere.* Amherst: University of Massachusetts Press, 1998.

Unger, Harlow Giles. *Lafayette.* Hoboken, NY: John Wiley & Sons, 2002.

Vallentine, Alan. *Lord George Germain.* Oxford, UK: Clarendon Press, 1962.

Van Steeg, Clarence L. *Robert Morris, Revolutionary Financier.* Philadelphia: University of Pennsylvania Press, 1954.

Van Tyne, Claude H. *The Loyalists in the American Revolution.* Gansevoort, NY: Corner House, 1999.

Wickwire, Franklin, and Mary Wickwire. *Cornwallis: The American Adventure.* Boston: Houghton Mifflin, 1970.

Wilber, C. Keith. *Picture Book of the Revolution's Privateers.* Harrisburg, PA: Stackpole, 1973.

Wilkinson, James. *Memoirs of My Own Time.* New York: AMS Press, 1973.

Willcox, William B. *Portrait of a General: Sir Henry Clinton in the War of Independence.* New York: Knopf, 1964.

Williams, Glenn F. *Year of the Hangman: George Washington's Campaign Against the Iroquois.* Yardley, PA: Westholme, 2005.

Wills, Gary. *Inventing America: Jefferson's Declaration of Independence.* New York: Doubleday, 2002.

Windrow, Martin, and Francis K. Mason. *A Concise Dictionary of Military Biography.* New York: John Wiley & Sons, 1991.

Wood, W. J. *Battles of the Revolutionary War, 1775–1783.* Cambridge, MA: Da Capo Press, 1990.

Wright, Robert K. *The Continental Army.* Washington, D.C.: U.S. Army Center of Military History, 1983.

Zobel, Hiller B. *The Boston Massacre.* New York: W. W. Norton, 1970.

INDEX

ABOUT THE AUTHOR

Michael Lee Lanning is the author of seventeen nonfiction books on military history. More than a million copies of his books are in print in fifteen countries, and editions have been translated into twelve languages. He has appeared on major television networks and the History Channel as an expert on the individual soldier on both sides of the Vietnam War.

A veteran of more than twenty years in the U.S. Army, Lanning is a retired lieutenant colonel. During the Vietnam War, he served as an infantry platoon leader, reconnaissance platoon leader, and an infantry company commander. In addition to having earned the Combat Infantryman's Badge and Bronze Star with "V" device with two oak leaf clusters, Lanning is Ranger-qualified and a senior parachutist.

Lanning was born in Sweetwater, Texas, and is a 1968 graduate of Texas A&M University. He currently resides on the Bolivar Peninsula of Texas and in Phoenix, Arizona.